MW00638631

On This Day In
NANTUCKET
HISTORY

On This Day In

NANTUCKET
HISTORY

AMY JENNESS

THE
History
PRESS

Published by The History Press
Charleston, SC 29403
www.historypress.net

Copyright © 2014 by Amy Jenness
All rights reserved

Front cover: Color postcards appear courtesy of the
Nantucket Historical Association.

First published 2014

Manufactured in the United States

ISBN 978.1.62619.626.1

Library of Congress CIP data applied for.

Notice: The information in this book is true and complete to the
best of our knowledge. It is offered without guarantee on the part of
the author or The History Press. The author and The History Press
disclaim all liability in connection with the use of this book.

All rights reserved. No part of this book may be reproduced or
transmitted in any form whatsoever without prior written permission
from the publisher except in the case of brief quotations embodied in
critical articles and reviews.

CONTENTS

ACKNOWLEDGEMENTS

Nantucket is fortunate to have had so many who preserved its history, and it has been a joy to go back in time to meet the characters and learn the stories of the island's people. I'd like to thank the *Inquirer & Mirror* and the Nantucket Atheneum for recently creating the Digital Newspaper Archive, it is an invaluable resource.

I'd also like to thank the Nantucket Historical Association for its commitment to preserving Nantucket history and providing amazing research databases, the Barney Genealogical Record and cemetery information, which were key to writing this book. Special thanks to the photographers of the Historic American Buildings Survey, whose work is available through the U.S. Library of Congress.

Thank you to Nantucket Historical Association photo archivist Marie Henke for your cheerful assistance with my long list of photo requests. Thank you to Nantucket

Atheneum reference librarian Lincoln Thurber for your genial willingness to help me each time I parked myself at your desk with questions. And thank you to Tabitha Dulla at The History Press for your help and for giving me the opportunity to write *On This Day in Nantucket History*.

INTRODUCTION

Nantucket is an island, but it's also an idea. For more than three hundred years, people have looked to it, a triangular-shaped sandy chunk of land twenty-five miles off the coast of Massachusetts, as a place of refuge.

In 1659, nine English families moved to the island to establish a town where no white person had ever lived and to custom design their new community. Countless ship passengers, whose travel plans changed abruptly when they shipwrecked, have landed there under circumstances both tragic and heroic. African Americans found a measure of freedom not available to them on the mainland. Women excelled in leadership roles, due in part to the lack of men and in part to Quaker ideals. In the 1880s, tourists and summer residents came to Nantucket for its slower pace, clean air and beautiful surroundings. Today, the tourist industry is Nantucket's economic driver and still entices visitors with its beauty and a sense of having stepped back in time.

Of course, as much as it is a haven, Nantucket also requires its people to be self-sufficient, creative problem-solvers and adventurous—all qualities that served its mariners well as they hunted whales and proved themselves adept traders in ports all over the world. Long before the age of jet travel and Federal Express, island captains thrived in an eighteenth- and early nineteenth-century global market, and all eyes were on Nantucket.

But by the 1860s, Nantucket whaling was in decline. The combination of a devastating fire, a sandbar filling in the mouth of the harbor, the California gold rush and the Civil War all contributed to the loss of the island's core industry. Nantucket's long reach to the sea would continue to make it an important place. Both the U.S. Navy and the hugely successful Marconi Wireless Company capitalized on the island's geographical location.

The speed and noise of the Industrial Age seemed to rattle the island, and its people had trouble adjusting to electricity, bicycles, cars, steamboats and even a municipal water system. In time, the island fell in with the rest of the country, but change came slowly. Even into the new millennium, Nantucket does things its own way. But that may be the thing that has made it so beloved down through generations.

January 1

In 1946, publisher Harcourt Brace released a book of poems called *Lord Weary's Castle,* written by Robert Lowell. In it was "The Quaker Graveyard on Nantucket," a long, ambitious poem that Lowell acknowledged was inspired in part by Herman Melville's novel *Moby-Dick.* Lowell used the rolling open hills of the Quaker Burial Ground as a metaphor for the sea and the sailor's struggle as a symbol to oppose war. Very few Nantucket Quaker graves have headstones, and to this day, the Quaker Burial Ground, located at the corner of Madaket and Prospect Streets, looks like an open field, even though thousands have been laid to rest there.

Born into a wealthy Massachusetts family with a navy officer father, Lowell was a lifelong pacifist. At age thirty, he received a Pulitzer Prize for *Lord Weary's Castle*, which cemented his reputation as a major poet.

January 2

Lillian Moller Gilbreth, whose family was famously portrayed in the book and film *Cheaper by the Dozen*, died in 1972 at age ninety-two.

Gilbreth was a psychologist, an industrial engineer and one of the first female engineers to hold a PhD. She and her husband, Frank Bunker Gilbreth Sr., were efficiency experts whose children illustrated how they applied their work to running a large family in the novel *Cheaper by the Dozen*.

Lillian Gilbreth worked for Johnson & Johnson and Macy's. In 1930, she headed a women's committee to end "involuntary idleness" for President Herbert Hoover. She helped design a desk displayed at the Chicago World's Fair in 1933 and pioneered the kitchen "work triangle" and linear layout still in use today.

For more than sixty years, Lillian and her Gilbreth clan summered on Nantucket on Brant Point in a cottage called "The Shoe," which they made by joining two lighthouses together. In September 1949, a camera crew from Twentieth Century Fox arrived on island to capture scenes for *Cheaper by the Dozen*. Nantucket youth were shot playing baseball and tennis dressed in the styles of the 1920s.

After her death, *Good Housekeeping* magazine named Gilbreth one of America's One Hundred Most Influential Women, and in 1984, the U.S. Postal Service created a stamp in her honor.

January 3

In 1793, Lucretia Coffin was born on Nantucket to Thomas Coffin and Anna Folger. She was a descendant of three of the island's original English settlers. At age thirteen, her parents sent her to a coeducational Quaker school in New York, where she met her future husband, James Mott. After marrying in 1811, Lucretia and James moved to Philadelphia, where they would live for the rest of their lives.

Lucretia Coffin Mott had six children and soon became active in Quaker meetings, the equivalent of a church service. In 1821, she became a minister of the Society of Friends of Philadelphia.

The Quakers believed women should take a public stand on issues that mattered to them, and James supported his wife wholeheartedly. Mott spent her life pursuing social justice by speaking against slavery and in support of women's rights, as well as at yearly Quaker meetings. She often spoke with the noted reformers Frederick Douglass, William Lloyd Garrison, Lucy Stone and Elizabeth Cady Stanton. She witnessed the beginning of the women's movement at the Seneca Falls Convention in 1848 and was elected the first president of the Equal Rights Association in 1866. She made her last speech at age eighty-five at the thirtieth anniversary of the Seneca Falls convention in Rochester, New York. Her last visits to Nantucket were in 1869 and 1876. She died on November 11, 1880.

January 4

The African Meeting House, built at the corner of York and Pleasant Streets by the Trustees of the African Baptist Society, was consecrated in 1825. The society erected the modest square building to house a school, a church and a meeting place for the island's African Americans. Early teachers were itinerant Baptist mainland preachers and often doubled as both preachers and teachers.

The meetinghouse quickly became a central hub for African Americans on Nantucket, most of whom lived nearby in a section of town called New Guinea. In 1848, a former Virginia slave, the Reverend James Crawford, a Baptist, revitalized the church, but the congregation slowly diminished following his death in 1888. The building was sold in the 1920s and would be used as a workshop, warehouse and garage (pictured opposite, top in the 1960s). In 1989, the Boston-based Museum of Afro American History restored the building and opened it as a museum in 2000 (pictured opposite, on the bottom).

January 5

In 1959, the *Nantucket* lightship was blown eighty miles off its mooring in hurricane-force winds and fifty-foot seas. The vessel was out of communication for several days due to water-damaged electronics.

Serving aboard lightships, which were floating lighthouses anchored near treacherous shoals, was both monotonous and dangerous. They were manned first by members of the U.S. Lighthouse Service and then the U.S. Coast Guard. The Nantucket Shoals station, forty miles southeast of the island, was established in 1854, and a series of lightships (all named *Nantucket*) were anchored there for over one hundred years. Of all the country's lightships, the *Nantucket* was anchored the farthest from shore, the first American light seen by boats traveling from Europe. The safety of the *Nantucket* crew was vulnerable to other vessels traveling the busy shipping lanes, and collisions did occur.

In January 1934, Lightship No. 117 was sideswiped by the SS *Washington*, and in May of that year, it was rammed and sunk by the passenger ship RMS *Olympic* in a heavy fog.

In 1936, Pusey & Jones of Wilmington, Delaware, constructed Lightship No. 112, the largest lightship ever built. The ship cost $300,956 and was paid for by the British government as reparation for the deadly collision with the *Olympic*. During World War II, Lightship No. 112 was withdrawn from the Nantucket Shoals and used in Portland, Maine. Lightship No. 112 served Nantucket Shoal for thirty-nine years.

January 6

Under the title "Whale Fishery," the *Inquirer* in 1830 reprinted an excerpt from the *Commercial Reading Room* analyzing the state of U.S. whaling. It examined the number of whale ships in the Pacific Ocean and off the coast of Brazil and expressed concern about the future of the fishery.

The item reports that 79,835 barrels of sperm oil were imported into the United States in 1829. Of that, 37,788 barrels came from Nantucket ships.

The report's summary takes a foreboding tone:

> *It will be seen by the foregoing statement, that the whaling business is overdone. On Jan 1, 1829, the people of Nantucket had 60 ships at sea, now they have only 49, and 4 in port; and there has not been a time since 1816, that they have had so few ships employed as whalers, as they now have. The author concludes by expressing doubt that a recent whaling community settled on the Hudson River could succeed and states the industry cannot support any more boats.*

January 7

In June 1795, gold and silver coins valued at $20,000 were stolen from the new Nantucket Bank. The theft was the first major crime on the peaceful island and residents became obsessed with guessing who did it. Despite the lack of evidence, bank president Joseph Chase, based on others' accusations and a visit with an astrologer, charged bank board member William Coffin with the crime. In time, Chase also charged other board members.

Frustrated by Chase's unwillingness to entertain other possibilities, including a theory that the crime was committed by off-islanders, Coffin investigated on his own. He traveled to three states to obtain search warrants and searched the suspects' homes himself.

On this day in 1796, Coffin wrote a letter to his wife, saying, "I would have left the matter and returned home before now was it not for the persons who are suspected at Nantucket who I believe to be as innocent as angels of knowing anything about the robbery."

Coffin's efforts succeeded: two men confessed to the crime. However, Chase still did not bring charges. More evidence of the men's guilt still did not result in their arrest. Unsubstantiated allegations against the board members would hang over them for decades and the scandal set off a feud that affected everyone. Finally, in 1816, twenty-one years after the crime, a New York prison warden provided Coffin with a confession of the robbery from an inmate incarcerated there and the issue was officially resolved.

January 8

In 1865, the *Inquirer & Mirror* published a report on an effort to return the *South Shoal* lightship, a manned floating lighthouse, to its mooring.

The government hired a Boston-based steamer to tow it back from Edgartown, where it had drifted, even though a Nantucket ship was available. The report recounts a story of ineptitude and feud and concludes: "Those who undertake to save by sending strange steamers here, show how little they know about the true means required to do such work effectually and well. No inspector is to blame who has not been at the South Shoal himself in winter time...owners of the Nantucket Boat are not trying to overreach him, and that it is cheaper for the Government to have the aid of our Boat than to procure it at a price nominally less, but really much more exorbitant."

January 9

In 1826, the *Inquirer* ran a U.S. Treasury Department ad soliciting estimates for whale oil for use by "Light House establishments" in the United States.

Whaling was the first industry to hunt animals on a vast commercial level. Whalers sold baleen for corsets, ambergris for perfume and rendered the blubber and sperm oil into liquid. Of all the whale products, sperm oil was the most valuable. Found only in the interior of a sperm whale's skull, sperm oil is a thick yellow wax. A skull can hold up to three tons of oil, and it was the most sought-after commodity because of its bright, odorless flame and because of its excellent qualities as a lubricant.

By the early 1800s, sperm oil was used to illuminate lighthouses, street lamps and public buildings. The use of spermaceti candles became so prevalent that it created a new light standard called the lumen.

January 10

In late December 1908, a devastating earthquake in southern Italy leveled cities and killed hundreds of thousands. With no place to send the survivors, the Italian government put them on ships headed for America. On this day in 1909, almost 850 displaced Italian citizens boarded the SS *Florida* in Naples. On January 23, one day before they were to land in New York their ship struck the ocean liner *Republic* in a heavy fog twenty-six miles from the *Nantucket* lightship.

The *Republic* had just installed a new Marconi wireless station, and wireless operator Jack Binns used it to contact the Siasconset Marconi station forty-seven miles away. It would be the first time the new radio technology was used to send a distress message, and mariners would later credit the Marconi radio with saving almost all hands that day.

Binns was the first operator to use the CQD code, which meant "Is anybody there? Danger." For the rest of the day, the sinking *Republic* and Siasconset wireless stations would coordinate the evacuation of passengers from both ships. Using lifeboats, the crews transferred passengers from the *Republic* to the *Florida*, a tricky endeavor since the Italian émigrés on the *Florida* came close to rioting when they saw more people coming onboard. Later, another ship took the survivors to New York City.

In all, six people died from injuries sustained from the collision, and more than 1,500 passengers and crew members were rescued.

January 11

In 1883, the Muskeget Life-Saving Station was established. Muskeget Island, located off Nantucket's western end, is a tiny island situated in the middle of some of Nantucket Sound's trickiest shoals. Life-Saving Stations, a precursor to the U.S. Coast Guard, were located in coastal communities all over Massachusetts, including one on Tuckernuck Island and several on Nantucket Island. The stations were manned twenty-four hours a day by a crew that watched for ships in distress. As many as 250 ships a day passed Nantucket, and a succession of several particularly deadly wrecks in the 1830s spurred islanders to create "Humane Houses" and, later, manned Life-Saving Stations.

With each wreck, those on duty at a Life-Saving Station attempted to rescue the crew, either from the beach or by rowing small boats out to the distressed ship. The Muskeget Life-Saving Station burned down in 1889, reopened in 1896 and closed for good in 1928.

January 12

Under the heading "Temperance Topics," the editor in the 1878 issue of the *Island Review* reported more than 650 people attended a temperance meeting that week and a new group called "Reformed Men's Club" would begin meeting the following week. And, he noted, "It is said that some people in this town are so strictly temperate that they won't even allow a piece of 'corned' meat in their house." In its broad definition, temperance means either to abstain from alcohol or use it moderately. On Nantucket, the term came to mean drinking no alcohol of any kind.

Around the country, temperance reform gained popularity throughout the nineteenth century. In 1838, Massachusetts banned the sale of fewer than fifteen gallons of alcohol per household per year but repealed the law in 1840. In 1851, a Nantucket Friends of Temperance group called for a law based on the "Maine Temperance Law," the first state law of its kind. The Bay State did pass a similar law, only to have it struck down the following year by the Massachusetts Supreme Court. In 1855, a new Massachusetts temperance law was passed.

Temperance took root on Nantucket, and an October 1881 *Nantucket Journal* item noted, "Five years ago the great temperance wave which swept over the country reached Nantucket and made its influence for good felt in the community generally and in many a household in particular. Nearly one hundred men who were more or less addicted to drinking intoxicating liquor publicly renounced the practice and endeavored to overcome appetite."

January 13

The schooner *Minnie C. Taylor* wrecked in 1894 on the lee side of Great Point, north of Coatue. The Coskata Life-Saving Station crew rescued all aboard from the beach using a breeches buoy, which consisted of a line and pulley system with a basket. The Coskata crew fired a line from a gun that landed between the main and mizzen masts on the ship. One by one, the ship's four crewmen were hauled in the basket to shore.

The *Minnie C. Taylor* was carrying 1,500 barrels of lubricating oil. It left Martha's Vineyard the day before and anchored near the lightship *Cross Rip*. But a storm and high seas that night severed its anchor line, and heavy ice prevented the crew from raising the sails. The crew anxiously rode out the storm in darkness and also had to extinguish a small fire when the heavy seas ripped the binnacle light from its socket.

The *Minnie C. Taylor* struck ground at 8:00 a.m., and the crew was quickly rescued. By that time, a crowd had gathered on shore, and salvagers began to unload the cargo. By nightfall, they had piled eight hundred to nine hundred barrels of oil on the beach. The ship was owned by its captain, and both the vessel and its cargo were insured. Captain Quinlan sold the remains of the *Minnie C. Taylor* to a Nantucket captain, Swain, for fifty-seven dollars.

January 14

In 1843, an item appeared in the *Daily Telegraph*, a newspaper published in 1843 and 1844, under the title "The Harpoon."

It read, "We understand that, at the Whig meeting on Saturday Night, another attempt was made to identify this paper with the interest of the Democratic Party. We were charged with having printed and issued 'The Harpoon' a partizin [*sic*] sheet got up by the Democrats for electioneering purposes." The writer thanked his colleague at the *Inquirer* for informing the meeting that the charge was untrue and also said, "Other than to acknowledge the extent of our obligations to our contemporary we should not have mentioned this attack, but have let it pass with numerous others of a similar character, a thing of straw not worth a breath."

Elsewhere in that issue, the *Daily Telegraph* reported on recent elections and noted, "The acidities of party spirit, which, used sparingly give a zest to public life are now neutralized."

Election results show that in 1843, Nantucket voters favored the Whig Party, electing George N. Briggs as Massachusetts governor and Joseph Grinnell to the Twenty-eighth U.S. Congress. At the time, the American Whig Party ran a close second to the Democratic Party. In the 1850s, the Whigs lost members as the nation struggled with the issue of slavery. A new Republican Party began and was primarily focused on keeping slavery in the South. So many Whig members became Republicans that the Whigs, who had put two presidents in office, had disappeared by 1860.

January 15

Caleb Lyons Depung died of pneumonia at the U.S. General Hospital in Washington, D.C., in 1864. Depung was a Nantucket farmer who enlisted to fight in the Civil War in 1862 at age thirty-five. He joined the army as a private in July and fought at Antietam and made the grueling march to Harpers Ferry. In October 1863, Depung fell ill and had blood in his lungs, which the Nantucket comrades who fought with him blamed on the march. Depung was moved to the Sixth Veteran Reserves Corps and died three months later.

Nearly four hundred Nantucket men enlisted in the Civil War, and more than seventy were killed. The island sacrificed dozens of whale ships, some of which were sunk to block Confederate vessels and others destroyed by Confederate raiders. In 1891, the island's Civil War veterans formed a Grand Army of the Republic post (pictured here).

January 16

An item with the heading "Obituary!" appeared in the *Island Review* on this day in 1875. It was the fifth edition of the new newspaper, begun on January 2, 1875, by Isaac H. Folger and his partner, S. Heath Rich. It read: "Obituary! Died, this afternoon. Just as we were going to press, our ADVERTISING PAGE. The thick-headed individual who has been for some time engaged in carrying our page of type up to the building in which our press resides, by his carelessness let fall one of the forms, and 'pied' the whole business. Our readers are asked to be lenient toward us in our misfortune, and by Saturday our advertisements will again appear as usual."

The *Island Review* survived the debacle and continued on Nantucket until 1878, when Folger and Rich moved it to Brockton, Massachusetts, and started a Brockton newspaper known as the *Enterprise*. The *Brockton Enterprise* still publishes daily.

In 1874, Folger and Rich capitalized on Nantucket's growing reputation as a summer destination and published the *Handbook of Nantucket: Containing a Brief Historical Sketch of the Island, with Notes of Interest to Summer Visitors*. In it, Folger writes, "Our reason for publishing this book is because many of our summer visitors desire to have some accurate, condensed epitome of the Island, and also, because when arriving here, strangers to the place, they desire some guide as to how they shall employ their time pleasantly to themselves, with as little loss as possible."

January 17

Miss Elma Loines died in 1983 at age one hundred. Born in Brooklyn and a graduate of Bryn Mawr, Loines spent many summers on Nantucket. In 1959, Loines gave an eight-inch Alvan Clark telescope to the Maria Mitchell Association. Loines and her father had used the telescope at their private observatory in Lake George, New York.

The gift spurred the association to build a proper observatory to house the telescope, and on August 1, 1968—on the anniversary of Maria Mitchell's 150th birthday—the Loines Observatory was opened on Winn's Hill, off Upper Vestal Street. In 1998, the association added a second state-of-the-art twenty-four-inch telescope. Far out to sea and away from the mainland's light pollution, Nantucket offers some of the best stargazing in New England, and for forty-six years, the Loines Observatory has been used by both scholars and hobbyists to study the sky. The Maria Mitchell Association opens the observatory to the public during the summer for viewing sessions.

Loines also donated her Flora Street home to the Maria Mitchell Association in 1972 and stipulated that the proceeds from its sale be used to fund graduate student research on Nantucket. Off-island, Loines founded the Master School of Music in Brooklyn, which trained classical singers until it closed in 1927, and the Metropolitan Museum of Art in New York City added several of her photographs to its collection in 1961.

January 18

The editor of the *Inquirer* published an 1850 obituary that eulogized Josiah Sturtevant, a Nantucket resident who left for California in search of gold in March 1849.

According to the item, Sturtevant died at Mormon Island Diggings, where he and other Nantucketers had been mining. The obituary doesn't explain how Sturtevant died at the age of forty but does quote an eyewitness account: "After Mr. Sturtevant arrived at this place, he appeared to be well and often said he thought the climate agreed with him. He died on the 4th [of November, 1849], suddenly, and I think unexpectedly to himself. He died towards morning. No expense was spared at his burial; and services were also performed." Sturtevant left a widow and an eleven-year-old son on Nantucket.

Many Nantucket men left for San Francisco in search of fortune after the California gold rush began in 1848. Already damaged by the Great Fire of 1846 and the silting in of the harbor's entrance, the whaling industry declined further with the exodus of hundreds of able seamen headed west.

Mormon Island—or Mormon Island Diggings, as it was known in 1850—was a thriving gold rush camp during its peak, with 2,500 residents, four hotels, seven saloons and one school. As its name implies, the majority of the camp was inhabited by Mormons. As the gold rush declined, so did Mormon Island, and it was completely abandoned by the 1950s. In 1955, Mormon Island disappeared under the man-made Folsom Lake, although building foundations can still be seen during periods of extreme drought.

January 19

Edgar Poe was born in 1809. Poe, who later wrote under the name Edgar Allan Poe, was an author, poet, editor and literary critic. Famous for his macabre mysteries, Poe was one of the earliest American writers to embrace writing short stories. The only novel he ever published was *The Narrative of Arthur Gordon Pym of Nantucket* in 1838. The story is the tale of a young Arthur Gordon Pym, who stows away aboard a whaling ship called the *Grampus*. Pym has many adventures that include a shipwreck, mutiny and cannibalism, and his journey takes him all over the world.

Reviewers were not kind to *The Narrative of Arthur Gordon Pym of Nantucket*, and the book did not sell. The book's failure marked a turning point in Poe's career. He went to work as a magazine editor and began to focus on writing the short stories he would later become known for. But *The Narrative of Arthur Gordon Pym of Nantucket* had a strong influence on other writers. Herman Melville was a fan, and scholars note many similarities between their work. Some say the character of Ahab, Melville's obsessed captain in *Moby-Dick*, was inspired by Poe's short story "The Fall of the House of Usher."

French author Jules Verne published a sequel to Poe's *Narrative* in 1897 called *An Antarctic Mystery*. Notable authors H.P. Lovecraft, Henry James and Charles Romeyn Dake have also cited the novel as influential.

January 20

In 1892, the Coskata Life-Saving Station rescued the crew of the British schooner *H.P. Kirkham* in what is one of the most remarkable Nantucket rescue stories. Coskata station keeper Walter N. Chase and his crew were out for twenty-six hours in a twenty-three-foot open boat during a ferocious winter storm and saved seven men whom they found clinging to the ship's icy rigging.

The *H.P. Kirkham* left Halifax, Nova Scotia, en route to New York City when it went aground on the Rose and Crown Shoal fifteen miles southeast of Nantucket. Heavy seas tore off the bow within the first hour, and all the crew could do was light distress signals and wait. At daylight, the Sankaty Lighthouse keeper spotted the wreck and alerted the Coskata crew members, who reached the *H.P. Kirkham* around 11:00 a.m. Using superb seamanship, the lifesavers were able to get a line to the disabled ship and bring the crew onto their surfboat. Due to the extra weight, they discarded their sail and mast and waited out the storm for hours. Eventually, the crew, exhausted and hypothermic, rowed the fifteen miles back to shore.

A year later, the U.S. Treasury awarded Station Keeper Chase a gold medal in honor of his leadership and gave the rest of the crew—Surfmen George J. Flood, Charles Brown Cathcart, Jessie B. Eldridge and Josiah B. Gould—silver medals for their participation in the rescue.

January 21

A bitter cold front plunged Nantucket waters into a deep freeze in 1970 and kept the island locked in ice for a week. With no boat travel, three U.S. Coast Guardsmen on the buoy tender *Proud Mary II* were stranded on the island but found warmth and friendship at the Nantucket Angler's Club.

Club president Pete Guild invited the men to play the club's "ring game," but there was a stipulation. If the coast guardsmen lost the game, then the Angler's Club won ownership of their vessel. Thus began a long tradition of the Angler's Club claiming and renaming USCG ships as Republic of Nantucket Cutters (RONC)—all in good fun.

According to the tradition, the skipper of the newly won vessel renamed it with the RONC designation. The U.S. Coast Guard has on record seventy-one vessels that have called at Nantucket, competed and lost at the ring game and now have RONC names. In June 1983, the USCG Point Jackson Station commander staged an "invasion" of the Nantucket Angler's Club in an effort to retake ownership of his lost vessels. The Angler's Club was swiftly and cunningly defeated when the Coasties occupied the Angler's Club building and made its president Dan Kelliher walk the plank.

The Angler's Club was formed in 1969 and is a private, membership organization. Its headquarters are located on the waterfront, and the anglers host pond- and ocean-fishing tournaments throughout the year. Fun competition aside, the club prides itself on welcoming members of the coast guard who are either visiting or stationed on Nantucket.

January 22

Charles Sayles died in 1994 at age eighty-five. Born in Ohio, Charles Sayles shipped out of the Great Lakes on a tanker and landed in Gloucester, Massachusetts, where he worked on fishing schooners. While on a fishing trip in 1926, Sayles visited Nantucket. He quickly fell in love with the island, with its historic waterfront and storied captains, and moved here not long after.

"I followed the water here," Sayle told *Historic Nantucket.* "I went quahogging and scalloping. I was the last one to scallop here under sail." Sayle, who fished until 1938, used to catch bay scallops from a sailing dory and a small schooner. He caught quahogs from his skiff using a pair of fourteen-foot tongs.

In addition to fishing, Sayles was a master maritime craftsman and made ships' models and ivory carvings. During World War II, he was commissioned by the government to make ship models, which took him to New Jersey for a few years. Highly regarded as a maritime historian, he wrote a column about the waterfront for the *Inquirer & Mirror* for thirty-five years.

Sayles was also a commodore of the Wharf Rats Club, a private club started in an old fishing shanty on Old North Wharf. Wharf Rats members include U.S. president Franklin Roosevelt, justices, ambassadors, admirals, generals, artists, pilots, fishermen, businessmen and scientists who meet to share their ideas and opinions. Sayles, one of the longest-running commodores, served from 1985 until his death.

January 23

The lighthouse keeper at Sankaty spotted the Comet Innes in 1910. The comet had been discovered in Africa the week before and was called the brightest comet since 1882. After being alerted by the keeper, several hundred people turned out around the island to observe Innes.

The comet had appeared suddenly in the southern hemisphere, and a number of people claimed to have discovered it. But it is thought to have been first spotted by diamond miners in South Africa before dawn on January 12, 1910, by which time it was already visible to the naked eye.

The first astronomer to study the comet properly was Robert T.A. Innes at the Transvaal Observatory in Johannesburg on January 17, after having been alerted two days earlier by the editor of a Johannesburg newspaper. The comet was closest to the sun on January 17 and was visible in daylight with the unaided eye. After that date, it declined in brightness but became a spectacular sight from the northern hemisphere in the evening twilight, its noticeably curved tail reaching up to fifty degrees by early February.

After 1910, astronomers named the comet the "Great Daylight Comet of 1910" and judged it to be brighter than the planet Venus. Its discovery created such a stir that it upstaged the heavily anticipated arrival of a second comet—Halley's Comet—later that year. Halley's Comet was also visible on Nantucket during the month of April in 1910.

January 24

Funds to build a lighthouse on Brant Point at the entrance to Nantucket Harbor were approved in 1746. As Nantucketers began to depend on the sea for trade, the need for maritime navigation became more urgent. At a town meeting, sea captains asked voters to establish the lighthouse to protect their investments, and they approved two hundred pounds. It was the second lighthouse, after Boston Light, to be built in America.

The Brant Point Light either burned down or was knocked down by a storm multiple times between 1746 and 1795, when the federal government took ownership of it. It was rebuilt each time.

In 1856, the U.S. government built a $15,000 circular brick tower and attached dwelling that was considered one of the best on the Atlantic Coast. The sturdy tower supported a lantern on top made of cast iron with twelve plate-glass windows. Shifting sands once again required a new lighthouse, and the present tower, the ninth light to grace Brant Point, was erected in 1901, roughly six hundred feet east of the 1856 lighthouse.

Brant Point Light is now the shortest lighthouse in New England, with an elevation of twenty-six feet. The light was changed from white to red in 1933 so that it would not be mistaken for the increasing number of house lights near the harbor. The tower was renovated in 1983 and again in 2000, and its light was automated in 1965.

January 25

The last midwinter graduation of the Nantucket High School occurred in 1906. Twelve girls and four boys composed the class of 1906 and gathered at the Nantucket Atheneum, the island's public library, along with a standing-room-only crowd, for graduation ceremonies.

Before awarding the diplomas, school board chairman Arthur Gardner announced that the board was changing the school year to begin in the fall and end in late June due to the difficulty of finding a heated auditorium large enough to hold graduation exercises and informed the crowd that a local church could accommodate a late June graduation ceremony.

As part of the festivities, each graduate read an essay with subjects that ranged from debating the need for a larger U.S. Navy to the rise of public schools to a futuristic look at Nantucket in one hundred years. The class sang "Our Public School" and the class song, "With Songs of Triumph." Valedictorian Clara Louise Bowen delivered an address titled "Nantucket in the Whaling Days."

The next high school graduation occurred on Thursday, June 27, 1907. Eight girls and three boys received diplomas. The ceremony was held in the Red Men's Hall and was a success, according to an account in the *Inquirer & Mirror*. "The graduation of the class of 1907 was attended by a departure from the somewhat stereotyped form of exercises of other years, the program being so varied and interesting as to banish the least vestige of monotony, and the audience which packed the hall were most attentive."

January 26

In 1824, Peter F. Ewer wanted to know how long it took his horse to make the trip from Siasconset Village to town, a distance of roughly seven miles. As a way to measure his progress, Ewer placed stone mileage markers along the road, now known as the Milestone Road.

In the 1820s, trips to Siasconset, located at the island's eastern end, took most of a day. The January 26, 1824 edition of the *Inquirer* took note of Ewer's project with interest. In the nineteenth century, the Siasconset road changed course several times, and the milestones were moved each time. There is a tradition in the family that Peter F. Ewer's descendants keep the milestones painted white. The markers still remain along the Milestone Road, now the fastest road on the island with a posted speed of fifty miles per hour.

Born in 1800, Ewer would later be well known for another accomplishment: the invention of the camels, which were flotation devices designed to lift whale ships over the sandbar that blocked the entrance to Nantucket Harbor in the mid-1800s. The Nantucket Historical Association owns a portrait of Ewer, which shows him with a diamond-shaped tattoo between his eyes.

January 27

George Cannon submitted a petition to the United States Senate in 1830 and asked the government to reimburse him for money spent at the custom house at Nantucket. The U.S. Customs Service, established by the First Congress in 1789, is the oldest federal agency. It assesses and collects duties and taxes on imported goods, controls carriers of imports and exports and combats smuggling and revenue fraud. On Nantucket, the first customs house was opened in 1791. Most of the customs documents between 1791 and 1846—which include crew lists, bills of sale, coasting license bonds and vessel registers—were lost in the Great Fire of 1846. In January 1847, the U.S. Congress authorized money to build a fireproof customs house on Nantucket. The custom house closed in 1913, long after the island ceased to dominate the shipping industry.

January 28

Elisha Pope Fearing Gardner, known as the "Peanut Man," died in 1913, just shy of his eightieth birthday. Known in old age as one of the island's most eccentric citizens, Gardner left school at fourteen years old and left the island for Philadelphia at age sixteen. In his youth, he went on one whaling voyage and worked at a grocery store on Union Street.

Gardner was a veteran of the Civil War, where he was both a soldier and a spy, and was captured by the South twice. He worked many jobs off-island and returned to Nantucket in 1891, where he was known as the proprietor of "Poet's Corner." He entertained thousands of visitors at his home each summer, an eclectic place decorated with signs and Gardner's poetry. Known locally as "Elisha P.," Gardner submitted poems to the newspapers and wandered through town in the summer selling peanuts and poems.

January 29

Herbert Palmer Smith, the last island veteran of the Spanish-American War, died in 1972 at age ninety-four. Smith was born in 1877 and lived on Tuckernuck and Nantucket until he graduated from high school. He then graduated from the Massachusetts Nautical School in 1897 and enlisted in the U.S. Navy as the country entered the Spanish-American War. He served aboard the *Vulcan*, a repair ship traveling in Admiral Sampson's Flying Squadron based at Guantanamo Bay, Cuba.

In Cuba, Smith was wounded and given a disability discharge. He returned home and joined the U.S. Life-Saving Service—a precursor to the U.S. Coast Guard. Smith spent ten winters serving Life-Saving Stations in Chatham and Nantucket, Massachusetts, and Watch Hill, Rhode Island. At the start of World War I, he enlisted in the Naval Reserves, where he commanded the USS *Joy*, stationed at Woods Hole, Massachusetts, and the USS *Winchester*, station at Norfolk, Virginia.

After the war, Smith signed on to the U.S. Shipping Board in 1920. He served the *Bellebuckle* as second mate on a voyage through the Panama Canal to Australia. During that trip, the first mate deserted ship and the captain died, so the American Consul put Smith in charge and ordered him to sail the ship back home. He would serve the U.S. Shipping Board until 1926, when he retired and returned to Nantucket. On island, Smith served in several town government positions and directed the annual Memorial Day Parade for thirty-two years.

January 30

In the 1841 issue of the *Islander*, a letter writer signed "B" addressed controversial topics relating to abolitionism: "I have as often said as I have heard it, made this reply:—That if the term negro applied to such only as were uncleanly and debased,—whether white or black,—I had no disposition either to associate with them, to sit between them, or beside them; but if applied exclusively to those whose skin was colored, without regard to the intellectual and moral worth of the individual, I did not hesitate to say, that there were persons among them, with whom I would much sooner associate, than I would with some of my own color."

The letter writer speaks at length about how the Bible never mentions any differences between the races, and "B" concludes by calling on the island to allow African American students to attend the high school: "I have deemed it proper that the position of abolitionists should be understood in our community—a community, where the right of the colored man is denied, not only in our meeting houses [*sic*] and vestries, and public lecture rooms, but his privilege is wrestled from him even in our public schools—a school instituted for the good of the whole people, and with which we justly prize for our own children, as is the greatest blessing which our Republican Laws can confer upon them."

January 31

Margaret Fawcett Barnes, who died in 1980, was destined to a life onstage when she was born to screen and film actors George and Percy Fawcett in 1898. The family lived in New York and summered in Siasconset, an island village her parents had helped make famous as an artists' colony. After marriage, she spent more time here and eventually moved to Nantucket year round.

She married playwright Robert Wilson at the family's Siasconset cottage in 1937, and they opened a theater in 1939. The next year, it moved to Straight Wharf and became known as the Straight Wharf Theatre. They produced plays with Nantucket stories written by Barnes, her husband and another Nantucket playwright, Austin Strong, as well as plays with other themes. The Straight Wharf Theatre burned in 1975 and was never reopened. After a divorce, Margaret married Landon Barnes. Along with many plays, Barnes authored the book *Sconset Heyday* in 1969.

February 1

In the hopes of creating a state law to protect Nantucket's historic buildings from being demolished, sixteen residents traveled to the Massachusetts Statehouse in 1955 and asked legislators to create a Nantucket Historic District Commission (HDC). The commission would have jurisdiction over the exterior design of all downtown buildings and the village of Siasconset. George Jones, speaking for the Nantucket Historical Association, said, "Unlike Williamsburg, there is no need to rebuild or restore Nantucket. The only problem is to preserve what we have and to guard the Town against destruction of the native beauty by commercialism," according to the *Inquirer & Mirror*. The legislature approved the law, and the governor signed it.

In 1972, the HDC's jurisdiction was expanded to include the entire island as well as the outer islands of Tuckernuck and Muskeget. The town-appointed commission started with six guidelines, which have evolved to include state and federal preservation laws and National Trust for Historic Preservation standards.

The HDC has been controversial for most of its history. Homeowners and developers object to its tight control over the design of their property and many rulings have resulted in litigation. The HDC has also needed to protect the island's historic architectural fabric while grappling with technological advances and changing tastes in design. Yet the vision of the HDC founders was instrumental in making Nantucket popular with tourists, now the island's main source of income. And the work continues. In 2000, the National Trust for Historic Preservation placed Nantucket on its most endangered list because of the threat of development.

February 2

For the first time in sixty-five years, a sailing vessel larger than a catboat was built on Nantucket and launched in 1924. The sixty-foot *Native*, commissioned by H. Marshall Gardiner and Howard U. Chase, was built by the Nantucket Boat Works. Its launch attracted a crowd that morning, but the launch didn't go as planned. Supported by a wooden cradle, the *Native* slid toward the water a little and then rolled and lodged in the cradle. The launch was postponed until the next high tide. The crowd gathered again at 10:00 p.m. and watched it glide into the water "as pretty as could be," according to an *Inquirer & Mirror* account.

Between 1802 and 1859, six large sailing ships were built and launched on Brant Point. But then Nantucket shipbuilding was reduced to small dories and catboats. The decline of whaling and the rise of gasoline-powered ships revolutionized the shipping industry and ended the golden age of sail.

The *Native* fished for many years. In 1929, it made an emergency stop in New York City so the captain could have his arm amputated after an accident. In 1933, the *Native* brought up a discharged torpedo in its dredges while fishing for sea scallops. The crew speculated that the torpedo was from navy exercises or a relic from World War I.

February 3

Cyrus Plumer, Jacob Ricke and Charles Henry Stanley, three of five American men who led a mutiny on the whale ship *Junior*, were brought to Australian Court to answer to the charges of mutiny and murder in 1858. The men were found guilty and sent to New Bedford, Massachusetts, to face criminal charges.

The Australian American consulate asked Nantucket captain Alfred Gardner, who was in Sydney on business, to sail the *Junior* back to New Bedford. The consul also placed the mutineers on the ship, locked them in cells and sent an armed escort of six guards to watch over them.

The *Junior* had left New Bedford in July 1857, and the five mutinied on Christmas night. The men attacked the cabin and shot the captain with a whaling gun, stabbed the third mate and wounded the first mate. After five days at sea, they asked the first mate to sail the ship to Australia and escaped in whaleboats within a few miles of the coast. The first mate continued into port and alerted the authorities. Throughout much of January, Australian police searched for the mutineers and located them on January 20.

At a trial in New Bedford, Captain Gardner testified he believed the whole affair had been instigated by the ship's first mate. Nonetheless, Plumer was given the death sentence and two others given five-year jail sentences. The others were not charged. Later, U.S. president James Buchanan reduced Plumer's sentence to life in prison.

February 4

The island woke up in 1871 to discover the Maine schooner *Mary Ann* flying its distress flag and trapped in the ice. It had broken from its mooring off Chatham and was dragged to within two miles north of the island. The steamer *Island Home* left to help but could get no further than Brant Point. That night, eight men pushed two dories onto the ice under the cliff and cautiously began sliding them toward the *Mary Ann*. The five crewmen were alive but cold and exhausted. The ship was nearly on its side in ten feet of water. Both crews returned to the dories and made the dangerous trip back to shore. The Massachusetts Humane Society awarded the eight rescuers of the *Mary Ann* a silver medal.

February 5

The lightship *Cross Rip*, stationed on Cross Rip Shoal in one of the most dangerous parts of Nantucket Sound, was spotted by the keeper of Great Point Lighthouse broken from its mooring, trapped in an ice flow and being pulled out to sea. The tender *Azalea* and other vessels went to the area to search but found nothing. All six men aboard were lost. Based on wind and tide conditions at the time, many later searches were conducted for wreckage, but all were inconclusive. Rescuers surmised that a moving ice pack, along with currents and tides, had snapped the sixty-three-year-old lightship from its mooring and taken it out to sea.

In 1933, the vessel *W.L. Marshall* found parts of a frame, planking and windlass believed to be from the lightship. In 1957, wreckage and artifacts found on West Dennis Beach were thought to be from the lightship, and in 1987, a lightship bell was recovered off Nauset Beach. None of these finds have ever been officially confirmed as belonging to the *Cross Rip*.

Built in 1855 in Somerset, Massachusetts, the lightship was an eighty-foot schooner, made of oak, with a metal frame on deck to hold two lights and also had a hand-cranked fog bell. A series of eleven *Cross Rip* lightships were stationed northeast of Nantucket and served mariners from 1828 until 1963, when the U.S. Coast Guard replaced it with a buoy equipped with electronics.

February 6

In 1826, *Inquirer* editor Samuel Jenks published a satirical item titled "Tattle Month," which examined the island's nickname for February: "Jubilee of Tattlers." Noting a rise in mean-spirited gossip in February, Jenks cites the perennially iced-up harbor as the culprit, because it both prevented travel and prevented the arrival of mainland news. Isolated together on their little island, Jenks said, "Tongues that had long ached with mere idleness are now exhilarated with a prospect of backbiting—and characters hitherto unassailable, or unnoticed, are dragged forth to be duly mangled secundum artem [according to art]."

Jenks suggested there is a gathering among a group of Nantucketers who decide in secret which unwitting citizen to defame and form a plan accordingly. Jenks concludes by saying a good independent newspaper is the solution to the scourge of gossip: "These agreeable recreations (incendiary gossip) served to dissipate the tedious days and weeks of Tattle Month; but now, alackaday! The truth must be told, or we are ferretted out by that abominable newspaper!"

Despite modern advances, winters are still long, and harsh winter weather still isolates Nantucket. Late in the twentieth century, Nantucket adopted a new term to describe bad behavior that typically occurs in winter: "Hate Month." Typically, "Hate Month" happens in March and refers to mean-spirited gossip intended to ruin someone's reputation. Nantucket's "Hate Month" is now one of the many little facts about island life that Nantucket Nectars prints on its juice bottle caps.

February 7

Born in 1846, Rear Admiral Seth Ackley lost his father, Captain Enoch Ackley, when he was six. Like his father, Ackley turned to the sea when he came of age. He graduated from the U.S. Naval Academy in 1866 and mustered out to fight in the Civil War. He served for twenty-two years and retired in 1901 due to health issues. He was reinstated in the U.S. Navy in 1904 by an act of Congress and promoted to rear admiral in February 1907. Ackley was stationed at the U.S. Naval Observatory in Washington, D.C.; commanded the U.S. Naval Station in Cavite, Philippines; and was a hydrographic inspector of the U.S. Coast Survey and Naval Secretary of the Lighthouse Board. Ackley died in Washington on this day in 1908. Ackley was also a member of the Grand Army of the Republic (GAR), a fraternal organization of Civil War veterans that disbanded in the 1950s when its last member died.

February 8

Captain William Cash died in 1882 one of the island's wealthiest and most respected whaling captains. But his career got off to a shaky start.

Born on Nantucket in 1816, Cash first went to sea at age thirteen on a whale ship that was lost in a fire in Oahu. On his next voyage, the ship wrecked off Long Island. In 1839, he shipped out on the *Ganges*, which was burned by the crew off the coast of Chile. He didn't make his first complete voyage until 1844, when he successfully returned home after four years at sea. Things improved for Cash, and he took command of his first whale ship in 1844. He commanded whaling voyages from Nantucket and New Bedford, made his last voyage in 1865 just as the Civil War was ending and retired a wealthy man.

February 9

Charles A. Selden began delivering the *Inquirer & Mirror* at age fourteen and soon began to submit newspaper stories. He continued to report the news through college and grew up to be a respected newspaperman working for major national newspapers. Born on Nantucket in 1870, Selden died on this day in 1949.

After graduating from Brown University, Selden and his family moved to New York City, where he reported for the *Sun*, the *New York Evening Post* and the *New York Times*. He covered World War I from Paris and remained in Europe until his retirement in 1937. He wrote the book *Are Missions a Failure?*, an analysis of American missionaries, after traveling around the world for the *Ladies' Home Journal*. Selden retired to Nantucket and lived in the family home. He was a school committee member and active in many clubs and the Nantucket Historical Association.

February 10

Led by Captain John Gardner, the "Half Share Revolt" ignited in 1677 when Peter Folger was put in jail. Nantucket was already populated by the Wampanoag people when nine English families, known as proprietors, arrived in 1659 prepared to forge a new community, and they intended to keep ownership of the island between themselves. But as more white settlers arrived, mostly tradesmen brought in to help develop the town, they objected to their lack of voice in town government and to their inability to own land.

In 1677, Folger, a Wampanoag translator and town clerk, was ordered to turn over the town records to the proprietors. Folger refused and, fearing the records would be altered, asked Gardner to hide them. Folger was jailed for not cooperating, although ultimately the governor of New York exonerated him. Residents took sides and held grudges, and the in-fighting between the proprietors and the newcomers, known as "half shares," began.

For four years, the two sides fought over the issues. Finally, after intervention from New York state authorities, the opponents agreed that the "half share men" could purchase property and that all residents would have an equal voice in town affairs. But the dispute wasn't completely settled until 1686, when Tristram Coffin's grandson married John Gardner's daughter and joined the feuding families in marriage.

February 11

With very little notice to Nantucket, the first deer hunt began in 1935. The Massachusetts legislature created a law establishing the first state-sanctioned deer hunt on Nantucket when Fish and Game officials said the herd needed culling. With a population estimated at three hundred deer, the animals were in danger of starving to death, wildlife managers said. The law created a one-time provision for a February hunt to be followed by an annual December hunt.

The townspeople were outraged by the "gangs" of off-island hunters who brought chaos to the island and killed seventy-five deer. Opponents referred to hunters as "pseudo-sportsmen who hunt tame deer." They complained of cars covered with dead carcasses driving through town. The issue was debated at town meeting that year. Newspapers in Boston, Philadelphia and Vermont ran editorials calling for a repeal of the hunting law. Summer residents wrote in to express their opposition. Local clubs held information meetings, and island legislators were taken to task for allowing it to happen.

But the annual deer hunt remained and still occurs every December. In 2005, the state tried again to institute a February deer hunt to cull the herd, now estimated at 2,000 deer. Fish and Game officials said starvation was a concern, and others supported the hunt to reduce the incidence of tick-borne disease. Hunters from all over the country arrived and killed 246 deer in one week. Once again, the island erupted in indignation and outrage. Although game wardens considered the 2005 February deer hunt successful, they have never suggested a repeat, citing the island's strong opposition.

February 12

In 1952, the tanker *Pendleton* left Louisiana headed for Boston with fuel oil, and the tanker *Fort Mercer* also left Louisiana carrying kerosene bound for Maine. Six days later, both ships would break apart off Nantucket during a powerful winter storm, and saving the crews would result in one of the U.S. Coast Guard's most dramatic sea rescues of the twentieth century.

Battered by the storm, the *Pendleton* broke in half at 6:00 a.m. on February 18, leaving its crew trapped inside the stern. All morning of that same day, the crew of the *Fort Mercer* heard loud cracks and saw oil in the water. The captain radioed the coast guard for help. At noon, the *Fort Mercer* split in half. The bow began to sink, and the stern floated free. The crew was trapped in both parts, but the stern engines still worked and the nine crewmembers there steered it away from the bow.

While searching for the *Fort Mercer*, a coast guard plane discovered the distressed *Pendleton* forty miles away. Now aware it had two sinking tankers, the coast guard sent every resource it could from Chatham and Nantucket. A thirty-six-foot lifeboat from Chatham reached the *Pendleton* and saved all but one man onboard. Five men were lost on the *Fort Mercer*, and thirteen survived. The *Fort Mercer*'s stern was salvaged and refitted with a bow. Now forty feet longer, it was rechristened the *San Jacinto* in 1953.

February 13

Clinton Mitchell Ray, known as "Mitchy," learned to make lightship baskets from his grandfather and father and was considered the last of the old-time basket makers when he died in 1956. After working off-island as a young man, Ray returned home, began making lightship baskets and opened a shop on Starbuck Court.

Lightship crew members started the tradition of making lightship baskets. Lightships were floating offshore lighthouses, and the crew members turned to basket making to keep their hands busy during long watches. The baskets are oval-shaped and made by tightly weaving flexible oak staves. Originally used for utilitarian purposes, Ray and others helped establish the lightship basket for use as women's purses.

Ray's baskets often have a paper label that reads: "I was made in Nantucket, I'm strong and I'm stout. Don't lose me or burn me. I'll never wear out. Made by Mitchell Ray of Nantucket."

February 14

In 1931, the *Inquirer & Mirror* recalled that cranberry bog workers had discovered a buried "peat sled" twenty-five years earlier. The sled, including its rope, was perfectly preserved in the dense soil of the bog and had the name Peter Chase engraved on it, who, the article said, died in 1842.

Nantucket has several low, swampy areas where cranberries and other dense vegetation grow naturally. English settlers discovered cranberries as a source of food and also harvested peat from the bogs for heat when Nantucket was blockaded during the Revolutionary War. The peat was mined, dried and burned as a heating fuel. Settlers cut peat at the Taupawshas Swamp east of town in 1778 and built roads and a drainage ditch there to give them better access. In 1880, painter Eastman Johnson captured island bogs in his famous painting *The Cranberry Harvest, Island of Nantucket*, seen here.

February 15

In 1777, Reuben Chase, age twenty-one, set off for New Hampshire to join Captain John Paul Jones in fighting the British. Chase spent most of his life at sea and had a colorful career as midshipman, privateer, merchant marine and whale ship captain. Born on Nantucket on June 23, 1754, he died on this day in 1824.

On his first voyage, aboard the U.S. warship *Ranger* heading to France with Captain Jones, the *Ranger* tangled with the British, and all were captured. Perhaps it was because the *Ranger* was the first American ship to fly the new "Stars and Stripes" flag.

Chase returned to the United States in 1778 and returned to serve under John Paul Jones as a midshipman on the French vessel the *Bon Homme Richard*. Once again, his ship battled with the British, but this time the British crew was captured. After that, Chase began a career as a privateer on French ships and returned to the United States in 1781.

Back home, Chase commanded packet ships moving goods between New York and Europe. In 1788, he began whaling as captain of the ship *Union of Nantucket* and commanded whale ships for ten years. Toward the end of his life, Chase left the sea and returned to Nantucket, where he helped form a commercial shipping company.

The character Long Tom Coffin in J. Fennimore Cooper's novel *The Pilot* is said to be based on Reuben Chase's career.

February 16

John Murray Jr. was born in 1854 on Graciosa Island, part of the Azores Islands off the coast of Portugal. Murray's father, John Murray Sr., also from the Azores, came to Nantucket as a whale ship crew member, and eventually he commanded two whaling voyages. In 1869, on his last voyage, he returned to the Azores to pick up his son, John Murray Jr., and his wife. By the time they arrived, a

community of Azorean immigrants had taken root because of the whaling industry.

The Azores were often a whale ship's first stop after leaving port, and Nantucket captains took on locals for the remainder of the voyage. Highly respected by their fellow Portuguese Nantucketers, both John Murrays were influential in their community. They helped build Alfonso's Hall, on Cherry Street (now owned by the Catholic Church), where families gathered for the Feast of the Holy Grail and other celebrations of Azorean culture.

February 17

In 1824, two crew members of the whale ship *Globe* killed the man who had led a violent, homicidal mutiny. The Nantucket ship had taken on additional crew in Hawaii, and in late January, harpooner William Comstock and four of the new crew members killed the captain and officers. Bloodthirsty and deranged, Comstock mutinied in order to create his own kingdom on the Mili Atoll, part of the Marshall Islands. But the crew feared for their lives and decided to end his life when they reached the atoll.

By the end, only two men survived: William Lay and Nantucket cooper Cyrus Hussey. The two recorded an account of their journey, and Hussey wrote:

> *17th Feb.; Comstock was discovered at some distance coming towards the tent. It had been before proposed to Smith by Payne, to shoot him; but poor Smith like ourselves, dare do no other than remain upon the side of neutrality.*
>
> *Oliver, whom the reader will recollect as one of the wretches concerned in the mutiny, hurried on shore, and with Payne and others, made preparations to put him to death…he did not make his appearance until within a short distance of the tent, which, as soon as he saw, drew his sword and walked quick towards it, in a menacing manner; but as soon as he saw a number of the muskets levelled at him, he waved his hand, and cried out, "Don't shoot me, don't shoot me! I will not hurt you!" At this moment they fired, and he fell!*

February 18

Passionate abolitionist, poet and teacher Anna Gardner died in 1901. When Gardner was six, she witnessed her parents hide runaway slave Arthur Cooper in their attic. That effort to avoid a bounty hunter set Gardner on a lifelong path of fighting against slavery and for social justice. Born on Nantucket in 1816, Gardner organized three Nantucket antislavery conventions in the early 1840s. She was the secretary of the Nantucket Anti-Slavery Society and the second person on the island to subscribe to William Lloyd Garrison's abolitionist newspaper, the *Liberator*.

In her early twenties, Gardner taught at the African School but quit in protest soon after her star pupil, Eunice Ross, was denied entrance to the public high school. Over the next two decades, Gardner published poetry and essays, lectured frequently and continued teaching. At fifty years old, she left for Charlottesville, Virginia, where she started a free school for students of African descent.

February 19

In 1900, exterminators spent the week scattering poisoned corn in prairie dog nests all over the island. Ten years earlier, someone had imported two pair of prairie dogs to hunt rats, and within a decade, they threatened to overrun the island. When it appeared the prairie dogs had invaded the golf courses, the issue went to town meeting for a vote. The U.S. Department of Agriculture noted the infestation in its 1901 yearbook:

> *Mr. Outram Bangs wrote in December 1899 that when on a visit to the island during the summer and fall of the same year he counted 200 prairie dogs visible at one time in one colony and states that three or four such colonies existed besides many scattering pairs and small colonies.*
>
> *W.W. Neifert writing from Nantucket under date of February 12[,] 1900[,] states that…at a recent town meeting a committee was appointed with a view of exterminating them and an appropriation of $350 was made to procure poison. In a subsequent letter Mr. Neifert writes, "In addition to the $350 raised by the town about $200 was subscribed by farmers and others interested. The poisoning scheme was adopted and bisulphide of carbon was the drug. A bunch of old nigs was saturated and placed in the mouth of the burrow and the hole closed with dirt or sod. This method was simple and inexpensive but did the work successfully and now there is not a dog left to tell the tale."*

February 20

Two years after her parents arrived from England, Mary Coffin Starbuck was born in 1645 in Haverhill, Massachusetts. Her father, Tristram Coffin, was one of the first white men to settle Nantucket and moved his family there in 1660. In 1662, Mary married Nathaniel Starbuck, also an original English settler. Nathaniel and Mary shared February 20 as their birthday. Nathaniel was born in New Hampshire in 1634.

Mary gave birth to the island's first white child at age eighteen and had ten children, of whom eight survived. In 1701, at age fifty-six, Mary converted from Puritanism and began preaching. Her devout belief in Quakerism, which emphasizes each person's direct connection to God through his or her "inner light," helped make it the island's dominant religion during her lifetime. "Great Mary of Nantucket" wielded power and was known for moving and eloquent sermons. The Quaker faith took root at the same time that island captains and merchants began to dominate the whaling industry.

She organized public gatherings and town meetings, and for many years, both worship and political meetings were held in her home, known as "Parliament House." The first Nantucket Quaker meetinghouse, built for worship, was opened in 1711, but Mary did not live to see the official Nantucket Monthly Meeting, which was established on May 16, 1780. She died on Nantucket on September 13, 1717, at the age of seventy-two.

February 21

Ten people living at the Nantucket Asylum and Poor House died in a fire in 1844. In 1822, voters embarked on a social experiment designed to save money and rehabilitate the indigent. They decided to build an asylum and poorhouse in an uninhabited section of the island known as Quaise. Far from town on the island's northeast corner, the taxpayer-funded asylum and workhouse occupied 237 acres and opened in 1823. At the time, many other towns were also creating asylums and workhouses to cut the cost of subsidizing the poor. The unemployed were sent to the poorhouse for hard labor, in the hopes of reforming them into contributing citizens, and the elderly, infirm or mentally ill were sent to the asylum.

The 1844 fire resulted in the Quaise asylum's demise. On a bitter night, the keeper's daughter-in-law awoke to discover the blaze. Rescuers from the adjoining farm came to help but were too few in number. In addition, many of the patients were disoriented and confused. The town rebuilt the Quaise asylum in 1845 but dismantled it and moved it to Orange Street in 1854. In 1905, the building was renamed Our Island Home and was used solely to care for the sick and elderly. In 1981, a new nursing home, also called Our Island Home, opened, and the former asylum building was renamed the Landmark House and was converted into apartments for low-income, elderly and disabled residents.

February 22

Captain Thomas F. Sandsbury served as keeper to two Nantucket Life-Saving Stations and received many medals from the Massachusetts Humane Society for his bravery. He served the Muskeget station from 1883 to 1886 and the Great Neck station on Tuckernuck from 1891 until his death on this day in 1903.

One rescue, in February 1888, involved three schooners stranded near Muskeget, a small island located off Nantucket's western end. Sandsbury and his crew of "surfmen spent three days bringing all aboard to shore. The schooners *Alba*, from New Brunswick; and *Lyndon* and *Sammy Ford*, from Maine, all left Martha's Vineyard part of a large group of vessels. The larger vessels avoided getting caught in the ice, but the five schooners were trapped and swept towards Muskeget." On February 15, rescuers stationed at Muskeget awoke to discover them stranded along the beach. Other vessels rescued two crews and Sandsbury's men spent three days bringing the rest ashore.

February 23

In 1783, a Nantucket whale ship was the first vessel to fly an American flag in British waters. Nantucket whaling merchants had a very profitable trade with Britain at the time of the American Revolution and tried to stay neutral during the conflict, but it had a price. In 1775, when Nantucket pledged its loyalty to the Crown, the king exempted the tiny, but dominant, maritime powerhouse from a British fishing and trade embargo. This made Nantucket ships a target for the architects of the American Revolution, who seized island ships and prohibited the colonies from doing business with Nantucket.

Some Nantucket merchants relocated to the Falkland Islands so they could trade with Britain. Others negotiated an agreement with Massachusetts in 1779 that gave them permission to ask the British not to attack their ships—another action considered traitorous by supporters of the Revolution.

As the war wound down and a peace treaty between Britain and the colonies seemed likely, William Rotch put his dry-docked whale ship *Bedford* back in service, flew the new American flag and sent it to London with a load of whale oil. But Rotch soon learned that Britain now put an exorbitant tax on imported whale oil, supposedly to protect its own fledging whaling industry, but also probably in retribution for America's new independence. Once again, Nantucket whaling merchants had to adapt to political forces dictating profits. Some debated seceding from the new America and others relocated to Nova Scotia to continue to trade tax-free with England.

February 24

An item in the *Inquirer* in 1854 reports on a new New Bedford, Martha's Vineyard Nantucket Steamship Company that planned to offer commercial service to Nantucket. In addition, two railroad companies were also planning to establish a boat line. "A little opposition in steamboating here would be no disadvantage to our own community," the editor noted.

Commercial service began in the early 1800s, and the popularity of railroad travel in the 1880s helped grow the island's summer tourism industry. The 1870s brought the first regular winter service, as the steamers were now powerful enough to break out of icy harbors. But the boat lines notoriously lost money and were not reliable. Service became more chaotic in the 1900s as rail travel declined and later when the U.S. Navy took steamships for World War I and World War II. In 1948, the Massachusetts legislature established a steamship authority, which has offered steady service ever since.

February 25

Benjamin Lawrence was born in 1799 and shipped out as boatsteerer in the ill-fated whale ship *Essex* in 1819. In 1820, the *Essex* was rammed and sunk by a whale in the South Pacific. Twenty of the crew, including Lawrence, set out in three small whaleboats. After drifting at sea, they landed on uninhabited Henderson Island, where they remained for as long as possible.

But when food and water ran out, three men chose to stay and the rest departed. With no food on the boats, the men resorted to cannibalism in order to survive. On February 18, 1821, the British brig *Indian* rescued the three men in Lawrence's boat. They reunited in Chile with other *Essex* survivors Captain George Pollard and Charles Ramsdell. Lawrence Benjamin returned to Nantucket in June 1821.

News of the sinking of the *Essex* traveled quickly among the whalers, and soon Herman Melville, at sea on board a whale ship, heard the story. There were other cases of whales ramming ships, but most *Moby-Dick* scholars cite the sensational story of the *Essex* and its crew as the inspiration for Melville's classic American novel.

Lawrence went on to command ships from other ports. When he retired from the sea, he bought a farm in Siasconset. He was also keeper at the Asylum and Poor House, located in Quidnet, from 1823 to 1854. He had seven children and died in March 1878 at eighty years old.

February 26

In the final chapter of a deadly voyage, the brig *Ann Eliza* of Maine shipwrecked on Nantucket's western end in 1829. The *Ann Eliza* left Palermo, Sicily, bound for Boston with a cargo of wine in late 1828. It came upon the sinking French brig *L'aimable* and took the French captain and crew onboard. Near Fayal, in the Azores, the French crew jumped overboard and swam for shore, although the captain and mate remained. On the trip across the Atlantic, the *Ann Eliza*'s captain, William P. Barstow of Boston, was lost overboard. And, almost home, the *Ann Eliza* lost its sails in a severe storm in Boston Bay and began to drift.

At 8:00 p.m., the boat came ashore on Nantucket and filled with water. All but one of the crew members, including the French captain and mate, were saved.

The wreck of the *Ann Eliza*, along with others that year, inspired the editor of the *Inquirer* to call for a series of "humane houses" to be built on the island's shores. The editor argued that seven 1829 fatalities caused by shipwrecks might have been avoided if shelters were available. Humane houses were built on Nantucket and equipped with blankets, lanterns and wood for heat. These were patterned after other houses built by the Boston-based Humane Society, established in 1785 to aid shipwreck victims. In time, the U.S. Life-Saving Service, formed in 1871, stationed crews of "surfmen" at Life-Saving Stations around Nantucket and its two islands, Muskeget and Tuckernuck.

February 27

The arrival of the steamer *Nantucket* in 1904 was front-page news. Under the headline "The Agony Is Over," the newspaper announced that the steamboat arrived for the first time in fourteen days, bringing one passenger, seventy-eight sacks of newspapers and twenty-three letter pouches. Heavy ice prevented the steamer from entering the jetties, and the crew unloaded cargo into small boats, which island boys pushed across the ice to Brant Point. The lone passenger, Linus H. Long, walked ashore.

A large crowd turned out, eager for news of the mainland and curious to watch the spectacle of dory-delivered mail. Onshore at Brant Point, a group of five passengers waited to board the *Nantucket* and leave. The ladies were put in a skiff outfitted with blades and pushed to the steamer while the men walked beside. It took the postmaster and his clerks six and a half hours to sort and deliver the mail.

A week earlier, the *New York Times* had reported, "The ice situation about Nantucket was worse today than at any time this Winter, and the island is held firmly in the grasp of a fourth blockade. The immense floes are piling upon each other, and as seen from the life-saving stations the ice on the shoals is a least fifty feet high."

February 28

In 1906, teenager John Egle fled Latvia when his revolutionary activities attracted the notice of Russian Cossacks. Egle, with his friend Charles Duce, stowed away inside a freighter and settled in London. The next year, his brother Max, also an émigré who had settled in Boston, sent for the two men. In 1910, the Egle brothers came to Nantucket. John was a fisherman and boat captain and worked in Max's small engine repair shop.

In 1920, the brothers were hunting when Max mentioned feeling ill. Ten days later, Max died of pneumonia, and seven days after that, his thirteen-year-old son died. Still feeling the effects of the 1918 influenza pandemic, Nantucket papers in 1920 contain many notices of islanders perishing from the flu.

John Egle lived to be 101 years old and died on this day in 1988. He began painting in his 80s and created three hundred artworks between the ages of 86 and 98.

February 29

By the mid-1850s, Nantucket whaling was on the decline, as was the island's population. The whaling industry never quite recovered from a devastating fire in 1846, mariners struggled to get ships over a sandbar that had formed at the entrance to the harbor and large numbers of able-bodied men went west in search of a fortune in California gold. Nantucket made the 1840 U.S. census list of "100 Largest Urban Places" at number 42 with 9,012 residents. By 1860, the U.S. census listed 6,194 residents and by 1870 (shortly after the last whaling voyage left from Nantucket), 4,123 residents.

In an 1856 issue of the *Inquirer*, the editor addressed an upcoming vote deciding how to deal with the dwindling enrollment at school. Voters would decide the following day whether to close one of three grammar schools and split the students between the remaining schools. The empty school would be turned into a high school. The editor wrote in favor of the consolidation: "The number of scholars in our public schools is yearly diminishing, and we have been informed upon good authority that within the past four or five years the numbers of scholars in our public schools between the ages of five and ten years has decreased from 1,800 to 1,400 and continues to decrease."

March 1

In 1946, the Massachusetts Steamship Company took over the holdings of the defunct Island Line in New Bedford. It established service to Nantucket and immediately raised fares, which outraged the island. The boat line posted losses for much of its two years, and when it appeared yet another private steamship line would fail, the government created a committee to investigate ways to ensure dependable boat service to the islands.

Out of that came the New Bedford, Woods Hole, Martha's Vineyard and Nantucket Steamship Authority, a state agency charged with providing passenger, car and freight service to Martha's Vineyard and Nantucket. In 1948, the authority purchased the Massachusetts Steamboat Company's holdings for $1.3 million and began service. In 1960, the authority dropped New Bedford from its route as a cost-cutting measure. Gradually, the steamship authority purchased new boats that were diesel-powered and sold its last steamship in 1987.

March 2

In 1843, Nantucket whale ships were scattered across the globe, and their ship's logs report seeing a comet. On this day in 1843, the *Charles Carroll*, located in the Pacific Ocean, tersely notes in its log, "Saw the comet."

The *Washington*'s captain, James Coffin, in the Indian Ocean, wrote, "Saw a comet star ablazing."

On the *Nantucket*, master George Washington Gardner Jr. wrote, "March 4: Cruising on equator. Immediately after sunset saw something to the West that had the appearance of the tail of a Comet extending from the horizon up about 18 degrees and the comet appeared to be below the horizon but a short distance. March 5: At dark saw the comet very plain a most beautiful one with a tail about 15 degrees long."

Reuben Russell, master of the *Susan* off the coast of Rarotonga, wrote: "March 4: At half past 7 p.m. about 8 degrees above the horizon we saw a remarkable bright Comet bearing west of us the tail of which extended about 30 degrees upward…at 8 it disappeared in the western horizon.

"March 5: We observed the Comet again last evening at about 7 o'clock which showed very brilliant…the star itself was about 10 degrees above the horizon the tail of which extended about 20 degrees pointing upwards from the sun…it bore west of us and south from the moon about 20 degrees…they set about 8 p.m."

March 3

By the late 1700s, whalers traveled farther than ever from home in search of whales. In 1789, first mate Archaelus Hammond, a Nantucket mariner on the English-owned *Amelia*, became the first westerner to successfully

harpoon a whale in the Pacific Ocean and unwittingly started a new chapter in whaling history.

Fifty years later, thousands of men on board hundreds of whale ships fished in fifteen areas of the Pacific Ocean. Nantucket mariners, away for four years at a time, spent as much time at ports in Chile, the Sandwich Islands (now Hawaii), New Zealand and Tahiti as they did at home. They sailed into places previously unknown. Forever chasing the whales, ships also established whaling grounds in the Arctic. The Pacific coast towns traded with the whalers and flourished, including the businesses that catered to sailors: taverns, brothels and gaming houses. Records from Honolulu and Lahaina indicate those towns had full jails and busy courthouses during the whaling era, and Lahaina also established a hospital (pictured here) to care for American sailors.

March 4

On this day in 1861, Edwin M. Stanton stepped down as the twenty-fifth United States attorney general under President James Buchanan. The following year, new U.S. president Abraham Lincoln tapped him for secretary of war, a position he held for six years. Stanton grew up in Ohio in a Quaker family. His grandmother Abigail Macy was born on Nantucket and left with the family in 1774. A Democrat who opposed slavery, Stanton began his career as a lawyer.

In 1856, he moved to Washington, D.C., where he built a successful career, receiving a lot of notice when he successfully used an insanity defense during the sensational trial of politician Daniel Sickles in 1859. Sickles was charged with killing his wife's lover, Philip Barton Key II, the son of Francis Scott Key.

During the Civil War, Stanton's efficient strategies helped manage the North's massive military resources and helped guide the Union to victory. After President Lincoln's assassination, he served President Andrew Johnson as secretary of war during Reconstruction's early years. But Stanton opposed the new administration's leniency toward former Confederate states, and Johnson tried to dismiss him. That action ultimately led to Johnson's impeachment by the House of Representatives.

After retiring in 1868, Stanton returned to law, and in 1869, Johnson's successor, President Ulysses S. Grant, nominated him as associate justice of the Supreme Court; however, Stanton died four days after his nomination was confirmed by the Senate.

March 5

Crispus Attucks was killed in the Boston Massacre in 1770 and is regarded to be the first casualty of the American Revolution. Details about Attucks's life are unclear. He was of either Wampanoag or African descent, and he may have been an escaped slave or a free man. Historians are cautious in claiming to know much about him, other than that he died instantly. But eighty years later, abolitionists were less careful about the details when they made him a martyr and war hero.

In 1851, Boston abolitionist William C. Nell petitioned the legislature for $1,500 to build a statue in Attucks's honor. In the petition, Nell, using the memoirs of an eyewitness, retold the massacre's story. In it, an eyewitness identified Attucks as a Nantucket Wampanoag in port on a Nantucket whale ship. "Mr. Pierce...remembers Attucks distinctly, though he never saw him before. He also remembers that he had a large stick in his hand, and that he saw him early in the tumult harassing and abusing the sentry, poking him severely with the stick, and calling him 'Lobster,'" said Nell's petition.

Historians do agree that Attucks was a sailor on board whaling ships. He had just arrived on a ship from the Bahamas and was scheduled to leave on another bound for North Carolina.

Nell got the legislature to establish a "Crispus Attucks Day" in 1858, and in 1888, the state dedicated a statue to all the massacre victims on Boston Common.

March 6

Whaling master Charles Veeder left Nantucket in September 1848 in command of the *Nauticon*. During the four-year trip, the *Nauticon* would travel around the Cape of Good Horn to Chile, then to Oahu, Tahiti and north to the Arctic and then back to Nantucket. Veeder brought his wife, Susan, and their two boys, ages six and thirteen, on the trip. Susan Veeder kept a journal, entering information about life on board the *Nauticon*, and painted beautiful watercolor images from her travels. On this day in 1849, Susan gave birth to a baby daughter she named Mary Frances. In her journal, she notes, "And then I was confined with a fine daughter weighing 9 lbs. which was very pleasing to us both and so things went along about as they should."

But sadly, Mary Frances died on March 6, 1850, in Tahiti when she was given an unknown powder to ease the discomfort of her teething. Veeder wrote, "At 11 o'clock am she breathed her last. What shall be done with our darling was the next question with us both. Could we think of burying her in Tahita [sic]. No we could not. We must take her with us away, so we have had a lead coffin made and the corpse embalmed to take home with us."

March 7

The schooner *Mount Hope* left Nantucket on a whaling voyage in the Atlantic Ocean in 1812 and, on July 9, became the first Nantucket ship to be captured and burned by the British, a casualty of the War of 1812.

When the war began, most Nantucket whale ships were at sea. Some returned home when they heard the news. Others, however, were captured by British cruisers and privateers and sent to Barbados and Halifax, Nova Scotia.

Nantucket ships in the Pacific were seized by Peruvian corsairs who claimed to be allies of Great Britain. In Talcahuano, Chile, a bustling port that hosted whale ships from all over the world, twelve Nantucket ships were among a large number of American whalers that were captured. Joel R. Poinsett, who had been sent to Chile by the United States government to protect its interests, joined the Chilean army and helped retake the city and free the Americans in Peru.

Shortly after that, Captain David Porter in the frigate *Essex* put an end to the attacks on American ships. Porter, who became an admiral, captured many English whalers and used them to assemble a small squadron that swept the English and Peruvians from the area. During the War of 1812, Nantucket lost forty-six ships, which was about half the fleet. But by 1820, the Nantucket fleet had grown to seventy-two ships, and Nantucket went back to work hunting whales all over the world.

March 8

Born in Brooklyn, New York, in 1826, Roland Coffin was educated and received his love of the ocean on Nantucket. Like most of his island relatives, Coffin went to sea, and from 1850 to 1860, he captained the whale ship *Senator* and then joined the U.S. Navy to fight in the Civil War. During the war, Coffin was mainly stationed in the North Atlantic Blockading Squadron.

While off-duty, Coffin learned shorthand writing and, after leaving the navy in 1863, became a reporter for the *New York World* newspaper, for which he reported on marine news and yachting. He published short stories in the book *An Old Sailor's Yarns* in 1884 and *The America's Cup: How It Was Won by the Yacht* America *in 1851 and Has Been Since Defended*. Coffin died in 1888, and his *New York World* co-workers purchased his memorial at Prospect Hill cemetery as a tribute.

March 9

On this day in 1877, the bark *WF Marshall* of St. Johns, New Brunswick, ran aground on the south shore in a thick fog. The captain had no idea he was in shallow water until the ship was in the onshore waves, and then it was too late. Unable to get to land, patrolmen from the Life-Saving Station on the beach threw a line with a sling to the vessel, and the fourteen crewmen and a child were safely brought to shore using a rope-and-pulley system.

Twelve days later, the Italian bark *Papa Luigi* from Sicily wrecked a half mile south of the *WF Marshall*. Again, the crew made it to the beach with the help of the Life-Saving Station crew. The crew members reported that at 4:00 p.m., they passed by the *South Shoal* lightship, but the fog was heavy. Shortly after that, the vessel thumped heavily on something, and the crew soon discovered it was leaking. It struck the Nantucket shore at 9:00 p.m. Not even two years old, the 456-ton *Papa Luigi* was bought by local salvagers, who stripped the sails and rigging. On March 30, Henry H. Nickerson, a Nantucket member of the Life-Saving Station crew, fell from the main topsail yard while working on the vessel and died.

In July, at considerable expense, a Boston firm purchased the brand-new *WF Marshall* and tried to relaunch it, but a storm thwarted the effort. The new owners gave up and left the ship to be broken up by a wrecking crew.

March 10

Despite a 1789 Massachusetts law requiring towns to establish public schools for all, Nantucket did not adhere to the letter of the law until 1827. Leaders had been discussing access to free education since 1818 and established a segregated public elementary school for nonwhite pupils in 1825.

But newspaper editor Samuel Jenks argued that the state mandate was intended to serve all children and lobbied the state's attorney to enforce the law on Nantucket. In 1827, the town added four additional public elementary schools and allowed any island student to enroll. A public high school opened in 1838.

An 1818 study had revealed that three hundred children ranging in ages from three to fourteen did not attend school and the selectmen's call for taxpayer-funded free schools for all ages was unsuccessful. At that time pupils who did attend school were educated privately or for free at "charity schools.

Finally in 1827, Nantucket appropriated $2,500 to create public schools and a school committee, and 350 pupils enrolled.

Also in 1827, Sir Admiral Issac Coffin, a veteran of the Royal Navy, funded a school for descendants of Tristram Coffin, an original settler whose grandson was the admiral's grandfather. The Coffin School opened in 1827 with 230 students.

March 11

William Rotch and Samuel Starbuck traveled to Philadelphia, Pennsylvania, and submitted a petition to the U.S. Congress in 1782 seeking permission for Nantucket whale ships to sail unmolested by American ships fighting for independence.

Nantucket tried hard to stay out of the conflict caused by the war, but its neutrality made the island a target for both the British and the Americans. Blocked and harassed by both parties, soon the island was facing starvation. Islanders negotiated a special deal in 1780 with the British that allowed a few island ships to trade with England at a time when both sides were embargoing all transactions, which only caused American soldiers to target Nantucket harder.

Two years later, Nantucket's economy now hobbled by the war, Congress took up Rotch and Starbuck's petition. In its report, the committee found "that the inhabitants of Nantucket have been and still continue in a very distressed state owing to the destruction of their whale fishery." The committee recommended that Nantucket ships be "provided with a Certificate from the Selectmen of said Island that she is bona fide the property of the inhabitants of said Island and provided further that nothing be found on board her but the necessary whaling utensils provisions for the voyage and the product of the fish taken therein."

March 12

Artist Frank Swift Chase was born in 1886. Chase visited Nantucket in 1919 and returned the following year to open an art school. A founder of the Artists' Association of Nantucket, he taught and summered on Nantucket for thirty years, and historians credit Chase with establishing Nantucket as a mid-twentieth-century art colony.

In his twenties, he studied painting at the Art Students League in New York City and Woodstock, New York. While in Woodstock, Chase lived at Byrdcliffe, Ralph Whitehead's Catskills experiment in utopian living. He also helped found the Woodstock Artists' Association. But it was Nantucket that captured him, and he brought other renowned artists who worked in a variety of mediums. They, alongside local artists, spent summers creating art inspired by Nantucket's beauty and history.

In 1940, Chase founded the Sarasota School of Art in Longboat Key, Florida. He died in New York on July 3, 1958.

March 13

In 1861, the town learned of the death of the island's wealthiest citizen, Joseph Starbuck, in the *Inquirer*. Born in 1774, Starbuck owned the whale ships *President*, *Hero*, *Omega*, *Three Brothers*, *Loper* and *Young*. They made over fifty voyages, bringing

back more than eighty thousand barrels of oil valued at an estimated $2.5 million. In 1838, Joseph Starbuck built the last whaler constructed on Nantucket and named it after himself: the Joseph Starbuck.

In 1836, Starbuck hired Christopher Capen to build three brick homes on Main Street for his sons: William, Matthew and George. Now architectural icons that illustrate the magnitude of wealth that whaling brought to Nantucket, the homes, nicknamed "The Three Bricks," are of a transitional Federal–Greek Revival style. A departure from the plain Quaker homes the island was accustomed to and a symbol of Starbuck's wealth, the large two-and-a-half-story residences were bigger and more stylish than any other homes on Nantucket.

March 14

In 1846 on this day, the ship *Earl of Eglington* from Scotland, went aground at Tom Nevers. Captain John Niven described the event in an 1881 letter, writing:

> *When near noon finding the water shoaling and imagining in the absence of sights that we were seaward of Nantucket Shoals, I hauled up, but still we shoaled at noon. The ship slightly grazed the bottom and the boatswain, an old shellback of threescore years, fainted in the chains. As soon as we again reached deep water the best bower was let go and sixty fathoms of cable veered out but his Lordship barely tightened the chain when it parted and off we went in as dense a fog as is ever seen on the shoals.*

Drifting with six feet of water in the hold, Niven beached the vessel at Tom Nevers, and eight crewmen left for shore. The boats capsized, and all but two men drowned. A crowd on the beach and instructed the remaining crew how to set up a rescue line with a sling to bring each person safely to shore.

Nivens wrote, "Well everlasting thanks and unceasing gratitude are all that the principal actor in these scenes can render to the noble band of islanders who left their warm habitations on that tempestuous morning in March to rescue entire strangers and foreigners."

March 15

In 1775, Massachusetts governor Thomas Hutchinson attended Britain's House of Lords to witness a debate on the New England Restraining Act, Britain's retaliation for the American colonies boycott of English goods. Hutchinson was a prominent Massachusetts businessman and politician known for his loyalty to England, but his politics caused both sides to mistrust him. The act ordered the colonies to only trade with Britain. It also barred New England ships from fishing North Atlantic fisheries, a disastrous development for the burgeoning Nantucket whaling fleet.

Hutchinson wrote in his diary: "The first witness was Seth Jenkins a ship master of Nantucket who was asked a great number of questions, most of them impertinent and others improper, what he thought the people would do with their vessels if the whaling should be stopped, which the Bill provides against, and whether the people would not be likely to go to Halifax [Nova Scotia] if they could not maintain themselves at Nantucket. To which he answered No. Why not? Because they did not like the government. Why did not they like it? Because they had a notion of its being military, or something like it, as they had always troops there."

The king approved the act on March 30, and in April, it was extended to include colonies in the mid-Atlantic but did not include New York, North Carolina, Delaware and Georgia because the government mistakenly believed those colonies did not oppose taxes levied by England.

March 16

Robert Folger Walcutt was born on Nantucket in 1797. Walcutt attended Harvard Divinity School, where he would begin a lifelong commitment to ending slavery and to Unitarianism. He served as pastor to a Cape Cod Unitarian congregation briefly but was dismissed for his antislavery views.

A friend of William Lloyd Garrison, Walcutt joined the New England and American Anti-slavery Societies and adopted Garrison's nonresistance and anti-Sabbatarian views. He first served as accountant, and then Garrison appointed him general agent in 1846. Walcutt's new position made him one of the antislavery movement's most important administrators, a post he held until 1865.

Although less known to the public than his colleagues, Walcutt published and distributed the lectures and letters of abolitionist orators in the *Liberator* and in pamphlets under the antislavery society's book publishing arm, 21 Cornhill.

Walcutt died in Boston on March 1, 1884.

March 17

Henry Coffin was born on Nantucket in 1807, when the island was the world capital of whaling. After attending the Quaker Boarding School in Providence, Rhode Island, Henry and his brother Charles took over their father's shipping business. In operation for most of the 1800s, the fleet owned by the firm Charles G. & Henry Coffin consisted of some of Nantucket's most famous whale ships. The

1840 voyage of the *Charles & Henry*, a ship that sailed from New Bedford, had a young crew member on board named Herman Melville. Melville later wrote about this experience in his autobiographical novel *Omoo*.

Coffin was one of the largest landowners on Nantucket at the time and built a grand, brick home on Main Street for his new wife, Eliza Starbuck. They married in 1833 and had five children. His brother Charles built an equally grand home across the street. Coffin died at ninety-three in 1900.

March 18

Captain Charles Grant, the most successful whaling master on Nantucket, died almost penniless in 1906. Grant brought back a record fifty-two thousand barrels of whale oil. Many credit Grant's inability to hang on to his wealth to his extreme generosity. He was born on October 29, 1874, to a Nantucket mother and a Scottish father, who had landed on the island after a shipwreck and stayed. Captain Grant died on this day in 1906.

Captain Grant first went to sea at age eleven and spent fifty-six years traveling the world on whale ships. He received his first command at thirty. On his next voyage, his wife, Nancy, one of the first Nantucket wives to go to sea, joined him, and she sailed with him on many voyages for thirty-two years, until he retired in 1881. All three of their children were born during Pacific whaling cruises.

March 19

The first Nantucket newspaper began publishing in 1816. Several papers had started up and failed until 1821, when Joseph C. Melcher started the *Inquirer*. It grew quickly, buoyed in part by the writing and ability of its editor, Samuel H. Jenks. Many competitors attempted to cut into the *Inquirer*'s readership with varying degrees of success. On this day in 1840, Nantucket's fifth newspaper, the *Islander*, began publishing.

Island Democrats backed the *Islander* (the *Inquirer* took a conservative position and staunchly supported the Whig Party) and hired Charles C. Hazewell, a young reporter from the *Boston Post*, as editor. Hazewell was a prolific writer and put the *Islander* in the middle of the hottest topics of the day. Pushing the Democrats' agenda, the *Islander* engaged in a fierce political campaign. The next year, the *Islander* championed the abolitionist platform and helped defeat a group trying to prevent antislavery meetings from being held on the island.

The paper was printed in a building that stood on the corner of Cambridge Street and Coal Lane until March 1843, when it was discontinued. The equipment of the *Islander* was purchased by two young aspiring journalists who started the *Weekly Telegraph* in June 1844. The *Telegraph* became Nantucket's first daily newspaper, and soon after, the *Inquirer* followed. Ten years later, Edward Cobb purchased both newspapers, discontinued the *Telegraph* and continued publishing the *Inquirer*.

March 20

In 1687, Nantucket property taxes—a payment of either one lamb or two shillings—were due, and residents were to pay them to the state of New York.

Members of the Wampanoag tribe lived on Nantucket without much interaction with Europeans until 1602, when Bartholomew Gosnold, an English lawyer, privateer and explorer, spotted the cliffs of Sankaty Head while scouting new territories for the English. Once they knew about Nantucket, the English started buying land. In 1641, Thomas Mayhew, a Boston and Martha's Vineyard businessman, was the first white person to purchase land from members of the Wampanoag tribe.

In 1659, a group of nine New Hampshire businessmen bought Mayhew's share for thirty pounds and two beaver hats (one for Mayhew and one for his wife). The following year, the new settlers moved to Nantucket in the hopes of creating a community.

As the town grew, settlers purchased more land from the Native Americans, and the record books are full of court cases disputing ownership. In order to simplify, town fathers organized a general grant of the entire island, which was finalized in 1687. An elaborate document, the grant created a corporation called the Trustees of the Freeholders of the Town of Sherburne and put seven men in charge of its oversight. The trustees could purchase land from Native Americans and confirm the title and levy the tax.

An act of Parliament in 1692 transferred Nantucket, Martha's Vineyard and the Elizabeth Islands to Massachusetts. Nantucket had been a part of Dukes County but became its own county when it joined Massachusetts.

March 21

The Honorable Peter Coffin, eldest child of Tristram and Dionis, was born in England in 1631 and died in New Hampshire on this day in 1715.

Coffin was one of the original purchasers of Nantucket and, some say, the wealthiest. On Nantucket, he owned a large mill and had been a merchant in New Hampshire before moving to the island. He didn't stay on Nantucket long, moving back to New Hampshire, where he served as a lieutenant in 1675 in King Philip's Indian War, a legislator, a judge and a member of the governor's council.

Coffin was made a Nantucket magistrate, and early records show him buying land and gifting acreage to his eight children. The lumber for his son Jethro's house, now the oldest house still standing, was the product of one of his mills.

March 22

Four schooners left Chatham, Massachusetts, bound for New York on this day in 1829. Three voyages would end the same day, wrecked on Nantucket's eastern shore during a furious snowstorm. The schooner *Ranger*, carrying spars, hit near Squam Pond. Shortly after that, the *Ann*, carrying lime, came ashore near the *Ranger.*

The *Ranger*'s captain and mate were able to get off the ship and took refuge in a shed, but three crewmen froze to death on board. On the *Ann*, the captain and two men survived, but the captain's two sons and another died. Although able to make it ashore, the boys' strength had given out, and the captain carried them about a mile looking for shelter. However, both died before reaching it. Exhausted and cold, the captain crawled the final distance to a house.

The town took in the survivors and buried their dead. All the island's clergymen conducted the funerals, and their remains were brought to the cemetery in a procession of a hearse and two carts followed by many townspeople who attended the burials. Another schooner that had departed Chatham that day also came ashore on the eastern end but was able to get off when the tide and the wind changed direction. Later, the schooner was spotted without masts, taking on water, with no signs of anyone on board. Island mariners concluded that all hands were lost, and the ship broke up on the shoals off Nantucket.

March 23

The brig *Sarah Ann*, traveling from Savannah to Boston with a cargo of rice and cotton, went aground on shoals on the south side of the island, near Hummock Pond, on this day in 1828. The crew tried to refloat it by setting the anchors and then throwing the cargo overboard but still could not get the ship off the shoal. Heavy wind and surf drove the ship far up onto shore, and after several days of trying, the crew abandoned the rescue effort.

The *Sarah Ann* was sold at auction on March 28 to P.H. Folger, who invested $2,497. After the sale, salvagers were able to refloat the *Sarah Ann* and put it back in use. It was then sold in Boston to Obediah Woodbury in July for $2,736. Hearing the news that the *Sarah Ann* was back in Boston and ready to sail again, the New England Insurance Company, which had underwritten the disastrous 1828 voyage, disputed ownership of the title, claiming that the captain was not authorized to sell the vessel. A lawsuit followed, which eventually went to the Massachusetts Supreme Court.

The defense argued that very few vessels stranded on Nantucket's south and west shores are recovered intact, and so the captain, who made the call the abandon the rescue effort, had no way of knowing the *Sarah Ann* would survive. The court agreed with the argument and sided in favor of Woodbury.

March 24

The town celebrated when the Nantucket Atheneum hosted its first regular lecture on this day in 1847. Formed as a private institution in 1835 and intended to be a place of learning, the building and its contents were lost in the Great Fire on July 13 in 1846. Proprietors were able to raise money from every state in the Union to rebuild and opened the new building in January, just five months after the fire. With its impressive Greek Revival façade, the new Atheneum helped reestablish a downtown leveled by fire. In its coverage of the lecture, the *Inquirer* said, "It was a cheerful sight, last Thursday evening, to see the Atheneum lighted once more for a lecture—the first time since the fire. The well-wishers of the Institution, must also have been pleased with the large attendance."

The lecturer, Reverend Osgood, spoke about "The New England Home."

March 25

The Massachusetts legislature guaranteed that every child would have access to public school regardless of race in 1845. The ruling came about in part because of a petition submitted by a group of African American Nantucketers. Although they may have opposed slavery, the island's white islanders overwhelmingly supported a segregated society.

The island's African Americans boycotted the schools after many years of bitter town meeting debate about whether to desegregate. Most African Americans lived in a neighborhood called New Guinea. At the time of the American Revolution, there were about one hundred people living there. By the 1830s, fugitive and freed slaves had swelled that number to five hundred.

In 1845, African American leader Edward Pompey petitioned the state legislature, calling for an end to school segregation. Over one hundred Nantucket African Americans signed it. Some members of the white community responded with an anti-integration petition of their own, while others submitted petitions in support of desegregation.

Absalom Boston, a wealthy leader in the island's African American community, sued the town when his daughter was not allowed to attend public high school. When it became clear Boston had the financial means and the drive to pursue the matter in court, the town finally voted to integrate the schools.

March 26

Many historians believe Scandinavian explorers passed by or landed on Nantucket in the eighth, ninth and tenth centuries. But there is little evidence to prove that they did.

In 1602 on this day, a lawyer, explorer and veteran sailor named Bartholomew Gosnold left Falmouth, England, bound for the New World. Gosnold is considered to be the first European explorer to see the eastern shore of North America. Funded by his patron, the Earl of Southampton, he set out with a small bark and thirty-two men (eight sailors, twelve farmers and twelve adventurers) and stopped at the Azores before heading west. After crossing the Atlantic, he discovered a point of land with a wide bay. He anchored in calm waters, caught many codfish and named the place Cape Cod. He found the Native Americans to be helpful and bartered with them for weapons, furs and tobacco. He continued to sail south and soon saw other islands. Because it was late in the day, he decided to stay at sea one night and soon saw high white cliffs at the east end of what is now called Nantucket.

Gosnold continued south, where he eventually founded Jamestown in Virginia. European settlers did not pay much attention to Nantucket between 1602 and 1641. It became part of New York when that state was founded in 1624. In 1641, Thomas Mayhew, a businessman with ventures in Boston, purchased land on Nantucket, Martha's Vineyard and the Elizabeth Islands from the second Earl of Sterling.

March 27

Famous orator and reformer Lucretia Coffin Mott delivered a lecture at the Nantucket Atheneum in 1853. Mott was born on Nantucket, where she was raised in the Quaker faith. At age thirteen, she left the island to attend the Quaker School in New York and lived in Philadelphia as an adult, but she returned often to visit family and to speak. Mott was against slavery and for women's rights. She lectured in Nantucket Quaker meetinghouses, delivered the sermon at the Unitarian Church in 1846 and spoke at the Atheneum, then a private organization that housed a library and museum.

In 1843, Henry David Thoreau attended one of Mott's lectures in New York City and wrote in a letter, "Mrs. Mott rose, took off her bonnet, and began to utter very deliberately what the Spirit suggested. Her self-possession was something to see, if all else failed, but it did not. Her subject was 'The Abuse of the Bible' and thence she straightway digressed to slavery and the degradation of woman. It was a good speech, transcendentalism in its mildest form."

In between 1840 and 1850, Mott traveled the country delivering lectures, often with other noted reformers like Frederick Douglass, William Lloyd Garrison, Lucy Stone and Elizabeth Cady Stanton. Mott participated in the Seneca Falls Convention in 1848 and was elected the first president of the Equal Rights Association in 1866. She returned to visit Nantucket in 1869 and 1876 and died at age ninety-three in 1880.

March 28

In 1791, three brand-new ships set out from Nantucket on whaling voyages that would take them all over the world: the *Beaver* (different from the *Beaver* involved in the Boston Tea Party), the *Washington* and the *Hector*. They were joined by veteran ships the *Favourite*, the *Warren* and the *Rebecca*.

In 1789, an English vessel had been the first whaler to enter the Pacific Ocean, and two years later, Nantucket whaling master Paul Worth, in command of the *Beaver*, would be the first American to fish in the Pacific. He returned to Nantucket on this day in 1793 with 1,300 barrels of whale oil.

But the first ship to return home from the group was the *Washington*, commanded by Captain George Bunker, who was the first to fly the Stars and Stripes in Pacific waters, in Peru, in January 1792. Around the same time, the *Beaver* was ordered out of Lima, Peru, by the Spaniards.

All six voyages were successful, and the *Beaver* helped start a new chapter in American whaling, which took ships farther away than ever to hunt for whales. Soon, Nantucket sailors would provision in whaling ports in Chile, the Sandwich Islands (now Hawaii), Fiji, Tahiti and New Zealand.

The *Favourite*, commanded by Captain Jonathan Paddock, brought back to Nantucket two distinguished Chinese merchants in 1808. They returned for another visit in 1814, when they were seen wearing "rich costumes, cap and red button upon the cap that marks a superior position in their own country."

March 29

In 1782, the French American writer J. Hector St. John de Crèvecœur published a book titled *Letters from an American Farmer*. In it, de Crèvecœur devoted five "letters," or chapters, to describing the whale fishery and customs of Nantucket. In his writing, one woman named "Aunt Kesiah" was mentioned frequently. He was writing about Kezia Folger Coffin, who died on this day in 1798.

In the book, de Crèvecœur said: "[T]he richest person [John Coffin] now in the island owes all his present prosperity and success to the ingenuity of his wife…for while he was performing his first cruises, she traded with pins and needles and kept a school. Afterward she purchased more considerable articles, which she sold with so much judgment that she laid the foundation of a system of business that she has ever since prosecuted with equal dexterity and success…[She and her husband] have the best country seat on the island…where they live with hospitality and in perfect union."

Kezia Folger Coffin was a controversial figure. Born in 1723, she left the Quaker church in 1773 when she was disciplined for keeping a spinet (a type of harpsichord). A cousin to Benjamin Franklin, Coffin sided with England during the Revolution. Suspected of smuggling and profiteering, she was prosecuted for treason after the war. Though cleared of the charges, acrimony and litigation marked the rest of her life, which ended when she fell down a staircase.

March 30

Mary Coffin and Nathaniel Starbuck were the first English settlers to wed on Nantucket in 1662, and in 1663 on this day, their daughter Mary Starbuck was born, the first white child delivered on Nantucket.

Mary Coffin and Nathaniel Starbuck were wealthy and powerful citizens. Her mother, daughter to one of the island's founders, ran a store and is credited with helping the Quaker religion take root on the island. Her father invested in whaling. Starbuck and her seven siblings would grow up in Sherburne, the island's first settlement, witnessing most of the island's major political and spiritual gatherings, which occurred at the Starbuck home, known locally as the "Parliament House."

Mary Starbuck married James Gardner, and they had six children. Mary died at age thirty-three, and James would outlive three wives. He had a son with his second wife, Rachel Gardner, and no children with his third wife, Patience Folger Harker. James died at age fifty-nine in 1723.

March 31

The Atlantic Silk Company was incorporated by a special act of the legislature in 1836. England had long been interested in creating American silk factories and sent silkworms to Virginia in 1617. Georgia had a silk factory in 1749, and by 1830 Connecticut was leading the country in silk production. A booming European market for silk led to the "1830s Mulberry Craze," which resulted in thousands of mulberry trees being planted around the country to create "cocooneries" designed to feed silkworms.

On Nantucket local businessmen were eager to capitalize on the craze. In addition, abolitionists called on consumers to substitute silk for cotton, which was picked by southern slaves. Egged on by newspaper editorials, William H. Gardner and Aaron Mitchell opened the Atlantic Silk Company.

The men built a factory on the southeast corner of Gay and Westminster Streets. In granting seven silk companies approval that year, the legislature also put a tax of one dollar on every ten pounds of silk manufactured.

Once operational, Atlantic Silk made silk vesting and handkerchiefs. But there was trouble early on. Nantucket people didn't like the industrial processes required to manufacture and dye the silk threads, and the trees did not thrive. By 1844, the factory was closed, and Mitchell moved the machinery to the second floor of a warehouse next to his home on Sea Street. It was so heavy that the building collapsed. Shortly after that, the Great Fire of 1846 destroyed the warehouse and Mitchell's home.

April 1

While traveling to Nantucket in 1840, the Boston schooner *Ellen* was struck by lightning during a ferocious thunderstorm. Halted at low tide by a sandbar at the entrance to the harbor, the *Ellen* was waiting for the tide to turn so it could sail over the bar. The ship was carrying groceries and furniture in the hold and iron hoops on deck.

Lightning came down the mast, went through the deck and set fire to the goods stored there. By that point, the schooner, now in flames, went aground. Eventually, the burning ship made it across the sandbar and into Nantucket, and the flames were put out by the fire department. The damage to the vessel was slight compared to the loss of the cargo. Several other vessels also waiting at the sandbar were struck at the time, but no damage was done.

During the same storm, the fishing boat *Republican* of Nantucket, captained by Walter Allen, dragged from its anchorage at the east end of the island and went ashore at Sesacacha Pond. It was hauled off a few days later and towed to town by the steamer *Telegraph*. In rounding Great Point, a waterlogged *Republican* rolled over and lost its mast, but rescuers managed to bring the ship to Nantucket and repair it.

April 2

Alexander Pinkham began his career at sea in 1807 at age fifteen. Born and educated on Nantucket, he sailed on the whale ship *Chili*, commanded by his uncle, Captain James Bunker. In 1837, Pinkham recalled that voyage in a letter to Captain Bunker: "I was sixteen years old I have no doubt you remember it. The relations of our exploits amongst the monsters of the great deep are the more interesting the longer time that intervenes between that of their execution and the period of their being retold. The whole that I can say for myself is to sum the whole up into one mighty blast which is poured forth in a declaration that I struck the whole of the twenty seven sperm whales we got to our boat on the last voyage in the *Chili* out of which there were but two that I did not put both irons into."

Later, Pinkham joined the navy, eventually becoming a commander, and was superintendent of the Gosport Naval Shipyard. In 1829, he commanded America's first privately owned sailing training vessel for Nantucket's Coffin School. Pinkham sailed from Boston, Massachusetts, to Brazil with a crew of boys on the brig *Clio*.

Pinkham is also credited with restoring John Paul Jones's Scottish home in 1831. On a visit to the British Isles, he found the American Revolution naval hero's ancestral home in ruins and paid to have it restored.

April 3

In 1834, the Massachusetts legislature granted a group of Nantucket men permission to incorporate the Nantucket Atheneum, a private institution dedicated to "scientific and literary purposes." The Atheneum opened in a former Unitarian Church in 1835 and became an intellectual center for the island. It had a circulating book collection, a museum of South Sea artifacts brought home by whalers, and it hosted lectures on a variety of topics. The founders hired a young teacher named Maria Mitchell to serve as librarian. In the 1840s, antislavery conventions held there attracted famous abolitionists as well as women's rights advocates.

When the building burned down, along with most of the town, during the Great Fire of 1846, Atheneum proprietors appealed for help and collected donations from every state in the country. In 1847, just five months after the fire, a new building opened. With its Greek Revival architectural design, it became a symbol of hope to the island, whose residents struggled to reestablish the once bustling downtown.

By the end of the nineteenth century, as the idea of free libraries gathered momentum nationally, Atheneum proprietors considered joining the movement, but the membership voted it down. Turning the Atheneum into a free, public library came up for a vote several times in the 1890s, and finally, on this day in 1900, proprietors and the town settled on a plan to make the Atheneum a free public library.

April 4

In 1752, eighteen-year-old Peleg Folger left on the ship *Mary*, headed north to hunt whales. The *Mary* traveled with a group of other Nantucket ships and was gone for a month. The grandson of island founders and first cousin to Benjamin Franklin, Folger recorded his thoughts and observations in a journal kept during several whaling voyages. In 1752, he wrote: "This Day we spy'd Spermaceties [sperm whales] in the morning and toss'd out one Boat (the other being out after Waggins [sea ducks]). So we row'd about a mile and Half from the Vessel, and then a Whale came up under us; and Stove our boat Very much; and threw every man overboard save one. And We all come up and Got Hold of the boat and Held to Her til the other boat (which was a mile and a half off) came up and took us in, all Safe and not one man hurt, which was remarkable, the boat being threshed to pieces very much. The same day we got a Quarter of a Spermaceti with Joseph Swain and Now We Shall be headed homewards Pretty Soon having but One Boat to help ourselves which Yet was Enough to be a means of Saving our Lives when Stove through Mercy."

The *Mary* made it back to Nantucket on April 12, and Folger wrote, "This Day we hove up our anchor and Run Home and found all well there (Laus Dei)."

April 5

By the time he made his last voyage in 1807, Nantucket whaling captain Mayhew Folger had sailed around the world three times and served in every position from cabin boy to master. On his final voyage, he left Boston on the *Topaz* to hunt seals and, when he returned in 1810, quit the life of a sailor.

During that last trip, Captain Folger discovered the surviving mutineers of the English royal ship *Bounty* who had eluded British capture and colonized an unknown island in the South Pacific. In 1789, mutineers put their captain and others in a boat and set them adrift. They stole the *Bounty*, and for nine years eight Englishmen and a handful of Tahitian men and women lived on Pitcairn Island, completely hidden from the rest of the world. In 1795, the group saw a ship off shore, but no contact was made. It wasn't until the *Topaz* arrived in 1808 that they were discovered. Folger reported his find to the admiralty, but by the time the Royal Navy sorted it out, only one mutineer still lived, and he was granted amnesty in 1825.

Captain Folger, born in 1774, was Lucretia Coffin Mott's uncle and a distant cousin to Benjamin Franklin. He married Mary Joy in 1798, and they had six children. One of his grandsons, William Mayhew Folger, became a United States Navy rear admiral. Captain Folger relocated to Ohio, where he was his town's first postmaster, and died in 1828.

April 6

In 1918, three weeks before Nantucket voters repealed a controversial ten-year ban on automobiles, a letter signed "Old Fogey" appeared in the *Inquirer & Mirror*, saying, "The scrapping of the railroad has caused me to look backward. I remember when the railroad came, for I did not want it to come. How we did kick about it and how we predicted all sorts of calamities. But it came—and now we are all sorry it is going to leave us.

The letter continues to list other modern improvements that met resistance on Nantucket, like the water company, electric street lights, the telephone and the "auto-chemical" fire engines. In regard to allowing cars on Nantucket's streets, the writer says: "I'm almost tired of bucking against these modern inventions. They come in time and then we are glad they are here. Suppose it will be that way with the automobile after it gets here.

"Probably it will prove a blessing like the rest of the things we bucked against. I'm against it just the same from force of habit, for I've been against everything else that spells progress and guess this is about the last chance I'll have to kick, for my kicking days are almost over."

On April 24, 1918, Nantucket became the last town in Massachusetts to pass a law allowing cars to drive on its streets. Town voters debated the hot topic and repealed the ban by a narrow vote of 326 in favor and 286 against.

April 7

In 1863, the USS *Nantucket*, built that year as a coastal monitor, participated in a large Union naval assault on Fort Sumter, South Carolina. The armored, submerged ship was hit fifty-one times by Confederate gunfire during the attack but remained afloat. The attack was unsuccessful, and the Union fleet withdrew, leaving Fort Sumter operational.

The USS *Nantucket* was a 1,875-ton Passaic-class monitor, also known as an ironclad, built by the Atlantic Iron Works at Boston, Massachusetts, and launched on February 26, 1863. Measuring two hundred feet long and forty-six feet wide, it had a crew of seventy-five men and was equipped with a single turret armed with two guns.

The USS *Nantucket* was quickly repaired and played a key role in forcing the evacuation of Fort Wagner in September 1863. The USS *Nantucket* continued firing on Confederate forts around Charleston Harbor for the rest of the Civil War and was attached to the South Atlantic Blockading Squadron. It assisted in preventing Confederate monitors from entering Charleston and was useful in enforcing the Union blockade of the Southern coastline.

Once the Civil War ended, the USS *Nantucket* was decommissioned at the Philadelphia Navy Yard in June 1865. The USS *Nantucket* would be used over the next forty years patrolling Northeast waters and was stationed in South Carolina again during the Spanish-American War in 1898. But monitors became obsolete by the end of the nineteenth century, and it was decommissioned and sold for scrap in November 1900.

April 8

From September 1848 to March 1853, Susan Veeder sailed with her husband, Captain Charles A. Veeder, on a whaling voyage aboard the ship *Nauticon*. The journey took her around Cape Horn to Chile, Oahu, Tahiti and as far north as the Fox Islands in the Arctic. During the trip, Veeder painted watercolors and kept a diary.

On this day in 1849, while anchored off the coast of Chile, Veeder wrote: "To day we went on shore, Captain Folger went with. We got a few shells and when returning to the ships we caught a number of small fish. We have lowered our boats a number of times for humpbacks, since we have been here but have not been fortunate enough to get any but once. I have been onshore a number of times but not much to be seen for they is not any inhabitable land nor a green bush to be seen."

April 9

The Bath Iron Works delivered the steamer *Nobska* to the New England Steamship Company in 1925. The *Nobska* served New Bedford, Cape Cod and the Islands until 1973.

From 1928 to 1956, it was renamed the *Nantucket*. At 210 feet long, it was considered elegant and modern for its time, and the ship's sharply pointed bow helped cut through ice. Efforts to preserve the vessel in 2006 failed. The *Nobska* had been on the National Register of Historic Places, and the National Maritime Alliance and the National Trust for Historic Preservation listed it as one the country's most endangered maritime resources. It was a floating restaurant in Maryland for a time but was eventually scrapped. However, the ship's steam whistle survived and can be heard on Nantucket throughout the day when the *Eagle* arrives and departs.

April 10

Fourteen-year-old James Athearn Folger and his two older brothers left Panama City on board the Pacific mail steamer *Isthmus* in 1850 and set off for California to strike it rich in gold. But once the brothers reached San Francisco, J.A., as he was called, decided to stay in the city and help it recover from a devastating fire. He was hired by William H. Bovee to build a spice and coffee mill.

Born on Nantucket in 1835, Folger had already helped his father's business recover from a crippling fire. In 1846, the family lost a blacksmithing business and two whale ships during the Great Fire.

With the discovery of gold in California, James and his brothers, Henry (age sixteen) and Edward (age twenty), set out in the autumn of 1849 for Panama. After a raft and hiking journey across the Panama Isthmus, the brothers caught the steamer and landed in San Francisco in early May 1850.

At age twenty-four, Folger was a partner in Pioneer Steam Coffee and Spice Mills, and in 1860, he created the J.A. Folger's Coffee Company, popularly known today as Folger's Coffee. Folger survived bankruptcy in 1864 and went on to create a coffee dynasty. He pioneered the concept of preground coffee and developed packaging designed to keep it fresh. After Folger died in 1889, his son continued to run the business.

J.A. Folger's granddaughter, Abigail Folger, along with her friend Sharon Tate, was murdered by followers of Charles Manson in 1969.

April 11

In 1825, a classified advertisement in the newspaper referred to the African School for the first time, an indication that the African Meetinghouse was used as a school and a church.

In an 1826 newspaper account, the editor praised the school, writing, "The present number of scholars in the African School in this town, is 47; of whom 34 write, 30 read in the Testament, 2 in Spelling books and 5 in the alphabet-their writing would do credit to scholars whose opportunities would have been greater than those children have had, and their reading, spelling, exercises in arithmetic., etc., were very creditable both to their instructor and themselves." The article encouraged local philanthropists to support the African School. It expressed the belief that education was the best way for African Americans to achieve equality and was "the surest passport to honour and happiness."

April 12

Born in 1699, Elihu Coleman was a carpenter, Quaker minister and writer. His pamphlet called *A Testimony Against That Anti-Christian Practice of Making Slaves of Men* was published in 1733, making him one of  the earliest antislavery advocates in America. His house, the second-oldest house on the island, still stands (pictured here).

In his writing, Coleman said:

> *And now, although some may think it hard to have this practice spoken against that has been carried on so long pretty much in silence, I may let such know that I have found it hard to write against it, yet nevertheless believing it to be my duty to do. I have written according to the understanding I have had thereof. And, although I have written but little and in a very plain way yet I hope that those remarks I have made thereon may serve as a text for some to preach to themselves upon.*

April 13

The military architects of World War I used patrol planes to spot German submarines. Stationed at Naval Air Station Chatham, the first hydroplane landed in Nantucket Harbor near Commercial Wharf in 1918.

The next time it came, on April 17, the schools declared a holiday, and the children, along with most residents of Nantucket, gathered on Brant Point to watch its arrival. For most of the crowd, this would be the first time they saw an airplane on the island.

By June, large numbers of seaplanes, which were armed with guns and bombs and carried a homing pigeon in case the plane went down, were based in Chatham. By July, they were making up to twenty flights a day, and wrecks and engine failure were common. Several times, Nantucket boats discovered downed planes and towed them back into port. By now, Chatham was one of the navy's largest air stations, with seventy-five officers, 450 men, eighteen seaplanes, kite balloons and two blimps.

World War I ended in November of that year, but Nantucket had caught the bug for aviation and for seaplanes. A floating pier in the harbor was constructed for seaplanes to tie up. On May 17, 1927, a seaplane made the first round-trip flight from Boston to Nantucket. Later that year, the first airport opened in Tom Nevers, which provided a place for airplanes with wheels to land.

April 14

Matt Tierney was working the night shift at the Marconi wireless station in Siasconset in 1912 when he heard a faint distress signal from the *Titanic*. He relayed the message to New York and then worked for four day straight relaying other messages that provided key information about the survivors of the ocean liner tragedy.

The *New York Herald* installed the Marconi radio station in the village of Siasconset in 1901. A 186-foot mast on a hill served as the antenna, and the station crew operated equipment in a nearby cottage. The newspaper also installed wireless equipment on the *Nantucket* lightship, anchored forty miles south of the island. Two years later, the wireless station was sold to the Marconi Wireless Telegraph Company of America. The stations in Siasconset and on the lightship would play an important role in maritime communications in the early days of radio and at a time when 250 ships passed by daily. Ships reported their position and arrival times. Wireless operators informed ships of world events. In Siasconset, the wireless operators were also charged with passing along New York Giants baseball scores to the summer crowd.

In 1909, the Siasconset wireless station was instrumental in saving lives when two ocean liners collided in the fog sixty miles south of the island. By relaying distress calls to nearby ships, the station helped orchestrate the rescue of all passengers. As a result, Congress passed a law in 1910 making wireless radio mandatory on ships with fifty or more passengers and on those traveling more than two hundred miles from port.

April 15

Nantucket's first public high school opened in 1838 with fifty-nine students and Cyrus Pierce as principal. Born in 1790, Pierce was from Waltham, Massachusetts, and graduated from Harvard University and Harvard Divinity School as an ordained Unitarian minister.

He first taught on Nantucket in 1810 but returned to Cambridge to attend divinity school. He returned to the island and married one of his former pupils, Harriet Coffin, in 1816. Pierce taught off-island and returned again in 1831. He purchased a home on Orange Street and started his own school. For a time, his assistant was a young Maria Mitchell, who would become the Atheneum's librarian and eventually gain national fame when she discovered a comet in 1847.

For a brief time, Pierce served as principal of the new Coffin School, a private school for descendants of Nantucket founder Tristram Coffin.

One year after opening the high school, Pierce was chosen by education reformer Horace Mann to become the principal of the country's first "Normal School" in Lexington, Massachusetts. The experimental school was established to train teachers for a career in public education, and later, it became Framingham State College. The Pierces lived on and off Nantucket from 1842 until his death in 1860. When he died, pupils from the Normal School commissioned the monument over his Nantucket grave, a Celtic cross inscribed with the saying with which their teacher closed every class: "Live to the Truth."

April 16

In 1944, a German submarine located south of Nantucket spotted a convoy leaving New York City bound for Great Britain. The *Pan Pennsylvania*, a large tanker in the convoy, straggled behind, and the German *U-550* torpedoed it. The ship quickly caught fire and

began to sink. As the *Pan Pennsylvania* settled, the submarine maneuvered underneath its hull in an effort to hide from its military escorts.

The navy and coast guard rescued the tanker's crew and detected the Germans as they attempted to escape. The USS *Joyce* dropped bombs all around the submarine and severely damaged it, forcing it to surface. Above the water, German and American sailors exchanged gunfire while the USS *Gandy* rammed the submarine. Eventually, the USS *Joyce* picked up thirteen Germans, and the rest of the crew went down with the U-boat. The USS *Joyce* delivered the prisoners of war and the *Pan Pennsylvania* survivors to the authorities in Great Britain.

April 17

In 1917, the Navy League of Massachusetts sent a letter to state residents, which was published in the *Inquirer & Mirror*. It said, "The American flag has been fired upon only a short distance from the shores of the United States by a German submarine—the first act of war on this side of the Atlantic. Raiding of American commerce and a submarine blockade of American ports is predicted. America must be ready to meet such warfare, and that she may be ready, every man and woman must accept the full duty and burden of his citizenship and aid the country in every manner possible."

Intensifying German submarine attacks not far from America's coast rattled Nantucket citizens, who worried that the island's isolation made it a target. In response, the Naval Reserves sent a representative to Nantucket with a threefold mission: to recruit men, make sure residents were ready and assure them of their safety. Also that month, the *Inquirer & Mirror* announced that Woodrow Wilson's daughter planned to summer in Siasconset. An editorial in that same issue informed readers that Nantucket would remain calm and peaceful, especially with navy warships off the coast and the president's daughter coming in June.

But the island would feel the impact of World War I in other ways when the navy took command of the Marconi radio stations in Siasconset and on the *Nantucket* lightship and also appropriated local passenger and fishing vessels for the war effort.

April 18

In 1673, Francis Lovelace, governor of the Province of New York, named Nantucket's new English settlement the town of Sherburne. When the founding English families arrived, they scouted different locations to build their homes. They looked at Madaket Harbor at the west end but eventually settled on a protected inlet on the northeast side, which they felt had better access to the sea, and laid out house lots near Capaum Pond. The new Nantucketers paid taxes to New York and obtained rights to fish the island's ponds and ocean waters from New York authorities.

Ownership of the island switched to Massachusetts when William and Mary came to the throne of England and reestablished their American state boundaries. At the time, Nantucket requested to become a Massachusetts town, and in 1693, the switch was confirmed by law.

As the island's population grew, so did the little town of Sherburne. But the area around the island's large natural harbor, known today as Nantucket Town, blossomed into a commercial center. In 1712, Nantucketers killed their first whale, and within eleven years, the island was actively pursuing whaling. No longer just hunting from shore, Nantucket boats now went off shore for up to six weeks. The town built Straight Wharf in 1723 so ships would have a place to dock. Eventually, all of the island's business centered around Straight Wharf, and residents abandoned Sherburne to re-settle near the harbor.

April 19

In 1880, the Massachusetts legislature granted a charter to the Nantucket Railroad Company. Though little evidence remains, the railroad served Nantucket from 1881 until 1917.

By 1880, Nantucket was developing into a summer destination for tourists and demand for transportation to remote sections of the island grew.

By the spring of 1881, the track had been established to Surfside, the engine and cars had been purchased and the railroad had built a restaurant at Surfside. By the end of that first season, its proprietors estimated the train had carried over thirty thousand passengers and traveled nearly six thousand miles.

The summer people loved the train, and its popularity attracted a hotel and real estate development to Surfside. Railroad service was expanded to Siasconset in 1884. The railroad changed hands and changed the course of its tracks, but it couldn't make a profit and closed in 1917.

April 20

In 1957, almost three hundred years after the island was settled by the English, the town started sorting through a massive property ownership conundrum and purchased 570 sheep commons shares for $4,500.

In the 1600s, the island's nine founding families, called proprietors, purchased land for their homes and also set aside large tracts to be used in common for grazing sheep. Over time, the island's population grew, and the number of people with sheep commons shares, as they were called, also grew. As original shareholders sold or bequeathed their interests, the number of people who held the land in common grew into the hundreds.

In time, everyone with a sheep commons share got a vote on how the land was used, and those with more shares had more power. At the beginning of the nineteenth century, three large shareholders wanted to carve off two thousand acres from the commons and become its sole owners. The men took their claim to court and won, which caused others to follow.

In 1821, the owners decided to divide several large land tracts and allow people to buy out the interests of other shareholders. But finding them and clearing a title was a complicated prospect. One share passed down through generations might be split among ten or fifteen heirs. In 1910, the Massachusetts Land Court began hearing title cases on Nantucket, and landowners began the lengthy process of petitioning the court to obtain a clear land title.

April 21

Throughout the early 1840s, abolitionists doggedly fought to integrate Nantucket public schools. Town meeting voters had already voted down integration several times and opposed it again in 1843. The school committee, controlled by a majority of radical abolitionists, ignored the vote and integrated the schools anyway. On this day in 1844, Nantucket voters, furious that their majority vote had been reversed, put segregationists on the school committee and separated white and African American students once again.

In 1840, Eunice Ross qualified to attend Nantucket High School but was denied because of her race. African American citizens wrote letters to the editor accusing the island's white people of racism. Abolitionists and education reformers, both on island and off, latched onto Ross's case, and the battle polarized the community. When voters re-segregated the schools in 1844, the parents of the African American children refused to send them back to school.

In 1845, both sides petitioned the state legislature to create laws to either segregate or integrate the schools. Massachusetts lawmakers passed a law in 1845 that outlawed segregating schoolchildren, but Nantucket ignored it.

In 1846, an African American student named Phebe Ann Boston also qualified to enter high school and was denied. Her father, Absolom Boston, a prominent member of the island's African American community, threatened to sue the town. Motivated by the possibility of a lawsuit, town meeting voters elected a new school committee and voted to end school segregation for good that same year.

April 22

William Mitchell was born on Nantucket in 1791 and married Lydia Coleman in 1812. They had ten children. Mitchell had a passion for astronomy and studied the stars all his life. His daughter Maria Mitchell became a renowned astronomer and educator. In 1827, William was appointed principal to Nantucket's first public grammar school, and in 1829, he established his own school on Howard Street.

William left teaching and entered commerce in 1832. He was secretary of the Phoenix Marine Insurance Company and cashier at Pacific National Bank, where his family lived in the Main Street building's second floor. Always studying the stars, Mitchell built an observatory on the bank's roof. It was there that his daughter Maria found a comet in 1847, a discovery that earned her international recognition as one of America's early top female scientists.

Mitchell died in 1869 and was buried on Nantucket on this day.

April 23

On this day in 1821, the English ship *Surry*, rescued three crewmen from the whaleship *Essex* who had lived for more than three months on a tiny island in the South Pacific.

When an enraged whale sunk the *Essex* in November 1820, twenty men escaped in three open boats and drifted with no food or water until they came upon Henderson Island, now part of the Pitcairn Islands. After a month, all but three decided to return to the sea and keep moving.

The boats became separated, and in February, five of the seventeen men were rescued. Captain Thomas Raine of the *Surry*, in port in Chile, was ordered to retrieve the three men on Henderson Island. That brought the total survivors to eight. As the story of the *Essex* became known, whalers heard of the crew members' hardship and how some resorted to cannibalism to survive. A young whaler from New Bedford named Herman Melville met *Essex* first mate Owen Chase, who gave him a written copy of the events, which Melville used in his novel *Moby-Dick*.

April 24

The first automobiles arrived in 1900 and frightened horses so badly that buggy passengers feared for their lives. Nantucketers did not embrace the automobile, and in 1908, under pressure, the Massachusetts legislature passed a law banning cars from the island. The one exception was that cars were allowed on the state-owned Milestone Road. In 1913, mail carrier Clinton Folger had a horse tow his car from downtown to the beginning of the Milestone Road on days when he delivered mail to Siasconset.

By 1916, many summer people, accustomed to driving on the mainland, brought their cars and used them. When they got in trouble with the law, the Massachusetts Automobile Association represented them. Folger forced the issue several times by making very public, attention-getting drives through town. Once again, residents debated the issue and voted against it. Finally, on this day in 1918, town meeting voters narrowly elected to repeal the ban on automobiles.

April 25

In 1967, a U.S. Air Force plane had just taken off on a routine mission from Otis Air Force Base on Cape Cod when it crashed one mile off Nantucket. Fifteen air force personnel died and one survived. Nantucket resident Mike Lamb was flying his single-engine plane home from New York and witnessed the crash. In an interview with the *Boston Traveler*, he said, "I saw something that looked like a bright light about 2,000 feet in the air. It seemed peculiar, but I didn't realize it was a plane in distress.

"I called the tower at Nantucket Airport and they advised me of an emergency. They advised me to keep the plane in sight and I followed it. It made one turn about five miles from Nantucket and then proceeded northerly. Then it made a 180 degree turn and proceeded southerly to the west end of Nantucket. Just before hitting the water off Long Pond, there was an explosion in the plane and it plunged into the water and sank. I couldn't see any signs of survivors. All I can remember is that big ball of flame and seeing it sink."

Survivor Lieutenant Joseph L.H. Guenet later recalled that the moment the plane's left wing struck the ocean, the airliner burst into a fireball and skidded one thousand feet parallel to shore. He said there was instant silence as the roar of engines on full power had been extinguished.

April 26

William Hadwen visited Nantucket to attend the wedding of his cousin and met his future wife, the sister of the bride. Hadwen moved to Nantucket in 1820 and married Eunice Starbuck, daughter of the island's wealthiest

whaling merchant, in 1822. Hadwen and his cousin (now also his brother-in-law) opened Hadwen & Barney, which sold whale oil and manufactured highly prized spermaceti whale oil candles. William was listed in the 1852 issue of *Rich Men of Massachusetts* as being worth $100,000, a little less than his father-in-law.

In 1860, during a dentist visit, Hadwen was given an overdose of ether, which would have been fatal except that his doctor saved his life. However, the aftereffects of the ether caused William to suffer from partial paralysis of the heart, a condition he died from on this day in 1862.

Hadwen's candle factory is now the Nantucket Whaling Museum on Broad Street.

April 27

Born on this day in 1776 into a Native American family, Dorcas Honorable entered the world in a time of struggle for the Wampanoag people. Her mother had survived a devastating epidemic of smallpox in 1763. Out of the 358 Wampanoag living here at the time, 222 died of the disease that year. Before the epidemic, her grandfather ran a school for Native American children. He taught them to read and write in their own language using materials developed by John Eliot. During his visit to Nantucket in the 1770s, writer J. Hector St. John de Crevecœur noticed that several Christian texts translated by Eliot "are still very common on this island and are daily made use of by those Indians who are taught to read."

Honorable lived quietly, did domestic work and attended the Baptist church. She was the last full-blooded Native American from Nantucket when she died on January 12, 1855.

April 28

The lighthouse on Great Point, located on Nantucket's northernmost tip, was placed on the National Register of Historic Places in 1982. Four years later, it was removed when the stone building collapsed during a late winter storm. A new lighthouse stands there today, the third one since 1784.

Jeannette Haskins Killen moved to Great Point when she was thirteen. The daughter of the last civilian light keeper, Killen lived there with her family from 1937 to 1944. In April 1945, she wrote in a letter: "First I will tell you more of Great Point. I always loved storms and still do. The storms there are beautiful. The wind swept along the dunes and at the top of the house, but never came low in our little valley. I used to love to walk in the brisk wind along the beach and feel the sting of the sand. I was never lonely. I liked housework and there was always plenty to do. I learned to cook and sew. I found other things to do too. My sister and I collected shells and different things on the beach and made necklaces and bracelets. I used to love to take a book and read under the scrub cedars we called woods and my sister and I used to lie on top of the boughs watching the sky and look at the sky and talk."

In 1944, the Haskins family moved to Nantucket's eastern shore and became the keepers of Sankaty Lighthouse.

April 29

Horace Mann, considered the father of public education, delivered a lecture at the Nantucket Atheneum titled "Physiology" in 1847. Mann was a Massachusetts legislator and helped create the state's first education board. He also filled John Quincy Adams's seat in the U.S. Congress after he died.

Mann spoke at the Atheneum four times, and in 1837 his lecture on education reform at the Methodist Church made headlines. Representing the education board, he noted in an 1838 report that Nantucket and Taunton were two of the last towns to comply with state law and open a public high school: "It will be recollected that this class of towns takes precedence of almost all the others in wealth that they expend a far less proportion of money per scholar for the support of public schools than the poorer and more sparsely populated towns."

April 30

In 1902, the *New York Times* reported that equipment for a new Marconi telegraph station at Sagaponack on Long Island had been delivered. The equipment consisted of a 185-foot mast, which would elevate the antennae wires, and a one-horse power gasoline engine. The station was anticipated to be the principal Marconi station on the New York coast, as well as the first to speak with ships approaching New York.

The Marconi operator on the *Nantucket* lightship took over the Long Island station, which was also used as a training school. The Sagaponack site was selected so its operators would be within the radius of the Sandy Hook Station. The Sandy Hook station was the first to be built in 1890 so reporters could communicate with yachts racing in the America's Cup. The second station was in Siasconset and on the lightship *Nantucket* in 1901.

May 1

Massachusetts lawmakers adopted a state constitution in 1779. That document was amended at constitutional conventions in 1820 and 1853. In 1917, lawmakers organized another constitutional convention that would debate state legal changes on a wide range of issues, including Prohibition, capital punishment, regulation of public utilities and the creation of a public defender's office.

Nantucket voters were set for a May election to choose their convention representative, but the race grew contentious in April. The primary's loser, Charles A. Snow, claimed the two candidates on the ballot were there illegally. The two, both judges, were Reginald T. Fitz-Randolph and Henry Riddell, who Snow said were prohibited from holding an elected position since both already had governor-appointed jobs. Snow took his complaint to the Ballot Law Commission in Boston. After testimony from both sides, the commission denied Snow's request to remove the judges from the ballot, saying the convention delegates should decide the issue. But the commission did allow Snow to add his name to the ballot using a "sticker" campaign, a precursor to the write-in candidate, and the first example of its kind on Nantucket.

On May 1, 1917, Reginald Fitz-Randolph won the election easily, receiving 330 votes. Riddell received 168, and Snow received 104 "sticker" votes. The *Inquirer & Mirror* noted that Fitz-Randolph had succeeded because of strong support from the island's fishermen and farmers, as well as from a good showing of Siasconset voters. At the convention, Fitz-Randolph was given a seat on the committee on taxation.

May 2

In 1931, Josiah Fitch Murphey died at age eighty-eight. Underage in 1862, his mother signed the papers so he could fight in the Civil War, and he joined 80 other Nantucket men in Company I of the Twentieth Massachusetts Volunteer Infantry. In total, Nantucket would send 280 men to fight in the war.

Within six weeks of enlisting, Murphey was fighting at the Battle of Antietam. During the time he served, he fought at Fredericksburg, where he was shot in the face, and marched his way toward Richmond, Virginia. Throughout, he kept a journal and wrote down his experiences of seeing General Grant, capturing a Rebel and chatting about the war with him, being the target of sharpshooters and the agony of watching a fellow Nantucket soldier taken prisoner. Murphey left the army on July 16, 1864. On that day he wrote, "We leave for home today, yes, Home, the dearest spot on the earth to me, how it thrills my every nerve to think of going home."

He spent the rest of his life on Nantucket, as postmaster, town assessor and town clerk. He also served several terms as commander of Nantucket's Thomas M. Gardner Post 207 of the Grand Army of the Republic (GAR).

Two years before his death, he wrote, "*Boston Herald* said [after the battle of Fredericksburg] that Murphey who was reported yesterday mortally wounded might possibly recover.

"He did and lived to be over 85 years old. He is writing this."

May 3

In 1879, the *Inquirer & Mirror* ran an obituary from the *Republican-Democrat* in Ravenna, Ohio, for former Nantucket whaling captain Charles C. Russell. Russell was born on Nantucket in 1803. He began whaling at an early age and spent thirty-six years at sea, commanding five voyages as commander of the ship. He was shipwrecked twice, once in the North Pacific Ocean between California and Hawaii and again off the coast of Africa.

He married in 1826 and had two sons. In 1849, Russell and his brother bought farms in Ohio. But Russell returned to Nantucket shortly after to command his last whaling voyage. In 1854, he retired from the sea and settled on his farm in Rootstown, Ohio. In his final years, he relocated to Ravenna, Ohio. Russell outlived his wife and both his children. He died on April 27, 1878, and the pallbearers at his funeral were all from Nantucket, four of them former whaling captains. The article said, "The once numerous circle of Nantucket people residing at Ravenna and vicinity are passing away with marked rapidity. So time marks its changes, and new actors come upon the stage."

Between 1844 and 1845, at a time when Nantucket whaling was declining, twenty-nine island families moved to Ravenna and began farming. Of those, twenty-one families were headed by whaling captains. Nantucket-born citizens of Ravenna would help establish churches and schools, represent the town in state government and continue to work on the antislavery reforms so popular on Nantucket.

May 4

In 1847, the Nantucket Atheneum invited Ralph Waldo Emerson to deliver a series of lectures. In a letter to Ellen, his daughter, Emerson described the island this way:

> *This is a strange place, the island is fifteen miles long, but there are no woods and no trees upon it, and hardly any fence. As soon as you have walked out of the town or village of Nantucket (In which there are few little gardens and a few trees) you come on a wide bare common stretching as far as you can see on every side, with nothing upon it but here & there a few nibbling sheep. And if you walk on till you have lost sight of the town, and a fog rises, which is very common here, you will have no guide to show you the way, no houses, no trees, no hills, no stones.*

May 5

The first steam-powered passenger vessel to serve Nantucket was the *Eagle* in 1818. Submarine inventor Robert Fulton had proven the viability of steam-powered boats in 1807 when he made a successful run between New York City and Albany. The *Eagle* made its first trip to Nantucket with sixty passengers, many of whom were Quakers coming to attend a Friends meeting. Two weeks later, the *Eagle* visited again and on June 25 started regular trips between Nantucket and New Bedford.

The fastest trip recorded was on July 30 when the *Eagle* ran between Nantucket and New Bedford in eight hours and seven minutes. The *Eagle* was ninety-two feet long, had a figurehead and round stern and had two copper boilers that burned wood. The first steam-powered whale ship also arrived on Nantucket in 1818. The *George* returned from a Pacific Ocean voyage on July 24 with 2,016 barrels of sperm oil on board. The *Eagle* towed the *George* over the sandbar and around Brant Point as hundreds of townspeople gathered along the waterfront to watch.

The *Eagle* made regular trips to Nantucket for three months, but the venture proved unprofitable because of a lack of passengers and the high cost of running the boat. The owners sold the *Eagle* in September to a company that began ferry service between Boston and Hingham. Nantucket would not see steam-powered boat service again until 1824.

May 6

Phebe Ann Coffin Hanaford was born in Siasconset in 1829. Raised a Quaker, Hanaford was cousins with Lucretia Coffin Mott and showed an early interest in reform. She signed a temperance pledge at age eight. She was a published writer by age thirteen and teaching by age sixteen. Four years later, she married Dr. Joseph Hanaford, and they soon moved off-island.

While Hanaford raised their two children, she continued to write and published fourteen books. She also started preaching. Struggling with a crisis of faith following the death of her siblings, Hanaford decided to follow Unitarianism. While visiting Nantucket in 1865, she gave her first sermon at the little schoolhouse in Siasconset where she once taught.

Active in the women's movement, Hanaford was the first New England woman ordained as a Universalist and served churches in Massachusetts, Connecticut and New Jersey. She died in 1921.

May 7

In 1932, the Motor Vehicle Registry stopped requiring out-of-state drivers to obtain Massachusetts summer registration license plates or to take a driving test. Massachusetts now allowed out-of-state drivers to operate vehicles anywhere for thirty days. If a motorist remained longer, they were required to get a special permit. On Nantucket, a registry inspector came once a week for the day.

Although cars had been on the road for decades, not all states required a license to drive in 1932. And of the states that did require a license, few required a test. Early drivers were taught by car salesmen, family and friends or organizations like the YMCA.

Concerned about the damage created by incompetent drivers, Massachusetts was the first state to enact a law requiring motorists to carry auto insurance in 1925. The new law allowed the authorities to revoke a car registration if it was not insured.

May 8

By January 11, 1778, the U.S. Congress had not heard from its commissioners in France for four months and anxiously waited for Captain John Folger, of Nantucket, to deliver their correspondence. But all the congressmen received upon delivery was a packet of blank paper. The congressmen accused Folger of stealing the dispatches. A congressional committee interviewed him the following day and had trouble believing Folger's innocence, but it had to wait for word from Governor Caswell of North Carolina before issuing judgment.

Folger had arrived in America at Brunswick, North Carolina, in December, and Caswell was the first official he met. In his letter to Governor Caswell, the president of Congress, Henry Laurens, said, "The man's behavior is such as induces most of the members of Congress to believe him an Arch Knave affecting the Fool _ my private opinion is that he is a very stupid confused creature altogether unfit for the charge." Caswell's deposition from North Carolina arrived in February and failed to clear Folger, who was waiting in prison for the matter to be resolved.

However, new information from France indicated that the dispatches had been stolen by Captain Joseph Hansen of Maryland, who Folger had lodged with before leaving that country. On this day in 1778, the congressional committee issued a report saying there was "no proof of any guilt in Mr. Folger," and he was released from prison. Historians have since discovered that Hansen was employed by both the Americans and the British and did, in fact, steal the papers.

May 9

The Nantucket Historical Association was organized in 1894 and incorporated on July 9 of that year. It adopted a constitution and bylaws in November and had a charter membership of 179 life members and 161 annual members. At its first annual meeting in June 1895, the secretary reported that 4 more life members and 50 annual members had been added.

During its first year, there were eight meetings that were "chiefly for the transaction of business but having nevertheless a somewhat social character." NHA member Mr. MacElroy gave a lecture for the benefit of the association. Shortly after its incorporation, the NHA gained ownership of the Quaker meetinghouse on Fair Street, which became its headquarters. The association planned to raise funds in the summer of 1895 to pay the meetinghouse mortgage and purchase a historic house for the collection so that it could be restored and only used for NHA meetings.

May 10

Elizabeth Saltonstall, a nationally recognized lithographer, died at age ninety in 1990. A core member of the Nantucket Art Colony, she came in 1922 to study with Frank Swift Chase. She lived on Old North Wharf and came every summer, except one, for sixty-eight years.

Saltonstall studied at the School of the Museum of Fine Arts in Boston and later under the tutelage of noted lithographer Stow Wengenroth in Maine. In Nantucket, she took classes in plein-air oil painting from Chase and exhibited at several galleries. She was one of the first artist members of the Artists' Association of Nantucket and a founding member of the Boston Society of Independent Artists and the Boston Printmakers. Saltonstall taught art at Milton Academy for thirty-seven years. Descended from the Brahmin Saltonstall family of Chestnut Hill, she was a cousin of Massachusetts governor Leverett Saltonstall.

May 11

Noting that novels have "some moral and intellectual value," an 1878 editorial in the *Island Review* called for the inclusion of novels in public libraries. The editorial discussed a recent conference of librarians in London who had debated whether to exclude fiction from library collections. One paper's author had called for banning novels, but others were for it. The editorial notes, "His view was opposed by no less a personage than the Librarian of the Bodleian, who held that the real use of fiction was to supply imagination to those who have it not. Moreover, he argues that librarians (or managers) would be travelling out of their sphere and, without authority, acting as censors of morals, in excluding this or that, according to their own views."

The editorial said novels preserve culture, events and public sentiment. "As such they are history—often, it is true, in a crude and undigested form, but history still."

The editorial lists the many great men who read novels and quotes other newspapers that have published editorials defending the reading of novels. The writer concludes, "If public libraries are made up of books of a solid and serious turn exclusively—what are called useful books—they will be public merely in name. Their object specifically is to encourage reading, not necessarily as a duty, for that would be to encourage study, but as harmless and generally profitable amusement, calculated to keep readers out of mischief and indirectly to refine their manners and tastes and habits."

May 12

The USS *Nantucket* arrived in Washington, D.C., in 1924 on the first leg of a training cruise to Europe. The U.S. Navy gunboat served the country from 1876 to 1920 and then was a training ship for students at the United States Merchant Marine Academy until 1940. It was scrapped in 1958, but the engine, which is the only one of its type still in existence, is on display at the American Merchant Marine Museum in Kings Point, New York.

A steamer that was also fully rigged for sailing, the USS *Nantucket* was first named USS *Ranger*, then USS *Rockport* and finally for the island in 1916. Commissioned and launched in Pennsylvania, the ship served American interests in the Pacific Ocean, Latin America and Mexico and protected seal hunters in the Bering Sea. It also patrolled American waters in the Puget Sound and off New England. The navy sent it into battle during World War I, and it was also a training ship for navy midshipmen. The USS *Nantucket* returned to Massachusetts after the war and served as a school and museum ship until it was scrapped.

As a school ship, the USS *Nantucket* sailed annually on a foreign voyage. In 1924, students sailed from Boston to Washington, D.C., and on to Norfolk, Virginia. The ship crossed the Atlantic Ocean and stopped at the Azores, Portugal and Tangiers and sailed back across the ocean to Bermuda, stopping at Nantucket and returning to Boston in mid-September. The cruise covered 10,573 miles, and 116 cadets participated.

May 13

At the beginning of the 1800s, almost half the island worshipped at the Quaker Society of Friends meeting, although the church was losing members, in part due to the wars in 1775 and 1812 and due to austere—some thought harsh—rules that caused parishioners to leave and worship elsewhere.

In 1827–28, simmering disagreements about doctrine erupted at the Philadelphia yearly meeting and permanently divided Quakers into different camps. Orthodox Quakers called Elias Hicks a heretic because his preaching questioned the absolute divinity of Christ. His followers, called Hicksites, called for more free thought within the church.

By the late 1820s, the Nantucket Meeting had also split into factions, and all held separate meetings, which effectively shattered Quaker unity. In 1829 on this day, the Quaker Society of Friends membership closed its meetinghouse on Broad Street and transferred its members to the meetinghouse on Main Street. By the late 1860s, there were only a handful of Quakers on the island, and by 1900, some historians believe there were none.

May 14

The *Nantucket Inquirer & Mirror* announced in 1927 the first air passenger service between Nantucket and Boston. The Briarcliff Trust Company, which owned a landing strip in Tom Nevers, and the Boston Airport Corporation would provide the service. The partners said they planned to begin June 15 and offer one flight a day. The three-engine plane would be able to carry four passengers and three hundred pounds of luggage.

The May 21 edition reported on a test run executed earlier that week. The Stinson-Detroiter airplane flew in from Boston and instantly generated a lot of excitement on the island. It was painted blue with silver aluminum wings. Inside, the passenger chairs were made of wicker and had blue leather cushions. The paper noted that occupants didn't have to wear goggles or other paraphernalia.

The first Nantucket passenger to travel to Boston was seventy-year-old Herbert G. Worth. A large crowd gathered to witness his flight take off, and the paper noted the group included the board of assessors, selectmen, finance committee members, a bank president, the postmaster, president of the water company, a clerk of the courts, the custodian of the dump, the tree warden and a large representation from island merchants on Petticoat Row.

After landing, Worth reported by telephone that the flight had gone well and had taken one hour and five minutes. Dick Sears, a Boston-based news photographer, filmed the day, and the next morning, his footage was on the movie newsreels shown in Boston movie theaters.

May 15

In 1935, the British luxury ocean liner *Olympic* accidentally broadsided the lightship *Nantucket*, a floating lighthouse moored forty miles south of Nantucket. Unable to see it in a heavy fog, the *Olympic* split the *Nantucket* in half. Both sections sank quickly, and seven of the eleven crew members died.

In 1911, White Star Lines introduced the world to the largest ocean liners, the *Olympic*, and its sister ships, the *Titanic* and the *Britannic*. The *Titanic* hit an iceberg and sank in the North Atlantic in 1912, and the *Britannic* triggered a mine and sank in the Mediterranean Sea in 1916. Built with the most luxurious features at the time and almost identical to the *Titanic*, the *Olympic* had a long career as a yacht and as a troop transport ship during World War I.

Britain paid for a new lightship to be built and installed on Nantucket Shoals.

May 16

William Rotch died in 1828. Born on Nantucket in 1734, Rotch was a Quaker businessman who owned a large whaling and shipping business at a time when Nantucket was the third-largest port in New England. In 1773, two ships he chartered to the East India Company—the *Dartmouth* and the *Beaver*—were raided during the Boston Tea Party. His ship *Bedford* was the first vessel to carry the American flag into a British port in 1783.

But the American Revolution was hard on Nantucket and on Rotch's whaling business. Both Britain and America refused to let Nantucket ships trade goods and mistrusted islanders, whose adamant neutrality prevented them from taking a side. In his memoir, Rotch remembered it this way: "From the year 1775 to the end of the war we were in continual embarrassments. Our vessels were captured by the English, and our small vessels and boats sent to the continent for provisions denied and sent back empty under pretense that we supplied the British, which was without the least foundation. Prohibitory laws were often made in consequence of these reports, unfounded as they were. By this inhuman conduct we were sometimes in danger of being starved."

Finally, after Rotch made a personal request, the Continental Congress allowed a handful of Nantucket ships to sail. When the war ended, Rotch transferred his whaling operations to France. In time, Rotch's son moved it to Wales. Rotch returned to America in 1795 and settled in New Bedford, where he continued to own whale ships.

May 17

In 1924, town meeting voters set aside $1,500 to dredge the harbor near the Yacht Club, off Brant Point in front of the Steamship Authority pier, as well as around other small piers. The project had several objectives, including deepening the harbor to better allow small boats to anchor and reusing the dredged soil to fill in the marshes and improve Children's Beach (pictured here).

The $16,000 project was jointly funded by the state, the town and private parties. On May 17, a Boston-based dredging boat arrived, and the locals found its electric-powered suction system intriguing. Previous dredging operations had involved digging with a clamshell or scoop-shaped implement. In the May 31 edition of the *Inquirer & Mirror*, the "Waterfront" columnist asked, "Have you been down to watch the dredger sucking up mud and sending it ashore through several hundred feet of pipe?"

May 18

Married to Nathaniel Barney on this day in 1820, Elisa Starbuck Barney was the daughter of wealthy whaling merchant Joseph Starbuck and Sally Gardner Starbuck. She met Nathaniel Barney at her sister's wedding when he traveled here stand up for his cousin. Elisa worked on a genealogical record of more than forty thousand Nantucket families spanning over two and a half centuries, a work started by Benjamin Franklin Folger.

She was deeply involved in both the women's suffrage and antislavery movements. Frederick Douglass was among the many prominent guests at 100 Main Street, the Barneys' home. The Barneys lived at 100 Main Street until 1862, then moved 94 Main Street and finally relocated to Poughkeepsie, New York, to be near their children.

Elisa moved back to Nantucket after the death of Nathaniel. She stayed with her son Joseph until the home he built for her at 73 Main Street was completed in 1872. Eliza was eulogized as a "lifelong Quaker, liberal in her views and tolerant of the tenets of others."

May 19

In 1916, the U.S. Congress proposed to amend the U.S. Constitution to allow women to vote and stated, "The right of the citizens of the United States to vote shall not be denied or abridged by the United States or by any State on account of Sex."

The proposal came more than sixty years after women first called for the right to vote at the Seneca Falls Convention. The 1848 convention was organized by a group of Quakers, including Lucretia Coffin Mott, a native of Nantucket. Among the many resolutions debated at Seneca Falls was the idea of giving women the right to vote. The convention issued a "Declaration of Sentiments," which became the blueprint for the young movement.

On Nantucket, an island comfortable with having female leaders, the suffragette movement had many supporters. In 1853, famed orator Lucy Stone gave one of her first speeches on women's rights at the Nantucket Atheneum.

May 20

When the island's first steamboat service failed in 1818, most people concluded that it was not feasible to operate commercial service between Nantucket and the mainland. But Captain R.S. Bunker, a Nantucket native, refused to give up on the idea. Bunker wanted to prove to Nantucket that steam-powered boats would be better than sailboats, and he speculated that island investors would back him. In 1824, Bunker brought the steamboat *Connecticut* to Nantucket. But Nantucket mariners and investors were unimpressed, and the *Connecticut* venture failed.

In noting the *Connecticut*'s lack of success, the *Inquirer* said, "It is hoped the little specimen of steam navigation lately exhibited to the citizens of this town will remove all doubts, if doubts may still remain, of the utility of a steamboat to ply between Nantucket and the continent."

Captain Bunker tried again in 1828, and the *Connecticut* arrived on Nantucket with a dredging machine in tow. The dredger had a twelve-horsepower engine and removed a ton and a half of mud a minute. But because of a lack of funding the machine only dug one hundred feet. The day after its arrival, the *Connecticut* started for Falmouth with three hundred passengers but went only a short distance and had to return to port because of rough conditions. It returned to New York on May 29.

In 1830, the popularity of steam-powered vessels on Nantucket finally took hold, and a succession of private passenger vessels served Nantucket until the state formed the Steamship Authority in 1948.

May 21

In 1913, Nantucket's last living whaling master, Thaddeus C. Defriez, "dropped anchor at the ripe age of 90 years and 7 months," according to an obituary in the *Inquirer & Mirror*. Defriez first sailed in 1840 as a cooper on a Nantucket ship that left from Edgartown because it couldn't get past the sandbar at the entrance to the harbor. On his next trip, he worked as a boat steerer on a voyage that went to the northwest coast. On this trip, he was promoted to first mate when the ailing captain left the ship. In 1852, he was given command of the *Richard Mitchell* and set off for the Arctic Ocean to hunt bowhead whales. The *Richard Mitchell* came back mostly empty, but Defriez was given another ship in 1858, the *Sacramento* out of Westport, which had better success.

Returning home in June 1863, Defriez was aware of privateers destroying ships loyal to America and skillfully used a heavy fog to bring his ship home. It would be his last whaling trip.

On Nantucket, Defriez was an agent for the Nantucket Fishing Company and in 1868 was asked to fill in as register of the probate court. Later, he became the collector of customs for Nantucket, a position he held until 1873 when he resigned to become judge of the probate court. He served as a judge until 1908, when he retired. In retirement, he was a notary public and treasurer for the Prospect Hill Cemetery Association.

May 22

The *Inquirer & Mirror* in 1909 reported that the telegraph cable that connected Nantucket to the mainland had been acting "cranky." The Postal Telegraph Company sent a cable expert to troubleshoot, and he discovered a break about five miles off shore from Nantucket.

The island tolerated marginal telegraph service until 1917, when a new cable from Wood's Hole to Nantucket was installed. It was the longest submarine cable in the United States and took advantage of the most modern technology. Twelve railroad cars carrying twenty-four miles of cable were delivered to the cable-laying steamer *Robert C. Clowry.*

The cable followed the same route as the telegraph wire, going from Wood's Hole to Martha's Vineyard and then to Nantucket. The installers looped a portion of the cable into a figure eight and floated it into the most treacherous section called "Middle Ground." The cable ended fifteen feet off Nantucket and was accessible through a small box.

In total, the project laid down 550 miles of steel wire, weighing over three-quarters of a million pounds and costing about $100,000. In its report, *Bell Telephone* magazine said, "The Nantucket people really became a part of the great continental telephone system with its nine million stations a matter of great rejoicing to the islanders and to the thousands of summer visitors." In 1946, AT&T installed the country's second ultrahigh-frequency microwave system and began transmitting telephone calls to the island through the air.

May 23

Azubah Handy Cash accompanied her husband, Captain William Cash, aboard the Nantucket whale ship *Columbia* on a four-year whaling voyage from October 1850 to May 1854. Traveling with the captain and their ten-year-old son, Alexander, thirty-year-old Azubah gave birth to a son on the trip in August 1851. She kept a journal and while hunting off the coasts of Siberia and Japan on this day in 1852, wrote:

> *Capt. Pierce of the Ship* Kutusoff *came on board while Capt. F.'s wife were here and he met with a great misfortune the night before. His boats were fast to two right whales, cow and calf, and had 3 boats stove very bad, and one boatsteerer killed (they did not get him) and his carpenter hurt very bad, and one other man. He looked very sad and it made us all feel so. He left his wife and little girl at Hilo (a place dear to my heart being the birth-place of my little Murray). He was glad she was not with him up here, for it was bad enough to be here himself. It must be very discouraging to shipmates. The boatsteerer was a coloured man and his first whale he ever struck.*

The *Columbia* returned to Nantucket in May 1854 with 1,634 barrels of whale oil and 19,400 pounds of whalebone.

May 24

In 1899, the *Los Angeles Herald* printed a story with the headline: "She Never Saw Her Husband—Both Are Blind and He Thinks of Her as Young."

> *Mr. and Mrs. Charles H. Chase of Nantucket are each nearly 70 years old and they have been married the greater part of that time, yet the wife has never seen her husband, for she has been blind since she was 5. He too has been blind since he was 18. A neighbor says of them: "No one would suppose that blind persons were the caretakers of their little home. Inside there is not a speck of dust to be seen. The floors are spotless and the windows are decorated with house plants. Both Mr. and Mrs. Chase are devout members of the Baptist church. They always decline guidance to the church, declaring that when doing their duty Providence will guard and protect them from all harm. When, however, the infrequent opportunity of going to hear music, of which both are very fond, comes they are glad of assistance, fearing, as they say, that in the pursuit of pleasure harm may come to them." Mr. Chase has been blind fifty-two years, but his wife lost her slight at 5 years of age and has never seen her husband. He, however, saw her at 18, and thinks of her now as still in the full flush of girlish beauty…The couple are much esteemed by the townspeople, who never allow them to want for anything that money can purchase.*

May 25

Annie Barker Folger was born on this day on Nantucket in 1852. Much of her childhood was spent in California, and she graduated from Vassar College in 1872. She was a founding member of the Art Students League of New York. She lived and worked in New York City and Nantucket and was known for her landscape paintings. Her work was exhibited at the Panama Pacific Exhibition of 1915. Folger continued to paint on Nantucket well into the 1920s and was an important link to the burgeoning art colony that developed on the island between 1900 and 1910.

Folger was a founding board member of the Maria Mitchell Association, a life councilor of the Nantucket Historical Association and a trustee of the Nantucket Atheneum.

An ardent preservationist, she purchased the Elihu Coleman House on Hawthorne Lane at a public auction. William Hosier had bequeathed the property to the town of Nantucket to be kept as a memorial to Elihu Coleman, carpenter, Quaker minister and author of a pamphlet written in 1733 denouncing slavery.

May 26

George Bunker was the son of William Bunker, a French Huguenot. He married Jane Godfrey in England in 1644, and the pair moved to America. He drowned in Topsfield, Massachusetts, on May 26 in 1658. Jane married Richard Swain four months later, and they were among the island's first white settlers. At the time of the move, the Bunker children included Elizabeth, twelve; William, ten; Mary, six; Ann, four; and Martha, twelve. Jane and Richard Swain had two more children. Jane (Godfrey) Bunker Swain died on October 31, 1662, and hers was the first recorded death on Nantucket.

Now famous as a Nantucket founding family, the continuation of the Bunkers fell solely on William. In April 1669, he married Mary Macy, and they had seven sons.

Upon marrying, William received land, part of which was later traded to the town to establish a public house, church and jail. In 1686, William Bunker was appointed keeper of the jail.

Sometime in the 1670s, sailors from a French ship broke into his house, took food and forced Bunker to help them sail through Vineyard Sound. He was released a day later and returned home.

William's heirs were active in education and local politics. James Madison Bunker (1811–1873) was town clerk before he became judge and teacher. Asa Bunker (1802–1869) was register of deeds. Augusta Bunker (1855–1886) married Walter M. Fee and moved to Washington Territory and Idaho to operate a ranch and teach school. Madison Bunker (1853–1916) became a veterinarian in Newton, Massachusetts.

May 27

In 1942, 340 miles north of Bermuda, a German submarine torpedoed and sank the Dutch ship *Polyphemus*. The explosions demolished the stern and instantly killed fifteen Chinese crew members in their quarters. Sixty people survived, including fourteen people whose ship, the M/V *Norland*, had been sunk by a German submarine five days earlier. The survivors abandoned the *Polyphemus* in five lifeboats, and soon the German submarine surfaced to question them. Satisfied with their answers, the Germans gave the lifeboats a carton of cigarettes, directions to New York and left.

The lifeboats became separated on the second night.

On May 29, one lifeboat was picked up by a Portuguese ship and its passengers dropped in New York. A fishing boat about fifty miles east of the *Nantucket* lightship picked up the crew of another lifeboat on June 1 and took the passengers to New Bedford.

The *Torvanger* picked up the crew of the third lifeboat about 130 miles east of Nantucket, and they landed in New Bedford on June 3. A Portuguese ship picked up the fourth crew on June 3 and took them to New York. On May 29, a different German U-boat surfaced to talk to the crew of the last lifeboat and gave them water and directions to the nearest port. On May 30, another U-boat spotted them, and that German crew gave them bread and a bottle of rum. Finally, the U.S. Coast Guard picked up the passengers of the fifth lifeboat on June 5 and took them to Nantucket.

May 28

In 1907, the *Inquirer & Mirror* published this small item:

O.C. Hussey went to Siasconset on Tuesday, to bring back a load of mattresses. A good stiff breeze was blowing and on the way down he chanced to light his pipe for a smoke. A frisky spark happened to drop on one of the mattresses behind him and soon a lively little blaze was in progress. One or two teams passed him and the drivers called out to Mr. Hussey that his load was afire, but the gale made the sound of their voices inaudible, and, thinking they were merely giving him a friendly greeting he continued on his way with never a glance behind him. It was not until he felt an unusual burst of heat that he realized his dilemma, but it was too late to save the mattresses, and hastily pulling them from the wagon he enjoyed a nice little bonfire by the roadside.

May 29

In 1775, the Continental Congress approved an order banning Nantucket from trading with any business outside Massachusetts. The order was included as part of a letter inviting Canadian citizens to join America in its fight for independence from Britain. Written by John Jay, the order states: "That no provisions or necessaries of any kind be exported to the island of Nantucket, except from the colony of Massachusetts Bay, the convention of which colony is desired to take measures for effectually providing the said Island, upon their application to purchase the same, with as much provision, as shall be necessary for its internal use, and no more.

"The Congress deeming it of great importance to North America, that the British fishery should not be furnished with provisions from this continent thro' Nantucket, earnestly recommend a vigilant execution of this resolve to all committees."

Nantucket made both the colonists and the English nervous. The island was home to both English Loyalists and those who supported independence. Its predominant religion, Quakerism, demanded pacifism instead of war. And the booming whaling industry kept Nantucket ships sailing all over the world.

But the impact of the congressional trade embargo was a harsh one for Nantucket citizens. Harassed and prevented from sailing any ships by both sides, island residents were starving without food and freezing without any heating fuel.

Some island leaders tried appealing to the British and to the Congress for relief. Others resorted to smuggling or moved off the island.

May 30

Nantucket purchased a new steam-powered fire truck in 1896. The fire truck was the first one not pumped by hand and had undergone rigorous testing to make sure it would accommodate the island's needs. On the first day of trials, schoolchildren were let out early and a large crowd turned out. The truck set up on Orange Street, and fire crews sprayed water thirty feet past the lightning rod on the Unitarian Church tower. They added 1,000 feet of hose and the new engine was able to pump water 170 feet in the air.

The fire department continued to test the truck in different locations. Satisfied, selectmen convened a special session and approved payment. Manufactured by the American Eagle Company, the engine cost $2,750.

May 31

In 1837, during a New England Anti-Slavery Convention held in Boston, a former slave named Samuel Snowden rose to speak: "What I have to say on this matter comes right from the heart. I have got no learning to make a speech. All the learning I ever had was in the battlefield. Sir, the cornfield worked by the slave."

Snowden, now a Methodist minister, told of meeting of a southern slave owner named Wolfolk in Boston to recover his escaped slaves. The owner told him:

> *Last summer I bought forty and sent them to sell and the slaves rose upon the Captain and threw him overboard and I lost them. They was taken on board a whale ship after they rose upon the Captain and brought into Nantucket and some of them got to Boston and that was the reason Wolfolk come here to look after his burden. He knew it [slavery] was wrong and his conscience had made him promise to give it up and he acknowledged to me that his losing the slaves was a judgment of God.*
>
> *Wolfolk got five of the slaves here and there was one poor woman who had been advised to go out of the way because your liberty Constitution makes your Courts here give up the slaves to their masters when called for. But it was no use they steered as straight as a bee to a hive and took the poor woman. That I believe was all he got out of his forty slaves.*

June 1

In 1796, the British brig *Swallow* received a "Letter of Marque" to capture French ships. The Letter of Marque and Reprisal was a government license authorizing privateers to attack enemy vessels (Britain and France were at war at the time) and bring them before admiralty courts for condemnation and sale. In December 1803, the *Swallow* captured the French whale ship *Hero* off the coast of Portugal, and its captain, Stephen Rawson, and its first mate, William Morris, hailed from Nantucket.

In late 1802, the *Hero*, an American cargo ship, landed in Le Havre just as Napoleon Bonaparte was visiting. Napoleon bought the ship and refitted it as a French whale ship. In early 1803, the *Hero* went south on a whaling voyage with a mixed crew of Americans, Frenchmen and Englishmen.

After its capture, the *Hero* was taken to Britain, and Morris testified before the British Admiralty Court. On June 1, 1804, records state that twenty-five-year-old Morris "answers that He was born and has always resided, save when subject at sea, and now lives with his wife and family…at Nantucket." In his testimony, Morris said he was not an owner of the *Hero* but had the usual $\frac{1}{25}$ interest in the profits from the voyage.

After extensive testimony, the court claimed the *Hero* a lawful prize of war and condemned it. In September 1805, it was sold and renamed the *Atlantic*. By 1806, the *Atlantic* was a British whale ship captained by William Swain of Nantucket, who would have one of the longest careers in the British whale fishery.

June 2

A fire started in a Union Street ropewalk in 1838 and destroyed more than twenty buildings downtown. Among the businesses lost were two candle factories, two oil companies, five shops, a twine factory, two buildings at the head of the wharf and ten residences.

Hampered by a strong southwest wind, firefighters struggled to contain the fire. They used gunpowder to blow up six buildings and successfully stopped the flames from reaching the extensive C. Mitchell & Co whale oil business.

The June 6 edition of the *Inquirer* described the scene: "The immense quantities of oil which were at one time on fire, created so intense a heat, that it was scarcely possible to approach the scene of ruin; while tar, hemp and other similar ingredients mingled with it, threw up huge volumes of smoke, so dense as to threaten suffocation to all within its range.

"As the oil burst from the burning casks in the oil houses &c. it ran in blazing streams into the harbor and docks, continuing to burn upon the surface of the tide, and in some instances setting fire to property on Commercial Wharf. The whole scene to those who had leisure to contemplate it, presented a most awfully magnificent spectacle."

At a special town meeting held the same night, voters appointed a committee to investigate the fire, form a plan to help its victims and recommend new rules on limiting the height of wooden buildings.

June 3

A Canadian freighter picked up a lifeboat with thirty-two survivors of a German U-boat attack and brought them to safety in Halifax, Nova Scotia, in 1942. The German submarine had torpedoed and sunk the British freighter SS *Mattawin* the day before and sent seven lifeboats with seventy-one people adrift in northern Atlantic Ocean waters. A Canadian military plane spotted the lifeboats on the day of the attack and dropped food and distress flares.

On June 4, a lifeboat with twenty *Mattawin* survivors landed at Nauset on Cape Cod. And on June 7, the USS *General Green* rescued nineteen survivors and brought them to Nantucket.

Between May 12 and August 18, 1942, German U-boat captain Karlchen Thurmann and his crew attacked seven ships off the coast of Canada that belonged to the United States, Britain, Norway, Holland, Belgium and Sweden. Thurmann, who would receive the Knight's Cross of the Iron Cross in August for the attacks, sunk six ships and damaged one. The submarine had even successfully cruised up the St. Lawrence River and sunk two ships there. Almost out of fuel and rations by the time of the *Mattawin* attack, the submarine discovered an empty lifeboat near the site of wrecked freighter the day after it sank and helped itself to the boat's rations. Captain Thurmann stated in his report, "Lots of well-preserved bread and chocolate for two complete meals; and condensed milk, too, and good-tasting vitamin tablets of enormously satiating effect, enough for fourteen days, all very welcome."

June 4

In 1864, nineteen-year-old Union soldier Josiah Fitch Murphey wrote in his journal:

> *Today we are in the same place as yesterday and our life are in constant danger. Many of the dead and wounded lay between the lines where they have lain for three or four days. At night we crawl out to some of them and drag them in laying flat on our bellies to do so. The wounded we send to the hospital and the dead we bury in this way: when we get a number of them we dig a long trench say 10, 15 or 20 feet long 6 ft. wide and two or three feet deep, lay the dead in side by side, place a piece of cloth or blanket over the face and cover them up raising the ground in a long mound over them to the height of about a foot or eighteen inches.*
>
> *Sometimes this was so hastily done on account of the Rebs. Firing upon us that when the fall rains come they would wash away the earth and a foot or a hand would be seen protruding from the ground, when we were marching over fields that had been fought the year before; Many of the dead on this field were buried by being covered with earth thrown out in building breastworks, the men being killed when the charge was made and the breastworks built afterward.*

June 5

A contract to create Nantucket's first whaling company was drafted in 1672 between town proprietors and a man named James Loper. Yet there is no evidence that the townspeople or Loper ever actually killed any whales. It wasn't until 1690 that the proprietors successfully established a commercial fishery when they hired Cape Codder Ichabod Paddock to teach them how to do it.

In those early days, whales could be easily gotten close to shore. Paddock set up four areas on the South Shore, each with a lookout station and a crew of six men. One man stood watch while the rest stayed in small huts on the beach. When a whale was spotted, the crew members set out in small boats to chase, harpoon and kill it. They towed the animal to shore, and the trypots, large cast-iron pots used to boil down the blubber into oil, were set up on the beach.

Nantucket's whaling business really took off in 1712 when Christopher Hussey brought back the first sperm whale. Nantucket whalemen found that the oil rendered from a sperm whale was superior to other types of whale oil, and the market for it expanded quickly. In 1715, there were six Nantucket ships hunting whales. By 1730, there were twenty-five. In 1720, a Nantucket ship took the first delivery of whale oil to England, and in 1723, the town built Straight Wharf to give vessels a place to load and unload. By 1726, whales close to shore were scarce, and Nantucketers began sailing farther, and staying away longer, in search of their prey.

June 6

Husband and wife, and stage and film stars, George Fawcett and Percy Haswell Fawcett died on the same day, six years apart, in 1939 and in 1945. The two helped found the Siasconset summer actors' colony and moved here full time near the end of George Fawcett's life.

George Fawcett appeared in 151 films between 1915 and 1933. Trained for the stage at Sargent's School of Acting, Fawcett had thirty years of theatrical experience when he began a film career around 1914. At fifty-four years old, he was called the "Grand Old Man" of films and worked with D.W. Griffith on many pictures, including the director's final silent film in 1929.

In 1895, he married Percy Haswell, who first acted on stage as a child. She first appeared on Broadway in 1885. Haswell acted in two silent films and numerous plays staged in New York City, Washington and Boston. Fawcett and Haswell (pictured here with their daughter) both formed acting companies, and in 1925, Haswell directed the Broadway play *The Complex*.

June 7

Former U.S. president Grover Cleveland visited Nantucket in 1897. After his second election to the presidency in 1892, President Cleveland established the first "summer White House" at the nearby Grey Gables mansion in Bourne, on Cape Cod. The president was seen frequently around Cape Cod fishing and sailing.

A June 12, 1897 item in the *Inquirer & Mirror* under the heading "Incog." said Cleveland had visited Nantucket as a guest of Commander E.C. Benedict aboard the steamer yacht *Oenida*. Four years earlier, while still president, Cleveland had arranged for surgeons to turn the *Oenida* into a floating hospital, and they removed a large tumor located above the roof of his mouth. The entire procedure was kept secret so as not to panic the nation.

On Nantucket, President Cleveland and Commander Benedict were given a private tour, and the newspaper noted no one would have known of the visit except that the party stopped to send a telegraph to Mrs. Cleveland.

June 8

Education reformers submitted a letter to the Massachusetts legislature in 1827 in support of creating a new private school to be called the Admiral Sir Isaac Coffin Lancasterian School. Opened that same year, the Coffin School, as it came to be known, was founded by British navy admiral Sir Isaac Coffin, who had visited the island in 1826.

Coffin donated £2,500 for a school to give the descendants of Tristram Coffin, one of the island's first white settlers, a traditional English education. The school opened on the corner of Fair and Lyon Streets with 130 children. In 1846, the school was closed, most likely due to the island's declining population and economy.

It had opened and closed again by 1903 when, in partnership with the public schools, it offered high school students classes in the vocational arts. By 1941, Coffin School was a part of the public school system, and classes continued there until 1978.

June 9

In 1809, Abiel Folger noted in her diary, "the ship *Arora* [*Aurora*] got to the kay." Abiel and her husband, Timothy Folger, were among the fifteen Nantucket families who moved to Milford Haven, Wales, in 1792 to establish a whaling venture sponsored by the British government. The British offered Nantucket families political and financial incentives in exchange for developing a whale fishery in the southern oceans of the world.

At the time, Nantucket had been economically crippled by the Revolutionary War and then hobbled by a British tax on whale oil. The island families saw the Milford experiment as an opportunity to get reestablished and also avoid the tax. First proposed by Sir Charles Greville in 1783, the British government was slow to back the idea. Three prominent Nantucket whaling merchants—William Rotch, Timothy Folger and Samuel Starbuck Sr.—decided not to wait and relocated to France and Canada. In 1791, Greville got British funding to create a new town called Milford Haven. The Nova Scotia–based families, Folger and Starbuck, relocated there immediately. In 1800, Rotch's son Benjamin would move part of his whaling business there from France.

The Milford Haven whaling industry never really thrived, and the transplanted Nantucket families never abandoned their link to the island. The Milford Haven ships were provisioned in Nantucket and New Bedford because it was cheaper. Those ships carried Nantucket's world-famous spermaceti whale oil candles back to England. And Abiel Folger's diary records many visits by Nantucket ships stopping in at Milford to visit the transplanted islanders.

June 10

A ship carrying soldiers who had fought for the North in the Civil War under General William Tecumsah Sherman went aground on Smith's Point in 1865. The ship, SS *Satacona*, grounded in a thick fog near the head of Hither Creek. For some of the ship's passengers, this would be their second wreck in two days. The soldiers had been on the troop ship *Admiral Dupont* when it collided with the *Satacona* and sank off Cape May, New Jersey, on June 8.

The first word Nantucket citizens had of the mishap was when the soldiers marched through town and onto a steamship that was preparing to sail for the mainland. Citizens scrambled to provide food for the soldiers before the boat departed.

The *Admiral Dupont* was a former blockade runner that had been repurposed as a government transport ship. Originally named *Anglia*, it was renamed *Admiral DuPont* in 1863. The ship was an iron side-wheel steamship that served the North successfully until it was captured by Rebels in South Carolina in 1862. After adjudication by the U.S. Prize Court, the Admiral DuPont was sold to new owners in 1863.

June 11

Mabel Gardiner Hubbard, deaf and ten years younger than her groom, married Alexander Graham Bell in 1877. But things got off to a rocky start. In the summer of 1875 the pair had a falling out in Cambridge, Massachusetts, and Mabel left for Siasconset before they reconciled. Distraught, Bell followed her to Nantucket and sent a letter from the Ocean House Hotel (now Jared Coffin House). In it, he said:

> *Believe me I have not come to Nantucket to wound and pain you. I respect and honour you too much for that.*
>
> *I have come to show my confidence and my trust in you. Whatever those about you may do—I do not fear that you will ridicule the honest love I have for you—nor treat me lightly because I have offended you.*
>
> *I await your answer as to whether you will see me or not. Do not do so if you are afraid of me. There is only one question that I wish to ask you and that is that you will tell me frankly all that there is in me that you dislike, and that I can alter.*
>
> *Perhaps it is too much to ask of you—so you need not do so unless you care to do it.*
>
> *I would take it as a kindness if some good friend would do it for if you are afraid to speak.*
>
> *I wish to amend my life for you. Whatever may be the result of this visit—Believe me both now and ever*
> *Yours affectionately,*
> *A. Graham Bell*

June 12

Walter Folger Jr. was born on Nantucket in 1765 into a wealthy family that manufactured spermaceti candles. Directly related to two of the island's founding English families, Folger was a bright child who had a gift for math and all things mechanical. Mostly self-taught, he learned to navigate by the moon, mastered algebra and French and had a lifelong interest in comets and astronomy. A cousin to Benjamin Franklin and Maria Mitchell, Folger shared Franklin's curiosity and inventiveness and Mitchell's interest in the stars.

Folger established himself as one of the best mathematicians and engineers of his time when he created an ingenious clock that displays the year, the day and the times that the sun and moon rise and set. It also shows the earth's position around the sun.

He passed the bar, and he was appointed judge of the county court, known as the Court of Common Pleas, and served for six years. That began a political career that included representing the island in the Massachusetts House and Senate and serving two terms in the United States Congress.

Folger was a friend of Thomas Jefferson and elected as a Democratic-Republican to the Fifteenth Congress and the Sixteenth Congress (March 4, 1817–March 3, 1821). When not attending to congressional business, Folger could be found in the Patent Office pursuing his interests in mechanical designs. Folger co-founded a scientific association in 1826 called the Nantucket Philosophical Institution and died in Nantucket on September 8, 1849.

June 13

In an *Inquirer & Mirror* article on bicycling, Max Wagner wrote in 1893, "The miracle that the bipede has wrought all over the civilized world has probably been nowhere more pronounced than on this beloved sand heap of ours, that the world generally knows as the island of Nantucket."

The first bicycles on Nantucket were so heavy few people wanted to ride them. But in 1880, the Brockton Bicycle Club gave an exhibition of a new, lighter model, and a bicycle craze was born. "Two years ago the cyclist here flocked all by himself; now everybody, irrespective of age, sex or previous condition of laziness, rides—or wants to ride—a wheel," Wagner noted.

An increase in mishaps caused town voters to create a law in 1894 that fined bicycle riders twenty dollars if they didn't have a bicycle bell when they were riding faster than ten miles an hour, riding at night or riding on the sidewalk.

June 14

Nantucket's whaling era ended in 1870 when the last whale ship, the *Eunice H. Adams*, commanded by Captain Zenas Coleman, arrived back in port in 1870. Once the largest whaling port in the world, by 1870, the island had lost 60 percent of its citizens, and it would lose another one thousand people over the next five years.

A combination of seismic events contributed to the end of whaling on Nantucket: a devastating fire in 1846 destroyed the town and its wharves, shifting sands at the entrance to the harbor prevented large ships from entering, the allure of the 1849 California gold rush pulled many young men west and 280 Nantucket men left to fight in the Civil War. In addition, whale populations diminished and petroleum oil was discovered in 1859.

The 1860s was a difficult period for Nantucket, and after years of economic depression, 1870 would be a turning point for the island as it fashioned itself into a tourist destination. Island newspapers and steamship companies marketed Nantucket to potential visitors, and new hotels opened to accommodate the growing tourist trade. In 1874, United States president Ulysses S. Grant visited and cemented Nantucket's popularity as a travel destination.

June 15

Lizzie Coggeshall, daughter of Great Point light keeper George Coggeshall, wrote a letter to her cousin in 1862.

Dear Coz Henry,

I was very much disappointed when I opened your letter, not to find your picture. I think if you knew what a comfort it is to look at my friends, when I am out to the Point, and get entirely tired of seeing the faces of my family, you would send it. I think I shall retain the looks of the family as I had them before me so long. As regards the assistant keeper I would say he is very pleasant, but I think when father is removed from the Point, I shall have served an apprenticeship at light keeping as long as I care to. You think my experience in household affairs is very limited, but I will assure you I do not care to know more about this house keeping than I already do.

I am disgusted with this war for I can't see that we gain one inch of ground. I wish I was a man that I could go to see what was going on, for we don't hear anything here.

Grandma is at the Point.

I think Uncle Hiram will be of more consequence than ever if he returns. I think Liz C. is going to write today, so perhaps between us you may hear something. I am going home next week. I think I shall take my friend Mary Frank with me...

June 16

The *Daily Alta California* newspaper reprinted a letter from Mark Twain in 1867 that recounted a New York City dinner party he attended with a group of Nantucket residents. Twain wrote that party guests discussed at length how the island had suffered from a trade embargo during the American Revolution, and one dinner guest told Twain that Nantucket horses are "celebrated for their general worthlessness, imbecility, and marvelous slowness." The guest told the story of an island horse sold to a cavalry officer, who came back in a rage claiming he'd been swindled.

"How?" said the Nantucketer.

"Why, there's not a bit of 'go' in him—and yet you warranted him as a good war horse," said the officer.

"Yes, I did, and by George, he is a good war horse—he'd sooner die than run."

June 17

The *Nantucket Gazette* reported a mutiny on the whale ship *Potomac* in 1816. Captain Alfred Alley left Boston on June 5 with an almost all–African American crew and headed for South America to hunt whales.

According to the newspaper, the *Potomac* arrived on Nantucket on June 10, anchored off shore and the captain went to town to get provisions. Captain Alley, his first and second mates and the cooper were the only white men, and the rest of the crew consisted of eleven African American men. For unknown reasons, these eleven men refused to follow the first mate's orders for a time. Although they eventually returned to work, tension grew between the two sides, and African American crew members again refused to obey orders until the situation turned into a full mutiny. The mutineers armed themselves with knives, a gun, a carpenter's adze and iron poles and took control of the *Potomac*. The ship's mate escaped in a whaleboat and went to shore to inform Captain Alley, who organized a large group of island men to take back control of the ship.

Alley brought charges against two of the mutineers, who were jailed, and four more men stole a whaleboat and deserted the ship. The two jailed men—Richard Taylor of Boston and Robert Smith of Halifax, Nova Scotia—were moved to Boston and charged with assault. The pair did not contest the charge and were sentenced to ten days of solitary confinement and three years of hard labor.

June 18

U.S. secretary of the treasury Alexander Hamilton submitted the first report on lighthouses to President George Washington in 1790. In 1789, the ninth law passed by the newly formed Congress put the federal government in charge of operating lighthouses. At the time, Nantucket had a lighthouse on Brant Point and Great Point.

In his report, Secretary Hamilton requested permission to appoint Paul Pinkham as the keeper of Great Point Light (called Sandy Point Light at the time) and compensate him $250 a year. Five years later, Pinkham sent a letter to the Lighthouse Board requesting a raise. "Sir: It is my ardent request that you will be pleased to lay before the Honorable Senate and House of Representatives the enclosed, and make use of the utmost your Influence to carry it into effect, as the Smallness of the Sallary renders it very hard for me to subsist. The twelve cords of wood which was allowed me by the Legislature of this Commonwealth as part of my Sallary now costs $96 landed at the Lighthouse, provisions in like proportion & all other Necessaries of Life. Therefore you must know that the Small Sum of $250 without any other natural advantages is a scanty support for a Family thus far removed from all the other immolients whatsoever. Now Sir your earnest attention to this shall be regarded and ever acknowledged by your humble Servant, Paul Pinkham."

Pinkham remained keeper of the Great Point Light until he died in 1799.

June 19

U.S. president Franklin D. Roosevelt sailed the schooner *Amber Jack II* into Nantucket harbor in 1933. William Holland, of the Nantucket Democratic Town Committee, persuaded Roosevelt to come to Nantucket while the president was on a sailing vacation off the coast of New England. Followed by a convoy of destroyers and press boats, the *Amber Jack II* arrived on Nantucket in the late morning. The destroyers anchored outside the harbor, but coast guard and press boats followed the president's yacht in. The president remained on the boat for his entire visit but did receive a visit from Holland. According to newspaper reports, the president was in high spirits and announced that he did not plan to set foot on land for two weeks. He added, "But some time I am coming to Nantucket again. It is thirty years since I have been here and I realize that lots of changes must have occurred in the meantime."

June 20

In 1661, tribal chief, or sachem, Wanackmamack sold Tuckernuck, a small island off Nantucket's west end, to Tristram Coffin Sr. and his sons. In 1672, Wanackmamack's son Ahkeiman claimed ownership of the island in a court suit. A Registry of Deeds document dated June 20 states that Ahkeiman had no right to Tuckernuck but, because he was a sachem's son, ordered the Coffins to grant him land on Nantucket and the right to hunt whales.

When the English arrived, there were two Native American tribes on Nantucket. Each had a sachem, and they began trading and selling land to the English right away. Court documents from 1673 to 1754 are filled with transactions, disputes and settlements between the Native Americans and the English founding families.

Originally welcoming of the new island residents, the Native Americans grew wary when they realized how many white people were coming and felt the courts discriminated against them. Plus, the English settlers had trouble communicating the idea that the sale of property meant the natives had to surrender all claim to it.

In addition, the English seemed dismayed by the amount of alcohol the Native Americans consumed. Thomas Macy wrote a forceful letter to the governor in 1676 asking him to create laws designed to curb Native American drinking, but they had little effect.

In 1763, 222 of the island's 358 Native Americans died in a smallpox epidemic, and their population was never able to reestablish itself. By 1809, only a handful of Native American citizens remained on Nantucket.

June 21

In 1753, Peleg Folger left Nantucket on the whale ship *Grayhound*, headed north to the Labrador Sea (Labrador whaling camp pictured here). Folger's journal describes the bloody business of whaling:

June 21st, 5th of week: First part of this 24 hours fine weather. We Saw whales and Elisha hove out his Boat and Struck one and we Soon made her Spout Blood but She was a Long time a Dying but at last She dy'd and we Got her between both Vessels and Cut her head off; the Bone measures 8 foot 3 inches, as being a very large deep whale. So it Blew up a Little Chopling and we got our vessels apart and One Boat's Crew went on board Elisha and rafted some Blubber and we took it onboard our vessel. So they kept cutting upon the whale all the remaining part of the day.

June 22

In 1929, during an elaborate ceremony, the telephone company "cut over" from an outdated magnetic telephone system at its Fair Street building to a battery system housed in a new building on Union Street (pictured with a fancy kiosk in the 1960s here). The new system replaced hand-cranked telephones and alerted operators to an incoming call by turning on a light at the switchboard.

Officials and one hundred invited guests gathered on the night of the changeover. The first phone call came from Representative Arthur W. Jones to John Terry. In a conversation heard by all, Jones said, "We would like to have you come down and join us. There is some cooling refreshment in the room down below and some nice-looking girls at the switchboard, so if you feel that you would like to come down, we would all be glad to have you with us."

June 23

Botanist and ornithologist Eugene P. Bicknell spent eleven years studying Nantucket plants. Born in 1859, Bicknell published "The Ferns and Flowering Plants of Nantucket" in the *Torrey Botanical Club Bulletin* in twenty installments between 1908 and 1919. He was the youngest founding member of the American Ornithologists' Union and a member of the New York Botanical Garden and the Torrey Botanical Club. Bicknell has many plants and birds named after him, including the Bicknell's thrush and *Crataegus bicknellii*, a species of Hawthorn tree found only on Nantucket.

Several island people, most notably island historian and amateur botanist Grace Brown Gardner, sent Bicknell plant specimens throughout his study, some of which were preserved at the New York Botanical Garden. On June 23, Bicknell reports that Grace Brown Gardner discovered a *Lathyris latifolits* cluster in full flower in the south part of the town.

June 24

Summer residents Sidney Chase and David Noyes placed an ad in the *Inquirer & Mirror* in 1897 announcing a meeting to discuss the creation of a golf club. To their surprise, a large group of people attended, and within two months, the island had its first golf course. The new Nantucket Golf Club purchased land on low rolling hills on the north side of the island and built a nine-hole course that

grazing sheep and goats kept mowed. Two years later, the club replaced tents with a full-fledged clubhouse and eventually expanded the course to eighteen holes.

In 1949, professional golfer Oswald "Tup" Tupancy purchased the course and renamed it Tupancy Links. By that time, other golf courses had opened, and the course was a modest nine holes. Tupancy decided to close the course for good four years later. In 1976, Tupancy donated the former course to the Nantucket Conservation Foundation, which has preserved it as open space.

June 25

Seth Coffin was born on Nantucket in 1753 and started whaling at a young age. In 1800, while whaling off the coast of Brazil as commander of the ship *Minerva*, Coffin's leg was badly crushed while capturing a sperm whale. There was no doctor on board, but Coffin had once witnessed an amputation. He asked his mate to use a whale-cutting tool, braced himself and ordered the man to do the procedure. When he was finished, both men fainted. Seth Coffin lived to age seventy-seven and had seven children.

In 1823, Seth Coffin's twelve-year-old nephew Alexander Coffin, whose family had moved off-island when he was a boy, ran away to Nantucket and sailed on Coffin's last whaling voyage aboard the *Aurora*. Alexander, nicknamed "Long Tom" Coffin, eventually landed in New Zealand and first appears in records at the Rhodes Brothers Whaling Station in 1840. He also worked as a drover and laborer before setting up in farming at Okains Bay. He dabbled in poetry, acted as a veterinarian and raised his family on the farm.

Alexander Coffin was married in 1850 but spent most of his life with another woman, Caroline Henrietta Bathurst. They had fourteen children and named one of them in honor of his uncle Seth. Legally, children of unmarried parents took the mother's last name, but some of the Bathurst/Coffin children chose to also use Coffin as a surname.

June 26

In 1854, Nathan Manter left Nantucket as captain of the whaling schooner *William P. Dolliver*. Born in 1819, Manter spent his life on the water and went on his first whaling voyage in 1835. By the end of his career, he was a beloved whale ship and steamboat captain and a favorite portrait subject of the painter Eastman Johnson.

Manter followed the traditional path to captain, working first as boat steerer, then second mate and first mate until finally taking command of his first ship, the *William P. Dolliver*. While serving as mate of the *Java* on an 1848 cruise, he was mistakenly reported as killed by a whale.

After commanding the *William P. Dolliver*, Manter worked for the Nantucket Steamboat Company and remained there until his death in 1897. He captained the steamers *Island Home*, *Massachusetts* and *Telegraph*. He claimed to have rounded Brant Point forty thousand times in his lifetime.

June 27

Whaling Captain Obed Starbuck, famous for saving a ship and its crew from a pirate, died in 1882. Born in 1797, Starbuck was a mate on the ship *Hero* in 1818. While anchoring off the coast of Chile, the *Hero* was captured by the pirate Benevedes, and Starbuck was imprisoned in his cabin. When another ship came close, Benevedes believed it was a government vessel and unmoored the *Hero* so it would drift ashore. He then left most of the crew locked up and rowed to shore with Captain James Russell and a cabin boy. Starbuck, aware the ship was abandoned, broke down his door, freed the crew and took command. He sailed the ship to Valparaiso and alerted the authorities, who went after the pirates. Benevedes, in a rage over the loss of the *Hero*, killed Captain Russell and the boy.

Starbuck found Captain George Pollard in Valparaiso, as well as a few of the crew members of the whale ship *Essex*, which had been stove by a whale. News of the two disasters arrived on Nantucket before the survivors did, and on August 1821, the ship *Hero*, commanded by Starbuck, in the company of the ship *Two Brothers*, on which Captain Pollard was passenger, came into Nantucket harbor. They were greeted by a crowd of two thousand people. Starbuck commanded the *Hero* on two more voyages and discovered several islands in the Pacific Ocean.

June 28

In 1828, the *Inquirer* published a recap of the annual three-day sheep-shearing celebration, writing, "In addition to the ceremonies, cheer and hospitality, connected with those immediately engaged in shearing, there is a large number of tents pitched a little to the

northward of the sheepfold, for the special purpose of making pockets lighter and heads and stomachs heavier."

Islanders started shearing sheep in 1696, and by 1775, the flock had grown to fifteen thousand animals. The annual shearing became so popular with tourists that a festival grew up around it, and by 1828, many visitors came from off-island to enjoy the bustle of the sheep shearing along with food, games, music and dancing.

The sheep were herded from common grazing areas to Miacomet, where they were moved through an elaborate series of fences that allowed handlers to segregate the animals by owner, wash them in Miacomet Pond and then shear them.

June 29

Nantucket's highest-ranking naval officer, Vice Admiral Marcel Gouin of Siasconset, was born in 1900. During World War I, he was a member of the Student Army Training Corps and graduated from the United States Naval Academy in 1924. After serving on ships, Gouin entered navy flight training school in Pensacola, Florida. During World War II, Gouin served on the aircraft carrier *Hornet*, which was sunk during a battle in the Pacific Ocean, and later on the carrier *Saratoga*.

He was director of the Naval Air Test Center in Maryland in 1943 and was appointed commander of the aircraft carrier *Admiralty Islands* in 1944. Gouin continued to shift between teaching, testing and field leadership positions until he retired. He returned to Nantucket and served on the Nantucket Airport Commission and was a member of the Nantucket Historical Association and the Wharf Rats Club. He died on May 20, 1960.

June 30

A three-alarm fire at a New Bedford steamship dock in 1924 destroyed the steamer *Sankaty*. The fire spread so rapidly that Captain Manuel K. Sylvia, who was asleep in his room, and his crew of five had to jump overboard to escape it.

Believed to have been caused by a carelessly thrown match or cigarette, the fire began on the wharf near barrels of oil. The oil ignited, causing a small explosion, and fire quickly spread to a load of hay waiting on dock to be loaded for the next Nantucket trip. The fire then moved to the side of the steamer, and it burned completely in a matter of minutes. The total loss of boat and wharf came to $325,000, and the crew members lost all their belongings. The steamship company lost its wharf, buildings and all the records in them but was back running close to a normal schedule within three days.

July 1

In 1828, the Supreme Court convened on Nantucket, and a defense lawyer on the docket was the great Massachusetts statesman and orator Daniel Webster. According to his letters, Webster argued cases on Nantucket in 1827 and 1828. Samuel Lorenzo Knapp quotes him in *A Memoir of the Life of Daniel Webster*, saying, "The people of Nantucket are intelligent, for these whale ships, for nearly half the time while on their voyage, are in truth Lyceums where mathematics and natural history and general knowledge are taught. The log books and journals of these whalers are well kept, the hand writing in these books is good and the reckonings admirably made, and everyone does something towards making a minute history of the voyage."

Webster noted the need for a breakwater at the entrance to the harbor and petitioned the U.S. Congress to build one in May 1828. In a speech to the Senate, Webster said, "A vast coasting trade plies through this sound, which is a sort of defile, a narrow passage obstructed with rocks and shoals and deficient in convenient and safe harbors. The anchoring of a floating light vessel in the sound had furnished the means of ascertaining the number of vessels which passed through it annually and perhaps some members will be surprised to hear that that number does not fall short of sixteen thousand."

During his Nantucket visits, Webster also gave a speech at the Nantucket Atheneum and met with astronomer and mathematician Walter Folger.

July 2

In 1659, Thomas Mayhew issued nine Englishmen the deed to land at the western end of Nantucket: "Be it known unto all men by these presents that I Thomas Mayhew of Martin's Vineyard, Merchant do hereby acknowledge that I have sold unto Tristram Coffin, Thomas Macy, Christopher Hussey, Richard Swain, Thomas Barnard, Peter Coffin, Stephen Greenleaf, John Swain & William Pile all the Right and Interest I bought of James Forret Gentleman, Steward unto the Lord Sterling and of Richard Vines sometime of Sacho, Gent, Steward General unto Sr Ferdinando Georges Knight." The nine men paid Mayhew thirty pounds and two beaver hats. Six weeks later, the new owners held their first meeting on Nantucket and began the business of creating a new community. At that meeting, they decided that each could have a sixty-rod portion of land wherever they chose for the purpose of building a house.

On October 10, 1659, Mayhew deeded the rights to Tuckernuck Island, located off Nantucket's western end, to Tristram Coffin Sr., Peter Coffin, Tristram Coffin Jr. and James Coffin. The men paid five pounds for the island.

Prior to making their arrangement with Mayhew, the proprietors also received permission from the island's Native American sachems. In addition, the proprietors paid the Native Americans twenty-six pounds for portions of the island in 1660.

As sailors, tradesmen and adventurers started to arrive, the proprietors created a policy called the "half share" system, which granted new residents half the amount of land rights given to the original nine settlers.

July 3

George Nelson Macy, the son of successful Nantucket merchants and a Civil War hero, saw Colonel Paul J. Revere, grandson of the "Midnight Rider," get killed at the Battle of Gettysburg 1863. Macy assumed command of the regiment and faced Pickett's Charge that day. A minié ball shattered his left hand; the arm was amputated, and after recovery in Boston, he was fitted with an artificial limb.

Born on Nantucket in 1837, Macy graduated from high school and left for Boston to make his fortune. There he became friends with members of Boston's prestigious militia company, the New England Guards. When the war began, Macy and his friends enlisted in the newly formed elite regiment, the Twentieth Massachusetts Volunteer Infantry. In February, just prior to Gettysburg, Macy returned to Nantucket to marry his sweetheart, Mary Hayden.

Despite his missing arm, Macy returned to action. In 1864, he was shot in both legs in one battle and had his horse fall on him in another.

For his distinguished conduct, Macy, at age twenty-seven, was promoted to the rank of brevet brigadier general in 1865. Later, he was appointed brevet major general by General Ulysses S. Grant.

At the Grand Review of the Army that same year, Macy led the parade before President Andrew Johnson and General Grant. Macy survived the war, returned to Boston, had three children and worked in a bank. In 1875, he stumbled during a dizzy spell, which fired a small pistol in his pocket and killed him.

July 4

The Nantucket Railroad made its inaugural run in 1881. The railroad linked the town with the village of Siasconset. Established on a wave of optimism about the island's economy, the railroad was plagued by accidents and costly repairs and eventually

couldn't compete with the automobile. The line closed in 1917, and its track and rolling stock were sent to France during World War I. Years after the railroad was discontinued, the last railroad car left on the island was converted to a popular restaurant.

The first surveys for the railroad were made in 1879 and created a route that went south to Surfside and then east to Siasconset. To further entice people to ride the rails, a depot and restaurant opened at Surfside in July 1881, and later land developers tried selling house lots in Surfside. By the end of the first season, the train had carried over thirty thousand passengers and traveled nearly six thousand miles.

July 5

After almost fifty years of aiding mariners in distress, the U.S. Coast Guard closed the Surfside Life-Saving Station in 1921. Established in 1874, the U.S. Life-Saving Service, which had just been created, chose the location because of its unobstructed views and shore access. A precursor to the U.S. Coast Guard, the Life-Saving Service set up manned stations along coastlines to assist the crew of sinking vessels.

Charles Robinson, a notable Nantucket builder at the time, constructed the Surfside station. Loosely related to the "humane houses," which were empty buildings provisioned with food and supplies for shipwrecked sailors landing on Nantucket, Life-Saving Stations were larger and housed crews and heavy equipment.

The station was expanded in 1876 and remains unchanged. Listed on the National Register of Historic Places, the station has been home to the Star of the Sea Youth Hostel for the past fifty years.

July 6

In 1852, a year after publishing his novel *Moby-Dick*, Herman Melville visited Nantucket for the first, and only, time. Melville and his father-in-law stayed at the Ocean House (now the Jared Coffin House), and he visited with Thomas Macy, son of historian Obed Macy, William and Maria Mitchell and *Essex* survivor Captain George Pollard. Later, he recalled the encounter by saying, "I—sometime about 1850–53—saw  Capt. Pollard on the island of Nantucket, and exchanged some words with him. To the islanders he was a nobody—to me, the most impressive man, tho' wholly unassuming, even humble—that I ever encountered."

The encounter left a deep impression on Melville, and in 1856, he wrote about the captain in his poem "Clarel":

> *Never he smiled;*
> *Call him, and he would come; not sour*
> *In spirit, but meek and reconciled:*
> *Patient he was, he none withstood;*
> *Oft on some secret thing would brood.*

July 7

In 1905, Nantucket's Unitarian church hosted the popular "Nantucket Summer Meetings," which included sermons and lectures. In announcing the program, the *Unitarian* magazine said, "The popularity of the quaint old island thirty miles at sea, its salubrity, and the interest which its sturdy people always have for visitors assure those who have these meetings in charge of a good attendance."

A Universalist church was built on the corner of India and Federal Streets in 1810. That building was sold to the Atheneum in 1835. Displaced Universalists began attending the South Church on Orange Street, one of two Congregationalist churches on the island. In 1837, the South Church adopted the Harvard Covenant, which parishioners believed to be Unitarian in spirit. Over time, the church became known as the Unitarian Church, although its formal name is Second Congregational Meeting House Society, Unitarian Universalist.

July 8

Authorities discovered James Ramsdell had escaped from Nantucket's jail in 1888. Ramsdell and his wife, Pauline, were convicted for breaking into a house and receiving stolen goods. James Ramsdell was waiting to be transferred to Charlestown Jail.

Police found no clues as to how he escaped, and his brother's dory in Madaket was reported missing the next day. A schooner picked up the fugitive in Nantucket Sound. Suspicious, the captain took him to Martha's Vineyard intending to turn him in, but Ramsdell disappeared before the ship docked. Authorities alerted police in Wood's Hole, but the fugitive had rowed to West Chop and caught a schooner to New York City.

New York City police captured Ramsdell on July 17 when he returned to the docked schooner with its first mate. Nantucket police brought Ramsdell to Charlestown Jail, where he was again behind bars by July 21.

July 9

In 1780, prominent Nantucket businessman Timothy Folger sent a petition to the British naval commanders engaged in war with the colonies and asked them to allow Nantucket ships to hunt whales and provision the island. "The petition of the island of Nantucket humbly shews that at this time there is five thousand inhabitants on said island who through the unhappy dispute that hath taken place between Great Britain and the colonies are reduced to the most miserable situation imaginable. The soil will not produce a subsistence for one third part of the people. Wholly destitute of fire wood and but a little clothing such being their situation and circumstances your petitioners really apprehend that without some indulgences from your excellencies there will many people perish for want before the end of another winter...

"As the inhabitants of said island were heretofore wholly employed in the whale and cod fishery and at present every other means of subsistence being cut off they hope your excellencies will permit twenty fishing boats to fish round the island of Nantucket and four vessels to be employed in the whale fishery and ten small vessels to supply the inhabitants with wood and one to go to New York for some little supplies said vessels being put under such regulations as your excellencies shall see meet."

The English did not respond, but the following year, the colonial military did allow the Nantucket whale ship *Dauphin* to leave on a voyage, which gave islanders hope that they would thrive once more.

July 10

In 1901, the *New York Times* reported on a U.S. Navy training mission: "The movements of the North Atlantic Squadron in Nantucket waters were well under way today, the original programme of having the warships go to Boston for coal apparently having been changed. About 2,000 marines are now ashore, and their tents cover two of the hills of Coatue, a strip of land separating the sea from Nantucket Harbor.

"No time has been lost by the men. Since the vessels arrived yesterday men and tents, stores and ammunition have been coming ashore. All night the boats were kept moving from the great ships to the land and back again. To-day efforts were directed mainly to the work of fortification, that of transportation having been nearly completed. The marines have attacked the sand hills which swell out of the lower stretch of Coatue, and trenches and embankments have grown rapidly, until it has become apparent that the town of Nantucket is to be well-defended from the 'hostile' vessels which are expected to attack it."

The North Atlantic Squadron was a section of the United States and renamed the North Atlantic Fleet in 1902. In 1905, the European and South Atlantic Squadrons were abolished and absorbed into the North Atlantic Fleet, and in 1906, the navy's Atlantic Fleet was established, which combined the North and South Atlantic Squadron.

July 11

A burst of cannon fire, steam whistles and bells kicked off the final day of a three-day celebration in 1895 to commemorate the one-hundred-year anniversary of the town's name change from Sherburne to Nantucket. Hundreds of people visited during the centennial celebration, which included a parade, concerts, fireworks, a baseball game, bicycle races, swimming competitions, a lifesaving demonstration, literary exercises, boat races, a reunion, a banquet and a ball.

Businesses and homes exuberantly decorated their buildings with bunting, and some families displayed art and artifacts from Nantucket's whaling days.

Five arches bearing patriotic messages decorated the town: one with supports made to look like the Eiffel Tower was placed over Main and Federal Streets, another arch made of hoops was on Steamboat Wharf, an arch made of fishnets spanned Main and Orange Streets and there were also arches over Main and Centre Streets and across Main Street at the Pacific Bank.

SHERBURNE · 1795 · NANTUCKET

July 12

Benjamin C. Chase wrote to the Light House Board in 1851 praising the effectiveness of Sankaty Light. Erected in 1850, the light was equipped with the nation's first Fresnel lens, which magnified light by refracting it through a series of prisms. Two lights in New Jersey also were installed with Fresnel lenses that year.

Chase wrote: "Sankaty head shows a clear, brilliant light when the flashes are at their greatest power and may be distinctly seen (in clear weather) from the deck of a vessel of one hundred tons, twenty five miles distant…My business packeting to and from Boston gives me good opportunity to observe the lights on that route In coming from the north in clear weather we raise Sankaty Head light above Great Point the point being six or seven miles nearest."

Many sailors sent letters to the Light House Board that year testifying to the superior visibility and efficiency of Sankaty Light.

Charles H. Coleman keeper of the *Cross Rip* lightship said, "I believe it to be the general opinion of the seafaring community that it (Sankaty) is decidedly the best light on the coast respectfully."

In 1852, the Light House Board issued a report saying Fresnel lenses were four times more effective than any other lighthouse beacon, and by 1860, almost every light in the country had one. In 1944, the U.S. Coast Guard took over Sankaty's operation, upgraded the Fresnel lens and donated the original one to the Nantucket Historical Association.

July 13

In 1933, the *Inquirer & Mirror* ran an article that profiled Leeds Mitchell's Nantucket House at his farm in Illinois. Mitchell, a distant cousin to Maria Mitchell and a beloved summer visitor, had purchased land and was building a shingled farmhouse in the style of Nantucket homes, complete with a replica of the Macy front door.

Mitchell, a prominent broker in Chicago and president of the Chicago Stock Exchange, was also trustee of Nantucket Cottage Hospital, director at Pacific National Bank and commodore at the Nantucket Yacht Club.

In Illinois, Citadella Farms raised chickens, and the newspaper reported, "Even after a year's association with them, Mr. Mitchell feels both awed and impressed by the chickens. They are quite self-sufficient, he has discovered, and he puts that down to their high birth. They are highly pedigreed, every one of them, and they taste better, he maintains, than any other chickens in the middle west."

In April 1937, *Life* magazine featured one of Mitchell's chickens on the cover and ran a feature story on his 320-acre farm, where seven thousand chickens produced five thousand eggs a day. The article showed photographs of the chickens in a state-of-the-art coop complete with air conditioning.

A man of many interests, he was also heard playing the piano by Nantucketers during a radio broadcast on WGN in December 1924. The *Inquirer & Mirror* noted that two of his songs were performed in 1926, and he appeared in *Life* magazine again in July 1937 in an ad endorsing Hammond Organs.

July 14

In 1846, the worst fire in Nantucket's history began inside a stovepipe in William Geary's hat shop on Main Street. The fire burned out of control for hours, and by the next day, almost eight hundred people were homeless, more than 250 buildings were destroyed and total losses amounted to more than $1 million (the equivalent of approximately $24 million today).

The *Warder*, the only newspaper that survived the fire, published the following day and said under the headline "Awful Calamity": "Buildings were blown up but the fiery elements seemed to have gained the ascendancy, and for hours it appeared as though all human efforts to stop the destructive progress would prove futile. A scene of devastation meets the eye, that beggars description. Many persons have lost their all. We have no time for further comments."

Within days, the selectmen issued an appeal for aid since the island's supply of groceries had burned. In their plea, they said, "There is scarcely a Dry Goods, a Grocery, or Provision store left standing, and what more particularly threatens immediate distress, the stocks contained in them, so rapidly did the conflagration extend, are almost utterly destroyed. There is not food enough in town to keep widespread suffering from hunger at bay a single week."

The fire's impact ushered in the end of whaling on Nantucket. Two-thirds of the loss was not covered by insurance, and the island couldn't overcome the destruction of seven whale oil processing factories, a dozen warehouses and three of the town's four wharves.

July 15

In 1837, the African American newspaper of the day, the *Colored American*, announced that Captain Edward J. Pompey had been appointed agent on Nantucket.

A whaling captain of the New Bedford ship *Rising States* in 1836 and a storeowner in the New Guinea section of town, Pompey emerged as a leader in the island's African American abolitionist movement at a young age. While others worked to change things locally, Pompey also focused his efforts on distributing the leading anti-abolitionist newspapers of the day.

In 1832, William Lloyd Garrison appointed him Nantucket's agent for the *Liberator*, and he served as president of the Nantucket Colored Temperance Society. He helped merge the women's and the men's Nantucket Anti-Slavery Societies, and he represented Nantucket at the 1834 New England Anti-Slavery Conference.

Believing that the abolitionist press gave the oppressed a voice, Pompey continued his work for the *Liberator* and the *Colored American* into the 1840s and was instrumental in arranging a trip for the *Colored American*'s editors to visit Nantucket. "Before this article shall present itself to our readers," the editors reported on June 20, 1840, "we shall probably be more than one hundred miles from our post, working in some other department for the success of our paper...We hope the friends where we go, will be ready to meet us. We expect to visit New Bedford and Nantucket and many other places."

Born around 1800, Pompey did not live to witness the Civil War or the emancipation of his people. He died of tuberculosis on October 6, 1848.

July 16

In 1921, the *Inquirer & Mirror* reported on a two-day celebration marking the 150th anniversary of Nantucket's Masonic Union Lodge, the island's oldest fraternal organization. The *Inquirer & Mirror*'s report included a mention that members of the New Bedford Masonic Lodge got a bit tipsy and spent most of the night singing and staging their own parades through town.

Union Lodge, chartered in 1771, is the fifth-oldest Masonic organization in the country. In 1890, the Nantucket Masons built a hall at the corner of Union and Main Streets, which they still use today.

As part of the 1921 festivities, Nantucket surfmen demonstrated a breeches buoy rescue. Partway through the exercise, the crowd called for Massachusetts governor Channing H. Cox to be "saved." He gamely climbed into the airborne rig and was brought to safety and then did it a second time so the news camera could capture the moment.

July 17

In 1883, the 'Sconset Union Chapel was opened. The former fishing village of Siasconset (or 'Sconset, as the locals say) had become one of the country's first summer resorts by the middle of the nineteenth century. As it grew, residents there began to hold religious services in the schoolhouse and a hotel and in 1882 decided to build a chapel.

In 1882, chapel founders selected a lot in the heart of the village on New Street and decided to build a chapel in the Gothic Revival style. The land was consecrated at a moonlit evening ceremony with an organ brought from the schoolhouse to the property and "a lantern held by a friendly hand."

Over the years, chapel leaders made small changes and repairs to the tidy structure and in 1942 added four buttresses to its outer walls. In 1992, the chapel purchased an adjoining lot for a columbarium and meditation garden.

The chapel is only open in the summer and today hosts both Protestant and Roman Catholic services each Sunday. It is also a very popular spot for weddings. Records show that the Siasconset Chapel has also been home to a black congregation and Christian Scientists.

July 18

U.S. Army lieutenant and Nantucket native George Nelson Macy recruited twenty-two island men to fight in the Civil War in 1861. The men served in the Twentieth Regiment Massachusetts Volunteer Infantry, which fought in every battle except one.

In all, four hundred Nantucket men fought in the Civil War, and seventy were killed. Of the twenty-two recruited by Macy on this day, four were killed in action, four were taken prisoner and two deserted.

One widely admired recruit was Sergeant Leander Alley, a twenty-year-old Nantucket sailor who was killed at the Battle of Fredericksburg in 1862. Company captain Henry Livermore Abbott ordered four men to recover Alley's body, and he paid to have it brought back to Nantucket.

Private William P. Kelley, eighteen years old and listed as a scholar at the time of his muster, caught the attention of the army doctor, who admired his excellent physical condition. Four years later, after being wounded in 1862 and captured by the Confederates in 1864, Kelley died of diseases he acquired while a prisoner in Richmond, Virginia, at Libby Prison.

Benjamin Pease, an eighteen-year-old sailor, was wounded at Gettysburg, reenlisted in 1864 and was shot in the chest at the Battle of the Wilderness. The thick wad of recruitment papers in his breast pocket saved him from death. Those papers, which have a bullet hole in them, are now in the collection of the Nantucket Historical Association.

July 19

Joseph E. Ray, a harpooner aboard the whale ship *Edward Cary* from 1854 to 1858, kept a journal of his trip and, in 1857, expressed frustration to be working on a Sunday: "At it again. Laying off and on at Upola, what for I do not know. All I know about is they went off this morning with flying colours. So it is haul and pull all this blessed day and I hope if there is any religion to be had ashore that they will get a little for themselves for they need it bad enough. So ends by standing from the land with squally weather and wind from the ENE ship head North."

His unhappiness had begun in the prior day's entry: "I shall be glad when this voyage is up for the laying off and on has commenced again. Tomorrow is Sunday but the boats has got to be put in order for whaling, Sunday or no Sunday, It makes no difference it's got to be done. So you can see how this cruise has begun the two first Sundays everybody employed. Six days shall thou labour and do all thou art able and on the seventh break thy back in two or three several different places."

Ray's cruise of the *Edward Cary* came at time when whale populations were diminished. The ship came home with a modest 665 barrels of sperm oil. Later, Ray sailed on the *Meteor* of Mystic, Connecticut, and was lost at sea during a storm.

July 20

Whaling captain Edward C. Joy died in 1894. Born in 1806, Joy and his two brothers all served as whaling masters. As commander of the whale ship *Lydia*, Joy lost the ship to fire in 1835. Obed Macy recounted the story in *The History of Nantucket*: "Nothing remarkable occurred before the 31st of 1st month 1835 when…the ship was discovered to be on fire. The fire increased so rapidly that all attempts to extinguish it were unavailing. The crew left the ship in three boats about

one and a half hour after the alarm having saved but very few things and in about one and a half hour got on board the bark *Washington of Hudson*, William Clark master, and went into Payta."

According to Macy, the fire started in steerage between the decks and was first detected when it came through a hatch.

Joy also captained the *Constitution* from 1835 to 1839 and then retired to farm on Nantucket.

July 21

U.S. Army private Byron L. Sylvaro, who fought in France during World War I, died at age twenty-three as a result of his wounds in 1918. On the day that she received a telegram announcing his death, his mother, Nellie Sylvaro, also received two letters from him.

> *We are having very nice weather, but it is very hot in the middle of the day, and pretty cold at night and morning, which is pretty good for those that sleep at night, but we don't always get a chance to sleep at night. Sometimes we don't get any sleep at all. The first front I was on I did not get but six hours of sleep in four days, but I have had it pretty easy since then.*
>
> *I have been on three fronts so far. Those big guns are making some noise now, they jar this paper I am writing on…This country is not so bad. I have been in lots of towns over here, but most all of them are in ruins. It is a pretty sad looking place.*
>
> *I am writing this letter in a YMCA, in the front line. Don't worry about me. Just write to me as often as you can, because your letters cheer me up.*
>
> *Give my regards to all the boys that are left. I will close now, hoping to hear from you soon.*
>
> > *Your loving son,*
> > *Byron*

Almost two hundred Nantucket men enlisted to fight the Germans in World War I. Private Byron Sylvaro was the only one who died while serving.

July 22

A seventh child was born to master mason Christopher Capen, age forty-six, and his wife, Lydia, age forty, in 1856 and was named Warren in honor of another son who died in 1850.

Capen built five of the most iconic homes on Main Street during the island's whaling glory days. Between 1831 and 1840, Capen constructed brick homes at 75 and 78 Main Street for the Coffins and the "Three Bricks" at 93, 95 and 97 Main Street for Joseph Starbuck.

In 1849, twenty-two Nantucket incorporators formed a California mining company and appointed Capen treasurer. He bought a ship and sailed with it to San Francisco. But the business lasted only four months, and Capen returned to Nantucket, where he learned his son Warren had died while he was away. With few work opportunities on Nantucket, Capen moved his family to Connecticut in 1863.

July 23

In 1919, Mrs. Edith Ackley addressed the annual meeting of the Nantucket Historical Association and talked about the first time she saw Nantucket and her travels around the world with her husband, Nantucket native Seth Ackley. They married in 1879, and Ackley had risen to rear admiral in the U.S. Navy by the time he died in 1908.

> *We visited many* [islands], *lived for three years in one, before the Long Trail ended, and in all of them found the distinguishing characteristic which marks the people of this dear spot—steadfast affection and loyalty to the birthplace. They* [Nantucketers] *wander far and near over the face of the earth, but wherever one meets them they are always planning "someday to go back home." Once as we were steaming into the harbor of Ceylon, a stalwart man standing on the landing stage, put his hand to his mouth, as we made fast, and shouted, "Hello, Seth! Coming round Brant Point?"*
>
> *What an evening they had! Coatue, the Haulover, Madaket, Sankaty, and Tuckernuck sounded strange enough in that island where the warm dusk was heavy with the odor of a thousand spices, amid palms and orchids, snakes and Cingalese. And that was only one of many ports where we saw familiar faces from the old home town, sailors mostly, for Nantucket has always pointed out to her sons the glittering treacherous highway, and they have followed it, many to the "vast and wandering grave," many to success and achievement in far countries.*

July 24

Charles C. Dyer visited relatives on Nantucket in 1846, just one week after fire destroyed much of the town. He wrote in his diary, "At the Poor House there was a short time ago one each of five generations from Rebecca Swain down. The house looks neat and well kept—heated by 3,000 feet of iron pipe from 1 to 2 inch Bore passing through every room and filled with water heated by a furnace in the cellar to about 400 degrees F. Near the Poor House is the County Jail with no prisoners in it now. It is a strong wooden building with grated windows."

Dyer also writes about the fire scene:

I have been too somewhat through the burnt district and it does indeed look melancholy, and yet some are beginning to rebuild already. I think the people are beginning to take courage; provisions and furniture and clothing are sent over quite freely from the continent. The boat today had a great deal sent over as donations…went down into the Burnt district in the morning…I perceive the people are already clearing out the "burnt districts" and have begun several buildings—8 or 9 small wooden buildings are already up and nearly finished and 5 or 6 more are framing—the lumber is coming in like smoke—the wharves piled up with it and a vessel just coming in with lumber—they are now surveying for improving the streets and the mechanics all going to work and labourers too.

July 25

The Italian luxury liner *Andrea Doria* collided with the MS *Stockholm* off the coast of Nantucket in 1956. Bound for New York City, the *Andrea Doria* was struck in the side and listed so severely to the starboard that half of its lifeboats were unusable. Yet the ship's design allowed it to stay afloat for over eleven hours while 1,660 passengers and crew members were rescued. In all, 52 people died as a result of the accident. The luxury liner capsized and sank the following morning. It remains the worst maritime disaster to occur in United States waters since the sinking of the SS *Eastland* in 1915.

The maritime disaster occurred in heavy fog, and an out-of-court settlement agreement between the two shipping companies has kept the cause under wraps. Historians now believe that both ship captains made errors using their radar, which resulted in the collision.

July 26

Massachusetts governor Thomas Hutchinson, a prominent businessman loyal to England, wrote to his son from London in 1775 expressing concern for his family's safety. Just five weeks after the Battle of Bunker Hill, Hutchinson suggested several locations where his children and sister could go, including Nantucket.

The next summer will no doubt determine the fate of America and it is said the same force will be employed as if the inhabitants were French or Spanish enemies. I therefore think there is a strong probability that you and your sister and both your children and may be reinstated there. It will therefore deserve consideration whether your present safety may not be secured upon easier terms than a removal to so great a distance as England. Your aunt too, who must be taken care of, will find insufferable difficulties in such a removal. I know not what will be the state of Rhode Island, but hear whispers. If your families could be there with safety, you or they, will be near the two estates. What do you think of Nantucket? Or could you bear the cold winter of Quebec? If it was not for the difficulty crossing the sea I think I would have chose to spend the winter there rather than in London…The change in our condition has been great, sudden, and unexpected; and however adverse it is ordered by the Wise Governor of the World and we not only ought not murmur and repine, but to fortify ourselves against a depression of spirits.

July 27

The whale ship *Fame* left Nantucket in 1833 carrying controversial poisoned harpoons, but they were never used. For decades, whalers had considered methods to ensure that a harpooned whale would die quickly. They believed instant death would be a safer alternative to waiting for the animal to exhaust itself before delivering the final thrust. As early as 1810, Nantucket captain Frances Rotch suggested heating harpoons in order to raise the whale's blood temperature and kill it.

Whalers in Scotland developed a poisoned harpoon in 1831 to prevent a whale from diving under the ice and dragging the whaleboat with it. France had also been experimenting with a poison harpoon, and in 1845, the government issued a patent for one.

Historians know that two French-made poison harpoons were brought to Nantucket to be used as patterns. The two French poison harpoons are now on display at the Smithsonian Institution in Washington, D.C.

But one account states that William Coffin Jr. of Nantucket did make poison harpoons in the 1830s that were carried on voyages of the *Susan* and *Fame* of Nantucket and the *America* of New Bedford but were never used. Historian Alexander Starbuck notes that harpooners feared the poisoned harpoons and refused to use them. Historian James Templeman Brown said, "Mr. Samuel Tuck…of Williamsburg, N.Y., formerly agent of the *Susan*, says that a harpoon similar to the old double-barbed iron was made by a Nantucket blackmith, with slots for bottles of acid, but it was not used at all during the voyage."

July 28

The Honorable James Coffin, the fourth child of Nantucket proprietors Tristram and Dionis, died in 1720. Born in England in 1640, and with his last name originally spelled Coffyn, James came to Nantucket with the first settlers in 1659 but soon decided to live in Dover, New Hampshire. While in New Hampshire, he was a merchant on the ketch *Neptune*, which was captured by the Dutch. Coffin moved back to Nantucket in 1671, where he lived until the end of his life. He and his brother Peter Coffin together owned a share of Nantucket.

In 1671, he is listed as purchasing land from the Native American sachem Wanackmemack. Like his father, he was a judge, and his role as judge of the probate court for twelve years was perhaps his most important. The island's first court records are under his administration. He also served as selectman numerous times, as assessor twice and as an assistant magistrate and a representative to the General Court.

Coffin, with his eldest son, also named James, owned trading sloops that most likely carried wool and whale oil between the island and mainland.

Married to Mary Severance in 1663, Coffin fathered fourteen children, twelve of whom survived. This branch of the Coffin family remained loyal to Great Britain in the American Revolution and produced the English general John Coffin and Admiral Sir Isaac Coffin, who both fought against the colonies. Admiral Coffin later funded a Nantucket school for Coffin descendants. Lucretia Coffin Mott, born on Nantucket and famous for her Quaker teachings, is another of his descendants.

July 29

After collecting seal pelts off the coast of New Zealand and negotiating a deal to sell rice to New South Wales (now Australia), the captain of the Nantucket ship *Favourite* sailed from Sydney to Canton, China, in 1806.

Now known for hunting whales, at the beginning of the nineteenth century, Nantucket mariners also hunted seals for their lucrative pelts and sold them in China. Adept negotiators, Nantucket captains traded in ports all over the world.

During the 1790s and early 1800s, American, English and French mariners competed to open up and gain control of the new hunting grounds in the Pacific Ocean. In 1809, New South Wales surgeon James Thomson wrote: "Ever since I have been in service in New South Wales I have observed most of the commanders of the South Sea ships to be Nantucket men."

The first Nantucket whale ship to arrive in Sydney was the *Brothers* in 1805. But three other Nantucket ships had already been there: the seal hunters *Favourite* and *Criterion* and the *Rose*, a merchant ship bound for China. The Americans took note of the profitable English seal hunt, and the first Nantucket sealing expedition left in 1791.

The *Favourite* left Nantucket in October 1805 and rounded the Cape of Good Hope, and its crew was among the first to hunt seal in the remote Crozet Islands. *Favourite* master Captain Paddock also went to the South Antipodes islands to pick up more seal pelts from an American sealing crew stationed there.

July 30

In 1935, Massachusetts governor James Curley (pictured in white) made headlines when a yacht he was on became caught on rocks in Nantucket Harbor. In a letter to the *Boston Herald*, Daniel Snow said, "Isn't the fellow Dolan, whose yacht ran aground on Nantucket the other day with the Governor aboard, the same chap who solved his financial troubles with a seven cents on the dollar settlement? If it is, how can he still run a 90 foot cruiser."

Curley frequently visited Nantucket, but this was his first as governor. He arrived aboard the *Maicaway* and spent the day visiting with Nantucket people, golfing at Sankaty Head Golf Club and eating at the White Elephant. The *Maicaway* became stranded on submerged rocks as it headed out that evening. After much commotion, including a member of the party falling overboard, another boat pulled it off the rocks, and it departed.

July 31

After trying three times to obtain permission to use Hyannis as a port, the Woods Hole, Martha's Vineyard and Nantucket Steamship Authority finally got legislative approval, and Governor Francis Sargent signed the bill into law in 1969.

The new regulations stipulated that the Steamship Authority could operate from Hyannis from May 1 to September 30. The authority would run Nantucket boat service from Woods Hole for the remainder of the year.

The Steamship Authority first tried to offer Hyannis service in 1961 and tried again in 1968. Both efforts failed due to strong opposition from Barnstable voters. Governor Sargent said he signed the bill because it helped more people than it hurt. Formed in 1960, the Steamship Authority originally included New Bedford. In time, it shifted its operations to Cape Cod. In 1985, the Steamship Authority began offering year-round service to Nantucket from Hyannis.

August 1

Born in 1818 and raised before the age of public schools, Maria Mitchell displayed an interest in astronomy and a talent for mathematics at a young age. Her father, the prominent William Mitchell, also a talented astronomer, taught her himself.

In 1836, Maria Mitchell became the first librarian for the Nantucket Atheneum, and for the next twenty years, she pursued her interest in math and astronomy while employed there. Her discovery of a comet in 1846 was due in large part to her self-education. The discovery made her an instant

celebrity, and the king of Denmark awarded her a medal. She was the first woman elected to the American Academy of Arts and Sciences in 1848 and the first to join the Association for the Advancement of Science in 1850.

In 1862, she began teaching at Vassar College, where she taught until she retired at age seventy, and she died in 1889.

August 2

In 1973, the first case of a diagnosed tick-borne disease was recorded on Nantucket. Doctors diagnosed the illness as Rocky Mountain spotted fever, a bacterial infection carried by dog ticks. But that year, Harvard University researcher Andy Spielman made an important discovery. Nantucket's white-footed mice were covered in deer ticks carrying a never-before-seen kind of bacteria that, like the bacteria that caused Rocky Mountain spotted fever, caused malaria-like symptoms in mammals.

In the forty years since, Nantucket became ground zero for the study of tick-borne disease, as well as for a growing health crisis in parts of the United States. The Centers for Disease Control and Prevention has listed Nantucket among the top three Lyme disease counties since 1992.

There are three types of known disease transmitted by deer ticks: Lyme disease (named after the town of Lyme, Connecticut, where it was originally reported in 1975), babesiosis and ehrlichiosis.

Lyme disease is the most commonly reported, and in 2007, Nantucket Cottage Hospital recorded 189 positive tests for Lyme disease. By 2008, the hospital had recorded 411 positive tests for Lyme disease.

Tick-borne diseases are contracted when an infected tick bites a mammal in search of its blood. Nantucket's high population of deer, rabbits and mice contribute to its large caseload of tick-borne disease. On Nantucket, about 10 percent of deer ticks carry the parasite that causes illness, according to Yale researcher Maria Diuk-Wasser.

August 3

The U.S. Coast Guard stopped broadcasting its Canadian Loran signal in 2010 and terminated a fifty-two-year-old system that pioneered radio wave, accurate maritime and aviation navigation all over the world.

During World War II, the U.S. Navy constructed a top-secret Loran (Long Range Navigation) station in Siasconset at Low Beach in 1942. The facility was part of a chain that stretched from Delaware to Canada. Two stations were paired, and each emitted a radio signal that planes and ships could triangulate to determine their location. During the war, navy personnel lived at the newly constructed Tom Nevers base (pictured here), and the U.S. Coast Guard operated the station after the war.

In peacetime, Loran grew to provide highly accurate navigation to boats and planes. Made obsolete by modern electronics, the coast guard ceased the United States Loran signal in February 2010, the Russian signal on August 1 and the Canadian Signal on August 3.

August 4

The steamship *New Bedford* made its last trip to the mainland in 1942. Both the *New Bedford* and the *Naushon* served Martha's Vineyard and Nantucket for twenty years and were requisitioned in 1942 by the government for service in World War II.

The two steamships served as hospital ships in the English Channel and were part of the Normandy Invasion. After the war, they returned to commercial service, but not in Nantucket Sound. The *New Bedford* ran summer service in Rhode Island and was eventually scrapped. The *Naushon* served the New York City area and was scrapped in 1974. Two steamships continued to serve the islands into the 1950s: the *Martha's Vineyard* and the *Nobska*. The *Martha's Vineyard* sank in 1990. The *Nobska* was scrapped in 2006, although you can still hear its high-pitched whistle when the Steamship Authority vessel *Eagle* is in port, only the whistle is now powered by air, not steam.

August 5

A Teacher's Institute sponsored by the Massachusetts Board of Education closed its three-day session in 1853. The institute, intended to further the education of schoolteachers during their summer break, was held at the Nantucket Atheneum and featured lectures on science from two men whose legacy is still felt today: Louis Agassiz and Arnold Henry Guyot.

Swiss-born scientist Jean Louis Rodolphe Agassiz taught natural history at Harvard University and pioneered new scientific ideas and methods for researching and classifying material. A passionate teacher intent on changing the way science was taught, Agassiz influenced the brightest stars of the next generation. Through his students, he can be credited for a founding role in the formation of the Woods Hole Oceanographic Institute on Cape Cod and the Chautauqua Institution in New York.

Arnold Henry Guyot, also a Swiss-born scientist and a friend of Agassiz, taught geography and geology at Princeton University and collaborated with the Smithsonian Institution to create a national system for meteorological observations, which lead Guyot to found the United States Weather Bureau.

Teacher Institutes were held all over the country and in the nineteenth century were the chief source of continuing education for many. And although it was targeted to educators, a large number of Nantucket townspeople attended in 1853. Originally designed as an experiment in improving how school subjects were taught, the institute's popularity and huge attendance nationwide each year reflected the tenor of the times—a belief in the power of education to mold individual character and improve life.

August 6

The second match of the Nantucket-Siasconset tennis match series held at the 'Sconset Casino had to be postponed due to rain in 1909. Nine teams of mixed doubles played six matches before the contest was halted.

By 1900, Siasconset had grown from a sleepy fishing village to a summer resort with two thousand residents and was famous as an artists' colony. A group formed the 'Sconset Casino Association in 1899 and raised $3,000 to build a "Hall of Amusement" on New Street. In July 1900, the 'Sconset Casino opened and has served as the village social center ever since. Casinos were popular on eighteenth-century country estates and were used for recreational and sporting activities and later built as private clubs.

Over time, the 'Sconset Casino purchased adjoining land to add courts, and today, it maintains eleven tennis courts.

August 7

In 1859, after hunting whales off South America for four years, the whale ship *Nantucket* went aground hours from home on Nashawena Island, which is part of the Elizabeth Islands off Martha's Vineyard.

Almira Gibbs, wife of Captain Richard Gibbs, went on the voyage and kept a diary. Of the *Nantucket*'s last day at sea, she wrote, "Block Island was sighted at two p.m. A pilot was taken on board at four p.m., and he wrecked the ship on the southwest end of the Island of Nashawena. So ends a long voyage. Saved ourselves but lost the Ship after carrying us safely over thousands of miles by water we left her upon the Rocks."

In 1857, she wrote, "I went a-whaling with no romantic illusions at all—which was lucky, as the old ship was slow and uncomfortable. I can hardly walk about, I fetch up sometimes where I start for and sometimes somewhere else."

In May 1858, another ship captain's wife, Henrietta Deblois, met with Gibbs in a mid-sea visit called a "gam." Henrietta wrote in her diary, "The sail proved to be the *Nantucket*, Captain Gibbs. They came on board and spent the day. Had a delightful time. Very pleasant people. Under God, I am indebted to Capt. G. for the safety of my husband." Captain Gibbs had once saved Captain John DeBlois after his ship was sunk by a whale.

The *Nantucket* had taken a total of 976 barrels of sperm whale oil, 1,743 barrels of whale oil and three thousand pounds of whalebone.

August 8

Miss Caroline French purchased the Old Mill at auction for $885 and gave it to the Nantucket Historical Association in 1897.

Built in 1746 by Nathan Wilbur, a Nantucket sailor who had spent time in Holland, the Old Mill was used to grind grain into meal and today is the oldest functioning mill in the country. It is also the only surviving mill of the four "smock mills" that once stood overlooking Nantucket town. Smock mills have a fixed body and a rotating cap that spins so that the sails can face the wind.

By 1828, the mill was falling apart, and Jared Gardner, a carpenter, bought it for twenty dollars and restored it. It was sold again in 1866 to John Francis Sylvia, a Portuguese miller of Azorean descent, who operated it for many years until it fell into disuse in 1892. The Nantucket Historical Association still grinds corn during the summer for demonstration purposes.

August 9

In 1834, Hawaiian native John B. Swain left Nantucket on a four-year whaling voyage aboard the *Clarkson* bound for the coast of Japan. He had been brought to Nantucket from Maui by Captain Obed Swain in 1833.

Over the next twenty-six years, Swain served as a crew member on eight whaling voyages, seven from Nantucket and one from Westport, Massachusetts. He was one of many Hawaiian-born whalers transplanted from their native islands to New England on board whale ships. Locals called residents of the Sandwich Islands (now Hawaii) Kanacka (or Canaka), which is a derivation of a Polynesian word meaning "people" or "person." Most Hawaiian seamen arriving on Nantucket were given English names, and their birth names have been lost. Town records show some Hawaiian children attended Nantucket schools, some owned homes and those destitute ended up in the asylum.

For the Kanacka seamen, who did not hunt whales in their culture, life on a whale ship was a double-edged sword: they were exposed to disease and could be abandoned in a foreign port, but it also allowed them to see the world and acquire foreign goods and money.

Native Hawaiians brought their own traditions onto the whale ships, including ancient chants, stories, sayings and proverbs describing their cultural connection to whales. In native oral traditions, whales sometimes carried boys and men on spiritual journeys to become religious leaders or priests.

Kanacka John Swain died in 1861 in New Bedford, where he lived with his wife, who was born in the West Indies.

August 10

A German submarine surfaced in the middle of a fleet of thirty boats fishing off George's Bank and sank three of them in 1918. Over the next few days, sixteen of the sixty survivors would be picked up in their dories and brought to Nantucket.

Crew members reported that one German had danced with an American flag around his shoulders and that their armed captors had been hostile, forcing them off the ships without food or clothing. They were then ordered to get on the U-boat, where they were photographed standing against the conning tower. As they were being lined up for the picture, the Germans jeered at them and hit them if they failed to move fast enough. With the Americans back in their dories, the submarine crew looted and sank their boats.

One survivor told the *New York Times*, "The Germans were half drunk at least. You would have thought that too, had you seen the dance of the German officer, with the Stars and Stripes draped about his shoulders, and heard the cheering as the flag finally was flung down and stamped on, amid shrieks from our captors. Finding a side of fresh beef in our galley, they set up a roar that resembled that which comes from a crowd at a ball game. The way they cheered made me think they were half-starved."

Six of the survivors rowed 180 miles before they were rescued near the *Great Round Shoal* lightship, six miles from the island.

August 11

In 1841, Frederick Douglass, a fugitive slave, addressed an audience for the first time during an antislavery convention at the Nantucket Atheneum. "It was with the utmost difficulty that I could stand erect, or that I could command and articulate two words without hesitation and stammering," he later wrote.

Leaders in the Massachusetts Anti-Slavery Society invited him join their cause, and within five years, Douglass had an international reputation as a powerful orator. He wrote three autobiographies, edited several newspapers, took a leading role in the women's movement and served for over half a century as an untiring advocate for racial justice.

Douglass was born a slave in Maryland in 1818. His maternal grandparents raised him, and at age eight, he was sent to serve his master's relatives in Baltimore. There his mistress taught him the basics of reading, and he soon understood the power of literacy.

In 1838, Douglass disguised himself as a sailor and took a train to Philadelphia and then traveled to New York City, where he married Anna, a free African American woman he had fallen in love with in Baltimore. The couple continued their journey to New Bedford, where they lived.

Douglass returned to Nantucket to lecture four more times: at antislavery conventions in 1842 and 1843, on the Fugitive Slave Law in 1850 and in 1881 on his experiences in the abolitionist movement. He died on February 20, 1895, at seventy-seven years old.

August 12

Siasconset's new Marconi wireless station received its first signal from the *Nantucket* lightship in 1901. The lightship and Siasconset station established a connection, and then the Siasconset station asked the lightship crew, "How are you all? What's doing?" The lightship crew responded with the message, "Convalescent thanks. Foghorn going since last night."

The *New York Herald* had been publicizing the long-awaited first official message from the transatlantic liner *Lucania*, which had been selected for the honor. But the first messages received in Siasconset actually came from a German ship, *Lahn*, and a passing tramp steamer. On August 16, the *Lucania* finally sent the historic message to the lightship, which was transmitted to Siasconset, which then telephoned it to the *Herald*'s New York office and shipping authorities who were watching for the Cunard ocean liner.

The message was, "All well on board. We are 237 miles from Sandy Hook. Expect to reach New York Harbor Saturday." The first passenger message was from Carroll Payne to Clark Howell at the *Atlanta Constitution*: "Homeward bound. Passage rough. Though far from home, message sent thanks to the *Herald*'s enterprise."

The *Herald* predicted that its wireless station on the *Nantucket* lightship would shorten a ship's Atlantic crossing and that westbound passengers could communicate with the American continent hours earlier. The newspaper's predictions came true, but more importantly, the Marconi's system very quickly resulted in safer boating voyages. Within twenty-five years, every vessel was required to have one on board.

August 13

In 1867, the *New York Times* ran a column describing one columnist's quest for a "Polpis Squantum." Squantum was a popular word at the time to describe a clambake, but what the writer actually experienced was Nantucket clam chowder. He wrote:

> *Polpis, which only comprises a few farms, lies back from the sea, though a quarter of an hour's walk brings one to the inlet—a sort of harbor within the harbor— where we went, soon after depositing the greater part of our cargo, to dig clams.*
>
> *Willing to think my dinner earned I sauntered out to find whatever the sea might have thrown up for me. Very little indeed. Plenty of the pearl mussels—growing on the kelp in the sand. Scallops, fresh from the water, and snapping viciously as I touched them. The treasures of the deep were growing in the sand instead of cast up in various forms as on other beaches.*
>
> *"Too many cooks spoil the broth." But I never heard that the same was true of chowder. The kettle was steaming hot; the pork, cut fine, went in to add to its commotion; onions, chopped, made the fizzle and sputter subside to a steady bubble; and the clams, white, sweet and tender, fresh from their shelly coverings, went in to give flavor to these preliminaries. So, when the whole mass had been duly thickened, we lifted up our voices and pronounced it "good."*

August 14

Susan Emma Brock (third from left), daughter of a whaling captain and a founder of the Nantucket Historical Association (NHA), died in 1937.

Born in 1852, Brock traveled as a child aboard the *Midnight* with her father, Captain George H. Brock, to San Francisco. According to her journal, he took her on deck in a snowstorm and said, "Now look hard and try to remember what you see, for there are not many little girls who ever see Cape Horn."

Brock served as the NHAs first curator and donated many valuable artifacts acquired during her father's travels. In 1903, nine years after the NHA was incorporated, Brock addressed the membership, saying, "It has been well said that a historical society should be something more than a 'strongbox' to hold collections. It must be a living institution." Within a year, the NHA had raised the money to build a museum on Fair Street, one of the first concrete structures built in Massachusetts.

August 15

Abiah Folger Franklin was born in 1667 to Peter Folger and Mary Morrill Folger. One of the first generation of white settlers to be born on Nantucket, Abiah became the second wife of Josiah Franklin, a soap and candle maker from Boston, and had eleven children (one died young). Their seventh child and youngest

son was Benjamin Franklin. Josiah and Abiah married on November 25, 1689.

Josiah's first wife (mother of their ten children) died, so Abiah raised all twenty Franklin children. The Nantucket chapter of the Daughters of the American Revolution is named for Abiah Folger Franklin. A granite fountain and a bench mark the site of her birthplace near Madaket Road.

Benjamin Franklin called his mother "a discreet and virtuous woman" with "an excellent constitution." She died in 1752 and is buried at the Granary Burying Ground in Boston, Massachusetts. The Nantucket Historical Association maintains a memorial fountain and a bench (pictured here) on the site of the Folger home.

August 16

Northeast Airlines Flight 258 crashed while trying to land at Nantucket Memorial Airport in 1958. All three crew members and twenty-two of the thirty-one passengers were killed, among them Gordon Dean, former chairman of the United States Atomic Energy Commission.

The accident occurred at 11:34 p.m. in heavy fog. The plane flew into the ground a third of a mile short of the runway and caught fire. A Civil Aeronautics Board (CAB) investigation found that the captain of the aircraft failed to acknowledge radio transmissions warning him of the deteriorating weather conditions in the minutes before the crash. The board also criticized Northeast Airline's training and operational procedures, noting deficiencies in aircrew proficiency, recordkeeping and monitoring of company radio frequencies.

In its report, the CAB said, "The Board determines that the probable cause of this accident was the deficient judgment and technique of the pilot during an instrument approach in adverse weather conditions in failing to abandon the approach when a visibility of one-eighths mile was reported, and descending to a dangerously low altitude while still a considerable distance from the runway."

August 17

American Revolution hero and Boston silversmith Paul Revere sent a letter to the members of the Union Lodge, Nantucket's chapter of the Freemasons, charging them with clandestine behavior and not paying their dues and threatening to expel them from the organization in 1797.

The Freemasons started in medieval England and came to the colonies with the British. Established in 1771 and one of the oldest Masonic lodges in North America, Nantucket's Union Lodge records show island Masons assisting families during the Revolutionary War when they were starving because they could not engage in shipping. Revere, who was Grand Master of the Boston Lodge, was not immediately successful. The Union Lodge did not resume paying dues until 1801.

The Union Lodge was not without controversy locally as well. Quakers list Masons in their "Book of Objections," and members of the Friends were disbarred for consorting with the Freemasons. Quakers, staunch pacifists, may have rejected Freemasonry because of its secret rituals and because of members' support of the American Revolution.

The Union Lodge commissioned Revere in friendlier times to make a set of gold symbols used during ceremonies: a plumb, a level and a square. Those gold pieces and Revere's dunning letter are still proudly on display at the Main Street lodge.

August 18

A three-day Coffin reunion commemorating the 200th anniversary of Tristram Coffin's death ended in 1881. More than five hundred Coffins attended, and festivities included speeches, a banquet and a ball. Coffins wrote down generations of genealogical details for the records of the Nantucket Historical Association, purchased plates and mugs with the Coffin crest and paid fifty-cent dues to their reunion sponsor, the Coffin Association. During the reunion, Tristram Coffin of Poughkeepsie, New York, went to look at his ancestral home, the Jethro Coffin House on Sunset Hill, and was dismayed to find it falling down. Nantucket settler Tristram Coffin built the house as a wedding gift for his grandson in 1686. Coffin purchased the house and later donated it to the Nantucket Historical Association in 1924. Now called the "Oldest House," the NHA operates it as a historic site, and it is open to the public in the summer.

August 19

Mary Ellen Pleasant, an African American abolitionist, businesswoman and entrepreneur during the California gold rush, was born in 1814.

Raised in Philadelpha, Pennsylvania, and educated on Nantucket, Pleasant met William Lloyd Garrison in Boston and joined the abolitionist movement. After the death of her husband, Alexander Smith, Pleasant moved west. She continued her abolitionist work and met John Brown.

By the 1860s, she was living in San Francisco, where she owned a restaurant and was an investor. She owned 920 Washington Street (in the heart of today's Chinatown), the meeting place of some of the city's most prominent politicians. She helped shape early San Francisco and is thought to have covertly amassed a fortune close to $30 million. Pleasant challenged Jim Crow laws in the city during two highly publicized court cases.

At the end of her life, her schemes began to fall apart, and her enemies "scandalized her name." By the end of the century, the popular press had named her "Mammy Pleasant" and depicted her as both angel and arch fiend and madam and murderess.

She acknowledged the distortions of her character in the press, saying that though they (the members of the press) were smart, she was smarter. Mary Ellen Pleasant died in January 1904 and requested that the words "she was a friend of John Brown" appear on her grave.

August 20

In 1899, the office of the Light House Board wrote a letter to Serbian American inventor Nikola Tesla stalling a decision on his offer to establish a wireless telegraph on the *Nantucket* lightship. T. Perry, commander of the U.S. Navy, wrote, "From certain expressions used in it the Board fears there may be some misunderstanding, so in order to prevent you from going to any trouble to expense, the board desires to say that it has taken no action as yet toward providing any apparatus for using wireless telegraphy, as no appreciation is available for the purpose."

Letters between Perry and Tesla continued into 1900, with each side parrying for position on the issue of cost and with Tesla's letters sometimes sounding irritable and contradictory. Perry eventually offered Tesla the contract, saying the government preferred to use an American company, a veiled reference to Tesla's rival, Italian Guglielmo Marconi.

In the end, Tesla never set up the wireless, and the *New York Herald* installed a Marconi system on the *Nantucket* lightship in 1901. Historians view Tesla's inability to gain a lightship contract as one of the major blunders of his career.

Tesla was an electrical and mechanical engineer and a futurist, best known for his contributions to the design of the modern alternating current (AC) electricity system. A prodigy of Thomas Edison, Tesla's patented AC induction motor and transformer were licensed by George Westinghouse. Famous in his time, Tesla's work fell into obscurity after his death in 1943 but began to gain notice again in the 1990s.

August 21

In 1901, the U.S. Weather Bureau sent electrical expert Reginald A. Fessenden to Nantucket to study and conduct experiments at the Siasconset Marconi wireless station so the government could establish a wireless telegraphy system on the Farallon Islands in the Pacific Ocean.

The newspapers *San Francisco Call* and *New York Herald* also participated in the project. The newspapers pioneered the use of a Marconi wireless station so they could report the news faster and had been pressuring government officials for a Pacific wireless station.

Fessenden, considered the father of radio, was an inventor and head of the electrical engineering department of the Western University of Pennsylvania and worked under Thomas Edison at the time. Born in Quebec, Canada, he may have been the first to broadcast radio transmissions of voice and music. In his later career, he received hundreds of patents for devices in fields such as high-powered transmitting, sonar and television.

August 22

In 1814, a British warship anchored off shore, raised a white flag and sent a message to Nantucket selectmen asking for a meeting. Since the beginning of the War of 1812, the island's people had suffered at the hands of British privateers, government-sanctioned pirates charged with stealing enemy ships. Privateers cruising Nantucket Sound and the harbor entrance made it impossible for Nantucket ships to do business, and the island people, close to starvation, were foraging food from the land and sea and digging peat from the cranberry bogs for fuel.

Nantucket selectmen agreed to meet the British the next day, and a committee of townspeople boarded the English brig *Nimrod*. The captain proposed that if Nantucket residents took a neutral stand in the conflict, then the English would allow some Nantucket ships to import goods. The terms included an agreement that, for the duration of the war, townspeople would not fight the English, would give up their arms, would allow English ships to land on the island and would not fish in local waters. That evening, voters gathered on the street in front of the Unitarian Church for an impromptu town meeting. The communication from the British commander was read, and voters agreed to abide by the requirements. On August 28, an agreement was signed, and the British issued paperwork for five Nantucket ships to make provisioning voyages to Delaware and New York.

August 23

After almost 188 years under water, the wreck of the *Two Brothers* was discovered by a team of NOAA researchers in 2008 on the French Frigate Shoals in the Northwestern Hawaiian Islands, almost six hundred miles northwest of Honolulu.

The Nantucket whale ship ran aground on February 11, 1823. *Two Brothers* was under command of Captain George Pollard Jr., the Nantucket whaling master who had survived the sinking of the *Essex*. The *Two Brothers* also brought Pollard home from Chile in 1821 when he was rescued after drifting in the Pacific Ocean for ninety-five days. He was immediately given its command and set sail again on November 26, 1821—one year and six days from the date of the *Essex* disaster.

While cruising west of the Sandwich (Hawaiian) Islands, *Two Brothers* was caught in a severe gale. Stunned by the loss, Captain Pollard was reluctant to abandon the ship. The crew members pleaded with him and eventually convinced all on board to embark on two small whaleboats, to which they clung for survival throughout the night. They were picked up by the whale ship *Martha* the next day.

Captain Pollard retired from whaling after that. He became captain of a merchant vessel and later Nantucket's night watchman.

NOAA researcher Kelly Gleason and her colleagues have found trypots, harpoon heads, a grinding wheel, a blubber hook and fragments of china at the wreck site. The *Two Brothers* is within the Papahnaumokuakea Marine National Monument and is protected by law and will stay in place at the marine sanctuary.

August 24

The Nantucket Civic League hosted the Neighbors Fifth Annual Festival on Commercial Wharf in 1944. According to an *Inquirer & Mirror* article, 1,500 people turned out to look at displays of Nantucket crafts and paintings by Frank Swift Chase. There was a pavilion that featured a miniature bowling alley and "turtle races." A wagon full of gypsies was parked on the wharf, and nearby, a small orchestra played jigs and reels. Later, an accordionist played more music. One local mariner provided boat rides around the harbor. The Coskata Coast Guard Station showed how to save a drowning victim, and there were surfboat races between the Coskata and Madaket stations (Madaket won). There were paddle boat races for boys, swimming races and swimming lifesaving demonstrations from students of the swimming class. Wharf boathouse owners opened up their properties for tours. The Nantucket Civic League was founded in 1903 and has a mission of informing the citizens through participation.

August 25

In 1929, the *New York Times* ran a feature story on the historic round-the-world flight of the German dirigible *Graf Zeppelin* under the headline "From Nantucket to the Urals and from Tomsk to Tokio."

The article stated, "A great ocean was spanned, majestic mountain ranges, desolate plains...the last bit of land visible to the dirigible's passengers before heading across the Atlantic was the little island of Nantucket, Mass...Situated on the edge of the Gulf Stream and now known chiefly as a summer resort, Nantucket has had a prominent place in New England's maritime history...Today tidy clapboard houses, painted green or white, have replaced many of the shingled houses of Colonial days. Nantucket held out against the invasion of the motor car for many years before it succumbed to the inevitable, and now even an airplane appears, with newspapers and visitors, from the mainland."

Backed by newspaper mogul William Randolph Hearst, the *Graf Zeppelin*, a hydrogen-filled airship, left Lakehurst Naval Air Station in New Jersey on August 7 and flew around the world, arriving back in Lakehurst on August 29. It was the first successful transatlantic flight ever made, and over the next eight years, the Zeppelin Company set the standard for intercontinental travel. The venerated *Graf Zeppelin* flew more than 1,056,000 miles, made 590 flights and carried 13,110 passengers. However, the public lost faith in hydrogen-filled airships in 1937, after the explosion of the *Graf*'s sister ship, the *Hindenburg*, and the era of global airship travel ended.

August 26

The *New York Times* ran a newsy blurb about Nantucket in 1894 that reported unseasonably cold weather, work on a state highway to Siasconset village and an outbreak of forest fires and finished by saying, "Eastman Johnson of New York is occupying his cottage on the cliff."

Johnson was an American painter and co-founder of the Metropolitan Museum of Art in New York City. He was best known for his paintings of scenes and portraits from everyday life. Johnson first visited Nantucket in 1869 but soon purchased property on Cliff Road and lived on the island in the summer. Johnson painted one of Nantucket's best-known works in 1880: *The Cranberry Harvest*. It is a landscape that depicts people picking cranberries in the moors. Johnson also painted many portraits of Nantucket sea captains, town officials, neighbors and other artists.

August 27

In 1874, President Ulysses S. Grant arrived on the steamship *Island Queen* as Hill's New Bedford Band played music, the bells of several church steeples rang and cannons were fired from Commercial Wharf. Vessels in the harbor and the wharves were decorated with flags and bunting for the occasion.

The president, first lady and his large party boarded carriages, and a parade of horse-drawn vehicles started down the wharf and went to Main Street via Water Street. There the procession passed between two lines of Sunday school children who held flowers and evergreen wreaths. It continued on a winding route that took the party through most of downtown and ended at the Ocean House (now the Jared Coffin House). President Grant greeted the large gathering there, and the hotel musicians gave a concert. The group ate lunch and then returned to board their boat so that President Grant could next visit Cape Cod.

At the time of his visit, President Grant was attending a Methodist camp meeting at Martha's Vineyard and had viewed an illumination show at Oak Bluffs the night before he left for Nantucket. On his trip, he greeted thousands during his visits to Nantucket, Hyannis, Wellfleet and Provincetown. He then visited John M. Forbes, a prominent member of the Republican Party, at his summer home on Naushon Island.

Although it was brief, President Grant's ceremonial visit was a key factor in establishing Nantucket as a tourist destination in the late nineteenth century.

August 28

In 1855, a *New York Times* editorial dismissed the idea that California could become a whaling port, but did question the future of whaling:

We have seen frequent allusions to a statement by one of our contemporaries, to the effect that the whaling business was about to be transferred from the ports in New England, where it is now carried on so largely, to San Francisco, or to some other port on the Pacific...

But still we do not imagine that San Francisco will ever become a whaling port....Nantucket has been the fruitful parent of all the whalers in the world, who have sprung from two or three hardy families by whom that sterile island was first peopled...But Nantucket is no longer the chief whaling port of the world; her ships engaged in the trade do not now number more than fifty, while her offspring, New-Bedford, leads often this great business, and probably has more capital engaged in it than all the rest of the world put together. It has already become too dear to be used for the purposes of illumination, and even in Nantucket the inhabitants have had to resort to gas to light their streets and houses. The whaling business has now become so uncertain, it requires so large an outlay of capital, and its prosecution is attended with so many hardships and personal dangers, that no people will even engage in it who are not driven to it by the stern necessities of their position in life.

August 29

Local telephone service had been available since 1887, but the first long-distance telephone call occurred in 1916. The Nantucket Atheneum's hall was decorated with purple-and-white bunting and American flags, and every seat in the room was wired and equipped with watch-case telephone receivers. Mr. Philip Spalding, president of the Telephone Company, was present and delivered a speech.

Telephone Company general manager William R. Driver Jr. called from Boston. This was followed by a three-way conversation between Joseph Brock, president of the Pacific Club, speaking from the Captains' Room; William F. Macy, from his home in West Medford; and the Honorable William Crapo from his home in New Bedford.

Following that call, the group heard the national anthem over the phone from Boston, and the men spontaneously rose and sang. Later, Telephone Company representatives demonstrated how to use the long-distance lines, and islanders made calls to friends throughout Massachusetts.

August 30

Rowland Hussey Macy Sr., founder of the department store R.H. Macy and Company, was born on Nantucket in 1822. Macy was the fourth of six children born to a Quaker family. At age fifteen, he worked on the whale ship *Emily Morgan* and had a red star tattooed on his hand, which became a central part of the Macy's logo.

He married Louisa Houghton in 1844, and they had two children. Between 1843 and 1855, Macy opened four retail dry goods stores in Haverhill, Massachusetts, and they all failed. He moved to New York City in 1858 and established a new store named R.H Macy Dry Goods at Sixth Avenue and Fourteenth Street.

As the business grew, Macy's expanded and used publicity devices such as a store Santa Claus, themed exhibits and illuminated window displays to draw in customers. Macy's offered a money-back guarantee and only accepted cash into the 1950s. The store also produced its own custom-made clothing for men and women, assembled in an on-site factory.

In November 1902, the store moved uptown to its present Herald Square location on Broadway and Thirty-fourth Street. With the store's Seventh Avenue expansion completed in 1924, Macy's Herald Square became the "World's Largest Store," with more than one million square feet of retail space.

Macy died on March 29, 1877, in Paris of Bright's disease. Ownership of the store passed through the Macy family until 1895, when it was sold to Isidor and Nathan Straus.

August 31

In 1893, the U.S. Navy put the old ironclad USS *Nantucket* back in service but almost lost the historic Civil War–era monitor when it was being towed from New York City to Wilmington, North Carolina.

Hampered by deteriorating weather, the towlines connecting the USS *Nantucket* and the corvette *Kearsarge* broke off the coast of Cape Hatteras. The crew hunkered down inside the drifting USS *Nantucket* and rode out the storm as huge waves washed over the ship and it began to take on water. At one point, there was almost six feet of water inside the ironclad. The *Kearsage* tried in vain to keep the USS *Nantucket* in sight but lost it in the middle of the night. After using every resource they had to keep up with water coming in, the ship and crew survived, and Lieutenant H.H. Hosley managed to pilot the USS *Nantucket* into Hampton Roads harbor.

In his report to the navy, Hosley praised the ship, writing, "During the gale the wind blew with great violence and the sea was running very high. The vessel proved herself a very good sea boat, riding the seas surprisingly well, and were it not for the very unsatisfactory condition of the quarters below we would have been as comfortable as could be expected." But for the *Nantucket* to be seaworthy again, the monitor would need to be repaired to make it less leaky, Hosley reported.

Commissioned in February 1863, the USS *Nantucket* was sent to Charleston, where it participated in attacks against the harbor forts. The ironclad was condemned and sold in 1900.

September 1

President John F. Kennedy and his family went for a cruise on the yacht *Honey Fitz* and briefly visited Nantucket in 1963. The president and Jacqueline Kennedy, along with a party of friends, took a day sail across Nantucket Sound from the Kennedy summer home in Hyannisport, Massachusetts.

Moored in the harbor, neither the president nor the first lady got off the ninety-two-foot yacht, but seven children, including Caroline and John Kennedy Jr., were taken to the Brant Point Coast Guard Station. The outing also included four Secret Service men, a nurse and the Kennedy dog, a German shepherd named Clipper.

The children climbed the coast guard watchtower and were given a tour by the operator there. After wandering around the station grounds for twenty minutes, the party was taken back to the *Honey Fitz*. In total, the visit lasted thirty minutes but created a frenzy among local boaters, who circled around the *Honey Fitz* in the hopes of seeing the president and his wife.

Nicknamed the "Summer White House," President Kennedy used the family summer home in Hyannisport regularly from the time he was elected in 1961 to his death in 1963.

September 2

Captain Reuben Russell commanded the whale ship *Susan* on a voyage to the Pacific Ocean and back between 1841 and 1846. He kept a journal filled with hand-painted illustrations and written entries. This was Captain Russell's second voyage with the *Susan*. Captain Russell and the crew returned home with a modest 637 barrels of sperm whale oil, 1,405 barrels of whale oil and twelve thousand pounds of whalebone baleen, used as stays in women's corsets.

In 1842, Russell wrote, "Friday Sept 2 brisk winds of fine weather by up NE all sails out. Two men sick latter part continues moderate of firm ay 10 All spoke ship *Erie* ere Fair Haven 20 months out 800 bbl., saw my brother Shubael whom I had not seen but twice in 24 years."

Reuben Russell was born on Nantucket in 1799 and lived there until 1847 when he moved to Ohio. His younger brother Shubael was born in 1806 and eventually moved to the West Coast. In 1859, he was accidentally shot and killed while living in California.

September 3

In 1849, Jethro C. Brock compiled a list of Nantucket people who went to California and printed it as a broadside called *A Correct List of Persons Belonging to Nantucket, Now in California, or on Their Way There*, which was published by the *Mirror*. Brock wrote, "It will be seen that this list comprises the names of many persons who are natives of Nantucket, that have not resided upon the island for a number of years."

Nantucket first heard about the discovery of gold in California in late 1848. As it did in the rest of the country, the pull of glory and wealth took hold, and by the end of 1849, more than five hundred Nantucket men left to seek their fortunes. The exodus took a toll on the whaling industry. More than forty-two whale ships were withdrawn to be refitted to carry goods and passengers to the goldfields, and numerous whale ships in the middle of the voyage were lured to California or lost men who deserted in order to seek gold.

Sensing a new maritime business opportunity, several Nantucket companies organized to provide transportation to those heading west. In addition, Nantucketers also formed mining companies. The Astor Mining Co was formed on Nantucket and purchased the ship *Henry Astor*. The company's constitution banned alcohol and enforced a Sabbath worship. The *Henry Astor* crew consisted of the captain, three mates, forty-four seamen, a cook, a steward and a physician, plus fifteen passengers. It sailed in March 1849 and was among the first to depart from Nantucket.

September 4

U.S. secretary of the treasury Charles J. Folger died in 1884. Folger was born on Nantucket in 1818 and moved with his family to Geneva, New York, when he was twelve years old. In 1839, he was admitted to the bar and began his career as a lawyer, judge, state legislator and eventually U.S. secretary.

In 1844, Folger became a judge of the Ontario County Court of Common Pleas and in the course of his life served in the New York State legislature, rising to serve as senate president pro tem and as chairman of the Judiciary Committee; as assistant United States treasurer; and as a judge on the New York Court of Appeals, where he was made chief judge of the court in 1880.

In 1881, President Chester Arthur appointed Folger to serve as secretary of the treasury.

At the time, Folger presided over the greatest surplus the government had ever had. He observed that times had changed since the first treasury secretary in 1789 was charged with devising plans for the collection of revenue: "What now perplexes the secretary is not wherefrom he may get revenue enough for the pressing needs of the government, but whereby he shall turn back into the flow of business the more than enough for those needs, that has been drawn from the people." By 1884, the government surplus had dwindled considerably, and Folger's problem disappeared.

Folger died in office on September 4, 1884, at his home in Geneva.

September 5

Members of the Melville Society gathered on Nantucket for a three-day conference to honor the 150th birthday of Herman Melville in 1969. The theme of the conference was "Melville and the Sea," and it attracted one hundred members, who stayed at the Jared Coffin House and attended events at Bennett Hall. The events included a series of lectures presented by maritime historians, films, a concert of sea chanteys and a dinner where poet Maria Rukeyser read a poem written for the occasion.

Nantucket historian Edouard Stackpole delivered a lecture titled "Whaling and Nantucket," which provided the scholars with an overview. "The Quaker whalemen of Nantucket were the first Americans to launch that important phase of Colonial whaling known as 'whaling in ye deep,' and they became the greatest exponents of it in America. Before the advent of the Revolutionary War Nantucket was the greatest whaling port in the world," Stackpole said in his lecture.

Following his talk, Stackpole introduced Naval Academy historian Wilson Heflin, whose research revealed that Melville had sailed on the Charles & Henry whale ship of Nantucket. Historians had known that Melville worked on the whale ship *Acushnet*, of Fairhaven, Massachusetts, but had not realized he also sailed on a Nantucket whale ship.

The Melville Society was formed in 1945 and has a membership of historians and scholars who meet yearly. In 1951, the society met in Williamstown, Massachusetts, to celebrate the 100th anniversary of the publication of *Moby-Dick.*

September 6

In 1929, the *New York Times* reviewed a book about the importance of the Galapagos tortoise as a food source for New England whalers. The author was Charles Haskins Townsend, the director of the New York Aquarium.

The turtle is native to the Galapagos chain of islands off the coast of Ecuador and is the largest species of tortoise alive today. It can weigh up to 880 pounds and measure almost six feet in length.

According to the article, "The Galapagos were a stockyard to the American whalers. No sooner had the anchor chains stopped rattling than overboard tumbled into the dingy boats a captain or mate with a load of men seasoned in hunting tortoises. They called it terrapin, or turpin, or terpin. Hard work it was climbing up the hills bristling with cactus, tracking the turtles and bringing them in batches down to the boats."

Townsend read seventy-nine whaling voyage logbooks from libraries in Nantucket, New Bedford and Salem. They showed the ships making 189 visits to the Galapagos between 1831 and 1868. Sailors caught a total of 13,013 turtles.

The *Times* article concluded, "Sadly enough, 'turpining' is almost of the past. On some of the Galapagos the tortoise is no more." Galapagos tortoise populations dropped drastically, from 250,000 in the sixteenth century to 3,000 in the 1970s. Due to conservation efforts and a breeding program, their population now numbers around 19,000.

September 7

President Chester Arthur made an unannounced visit to Nantucket on the steamer *Dispatch* in 1882. His arrival was not kept secret for long, however. Town crier Billy Clark blew his trumpet and announced the president's presence. By midmorning, F.C. Sanford had invited Arthur to visit Nantucket as his guest, which the president accepted. President Arthur and a small party landed on Steamboat Wharf at noon as a large gathering of townspeople cheered. The presidential party had lunch at Sanford's home and toured the island in the afternoon. Although Arthur declined an invitation to turn his visit into a formal ceremony, he did speak briefly to a crowd gathered outside Sanford's home at the corner of Federal and Broad Streets. President Arthur thanked them for their kind welcome but excused himself from making a speech.

The presidential party visited Charles O'Connor, a one-time legal opponent of Arthur in their days of practicing law, on Cliff Road; visited prominent artist Eastman Johnson; toured the Agricultural Fair; drove past the birthplace of Arthur's U.S. treasury secretary, Charles Folger; and returned to town. From there, the president rode the new Nantucket Railroad to Surfside to view a proposed development. Finally, the party finished its tour at the Nantucket Atheneum, where President Arthur expressed interest in the library's collection of whaling artifacts, in particular a large whale's jaw. The group stopped at Sanford's house for refreshments and an impromptu concert from the Metropolitan Band of Boston, there to perform at the Agricultural Fair, and left the island to board the *Dispatch* at 5:00 p.m.

September 8

In 1913, Yale University, having failed to win a football championship and—worse—having lost to rival Harvard University, ended the tradition of naming a senior to coach the team and hired Howard Jones, its first salaried football coach. That September, Jones sent his linemen to Nantucket and his linebackers to Newport, Rhode Island, for a week of training.

Hiring a salaried coach proved controversial, with critics arguing that the game would lose its amateur status. But the decision came from team captain Henry "Hank" Ketcham, an All-American player who personally hired Coach Jones.

On Nantucket, the thirty men lived at the 'Sconset Cottage Club, located on Ocean Avenue, and practiced in a field north of Siasconset Village, where they worked on conditioning and drills. The football team was also welcomed at the Sankaty Head Golf Club and given use of the 'Sconset Casino.

September 9

In 1838, the whale ship *Napoleon* sailed for the Pacific whaling grounds. While visiting the island of St. Helena, ship cooper, Henry Plaskett Clapp, visited the grave of exiled emperor Napoleon Bonaparte and took three cuttings from a willow tree located there.

Clapp nursed the cuttings during his four years at sea and gave them to his mother when he returned. They were planted on the east side of Centre Street, where they grew until two were blown over in the 1890s and the third was cut down in 1918. The remains of the second "Napoleon Willow" were used for fill on Easy Street. A piece of that tree survived and grew up in the middle of the street, where it stayed until 1935. The willow cut down in 1918 sprouted again and regrew on Centre Street until the 1980s, when it was permanently removed.

September 10

In 1904, geographers from all over the world came to the United States for a sixteen-day International Geographic Congress. Up to that point, all meetings had been held in Europe. At the American gathering, the group traveled between sessions held in Washington, D.C.; Philadelphia, Pennsylvania; New York City; Chicago; and St. Louis, Missouri.

Professor F.P. Gulliver, of Southboro, Massachusetts, presented a paper on the geographical effect of erosion on Nantucket. Gulliver noted that shoreline exposed to the open sea experienced significant erosion, while other areas of the island seemed to be building up sand along the shore. He wrote:

> *Smith Point, extending from the southwestern corner of the island, represents the attempt of the sea to join Nantucket and Tuckernuck islands with Chappaquiddick and Martha's Vineyard islands. This uncompleted tombolo has gone through many changes of form since the first maps were made of this region, the currents having broken across it at many times. Muskeget Channel shows that the currents formed by wind and tide are too strong to allow the completion of this tombolo. The great irregularity of the shoals as mapped by the Coast Survey shows a constant strife between the sea on the one hand which tries to join all these islands with a sand bar and the currents working at right angles to the alongshore movement which try to keep the channels between the islands open.*

September 11

The Atlantic Yacht Club held a schooner race in 1903 with a 925-mile course that used lightships located off Nantucket, New York and New Jersey as race markers. The *Ingomar*, owned by Morton F. Plant, won the race in three days, twenty-two hours and eighteen minutes.

Yachting took hold of American culture in the 1850s, and the custom of using lightships as race markers for both East Coast and transatlantic races would last into the 1970s. When World War II prevented the popular Newport-to-Bermuda sailing race, its organizers planned a substitute race that sailed from Rhode Island, to the *Nantucket* lightship, to the *Cape May* lightship and back.

When racing off New York, the America's Cup frequently used the *Sandy Hook* lightship as the midway point where racing vessels turned and raced back to the finish.

September 12

Stephen Symonds Foster, a radical abolitionist and author of *The Brotherhood of Thieves; or, A True Picture of the American Church and Clergy: A Letter to Nathaniel Barney, of Nantucket*, died in 1881.

Foster, who was famous for his dramatic and aggressive style of public speaking, spoke at a Nantucket Anti-Slavery Convention at the Nantucket Atheneum in August 1842. During his lecture, Foster told the audience that, because members of the Southern clergy in the Methodist, Episcopalian, Baptist and Presbyterian churches held slaves and Northern members of those churches kept fellowship with slaveholders, they were all, by extension, guilty. The church, Foster proclaimed, was the "Bulwark of Slavery," its clergy "a designing priesthood" and its membership a "Brotherhood of Thieves."

His lecture riled a great many Nantucketers who were offended by Foster's criticism of the church. In addition, the town was in the middle of a tempestuous struggle to integrate the public school, and tensions were running high. The next night as the convention met, a hostile mob threw stones and rotten eggs at Atheneum windows and pursued attendees as they fled looking for a safe place to finish their meeting.

A year later, Foster published his "Brotherhood of Thieves" speech. As a youth, Foster had attended Union Theological Seminary but left when the seminary refused to accommodate a protest meeting. Convinced that American churches did not uphold genuine Christian principles, the embittered Foster became one of the most extreme and vitriolic of the abolitionists, and religious institutions were often his target.

September 13

Nantucket-born Moses J. Barnard, commander of the Voltigeur Regiment of the U.S. Army during the Mexican-American War in 1847, distinguished himself during an attack on the Chapultepec fortress by flying the Voltigeur colors as the regiment captured the stronghold. Barnard, a captain, was one of the first to scale the parapet during heavy gunfire. When the flag bearer was shot, he picked up the banner and planted it, getting wounded twice in the process.

On the recommendation of his general, Barnard was cited for "conspicuous gallantry" and promoted to major in 1848, and the citizens of Nantucket presented him with a sword in honor of his bravery.

The Regiment of Voltigeurs and Foot Riflemen was one of nine new infantry regiments authorized by Congress in 1847 for one year of service in the Mexican-American War. Intended to be composed of mounted soldiers and foot soldiers, the Voltigeurs turned out to be foot riflemen who were armed with the muzzle-loading rifles and also included a company of mountain howitzers and war rockets.

At the time of his enlistment, Barnard was living in Philadelphia, and he died on July 4, 1852 in Oregon City, Oregon. According to congressional records, he died from either the wounds he received or a disease he contracted during the war.

September 14

After visiting Nantucket, United States president Woodrow Wilson and his wife departed early on the yacht *Mayflower* in 1917. The Wilsons had stopped at Nantucket to bring their daughter, Mrs. Francis B. Sayre, to the island to reunite with her family in Siasconset.

The island didn't have much warning of Wilson's visit but still managed to offer him a grand welcome when he arrived on September 13. Schools were cancelled, businesses were closed and most of the town gathered on Steamboat Wharf to cheer the Wilsons when they landed at the Yacht Club pier. The president cheerfully waved his hat and acknowledged the greeting. The party rode to Siasconset in a horse-drawn carriage. At the Sayre cottage, the president and Mrs. Wilson visited with their grandchildren and stayed for dinner. They returned to town by 10:00 p.m. and were again cheered by a crowd as they returned to the *Mayflower.*

September 15

In 1961, Hurricane Esther gathered itself into a category-three hurricane as it moved north-northwest from the Cape Verde Islands. The storm peaked with sustained winds of 145 miles per hour and made landfall in North Carolina before it continued north and hit Nantucket on September 26. Twenty-foot waves plowed through Broad Creek Crossing in Madaket and created a channel that cut Smith's Point off from the rest of Nantucket.

In the days after the storm, local people assumed the channel would close up, but it did not. With a wide opening to the sea established, strong ocean currents continued to redefine Madaket's shoreline throughout the fall. By November, three homeowners had moved their cottages away from the eroding shoreline. The severed section of Madaket remained an island for more than twenty years and eventually became known as Esther's Island. In the mid-1980s, shifting sands reconnected Esther's Island to Nantucket.

September 16

Famed Nantucket whaling Captain Albert Wood was born in 1813. The youngest child of a whaling captain, Wood was ten years old when his father was lost at sea.

Wood was best known for his harrowing escape from the jaws of a sperm whale. While serving as mate on the ship *Ploughboy*, he was knocked from a whaleboat into a whale's mouth. Wood managed to escape from between the whale's jaws and got himself into the boat of his fellow crew members. He recovered from wounds to his head and the side of his body. The whale, which was killed, netted eighty barrels of oil, and Wood kept one of its teeth.

Later, Captain Wood commanded the mail steamer *Shamrock*, which traveled between Hong Kong and Canton, China. During one voyage, he discovered river pirates hidden on board who planned to take over the ship. As a result, Captain Wood surrendered the steamer to a British man-of-war, resigned his command and headed back to Nantucket by way of Manila. But he stayed in the Philippines as a shore superintendent and agent for Lloyds of London until 1867. He returned in 1868 after a fifteen-year absence. His dog Obed recognized his master, which was the only way his youngest son, John, whom he had never met, could identify him.

Captain Wood lived the rest of his life on Nantucket and died in 1884 at age seventy-one.

September 17

Austin Strong, step-grandson of Robert Louis Stevenson, playwright and founder of Nantucket's famed "Rainbow Fleet," died in 1952. Born in San Francisco in 1881, Strong spent his childhood in the South Pacific, first in Hawaii and later in Samoa. Austin and his parents lived with Robert Louis Stevenson in Samoa and the famed poet and writer of *Treasure Island* would sometimes help him with his schoolwork.

Strong wrote the successful Broadway plays *The Drums of Oude* and *Seventh Heaven*. On Nantucket, he created follies for Nantucket audiences and led campaigns against paving over the cobblestones on Main Street and prohibiting cars on the island. Strong created a sailing school on Nantucket for his many nieces and nephews, as well as the Gilbraith children, who were made famous in the book *Cheaper by the Dozen*. The school was called the "Rainbow Fleet" and was established in a wharf shack.

September 18

Photographer H. Marshall Gardiner was born in Canada in 1884. Gardiner learned the art of making hand-tinted photographs from his father, who had established successful photo studios in Michigan and Florida.

In 1910, Gardiner opened a summer photography shop on Nantucket, which provided the only photo finishing service on the island.

For thirty years, Gardiner created hand-painted photographs in Nantucket, Florida and Bermuda. His pictures of Nantucket are the most well known, in particular his colorful photo of the "Rainbow Fleet," a class of small catboats, sailing past Brant Point. An adept marketer, Gardiner painted the now iconic compass rose mural on the side of his store on Main Street. The compass rose includes distances to many famed whaling ports as well as to the sites of Gardiner's other stores in Florida and Michigan. The Nantucket Historical Association now holds a preservation restriction on the mural.

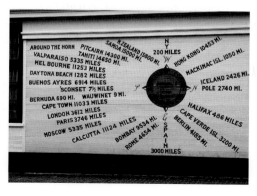

September 19

The Nantucket whale ship *Union* left port in 1807 bound for the coast of Brazil. Twelve days later, while under sail, the *Union* struck a whale so hard that it broke two timbers on the starboard bow. Captain Edmund Gardner, master of his first whaling voyage, ordered the boats to be lowered and readied in case the crew needed to abandon the ship. By midnight, two hours after the collision, it was clear the crew would need to evacuate. Sixteen men in two boats left the *Union* behind and began to row for the Azores.

"'Twas thick and dark with squalls, it was really a dark day, our water nearly exhausted, night approaching, my boat leaking so that one man was bailing water from the boat continually," Gardner wrote of the incident. "All but the man throwing the water from the boat and myself was laying down. I saw him who was bailing earnestly looking, the sail intervened prevented my seeing what he did. I asked him what he saw, his reply was 'I don't know, 'twas something black.' I then looked under the sail and saw the Land a more pleasant sight was never seen."

When they landed in the Azores, their provisions gone, they had been at sea for eight nights and had traveled nearly six hundred miles.

Later in his career, Gardner made history in 1819 when he and another Nantucket ship became the first American whalers to visit the Sandwich (Hawaiian) Islands.

September 20

In 1901, as the transatlantic passenger ship *Teutonic* approached New York Harbor, its captain redirected the ship's course so that he could pull alongside the *Nantucket* lightship and receive an update on the condition of United States president William McKinley. Those aboard the *Teutonic* were shocked to hear of the president's death. When the ship left Liverpool, England, the news from Buffalo, New York, had been promising.

McKinley, the twenty-fifth U.S. president, was shot and wounded on September 6 inside the Temple of Music on the grounds of the Pan-American Exposition in Buffalo, New York. The president was shaking hands with the public when he was shot by anarchist Leon Czolgosz. McKinley died on September 14 from gangrene caused by the bullet wounds.

McKinley had been elected for a second term in 1900. He enjoyed meeting the public and was reluctant to use security. The secretary to the president, George B. Cortelyou, feared an assassination attempt would take place during a visit to the Temple of Music and twice took it off the schedule. McKinley put it back each time.

The president initially appeared to be recovering but took a turn for the worse on September 13 and died early the next morning; Vice President Theodore Roosevelt succeeded him.

As the *Teutonic* left the *Nantucket* lightship, bound for New York, the English flag on its stern and the American flag on its foremast were lowered to half-staff.

September 21

After the Great Fire destroyed its building in July, the Episcopal Church dissolved in 1846 as a way to shed the burden of heavy debt left by the disaster.

In 1837, the Reverend Moses Marcus of New York had visited Nantucket and wrote in his diary, "I this day made my first visit to the Island of Nantucket Dec. 31 Preached in the Methodist Chapel in the morning, in the Second Congregational in the afternoon, in the First Congregational in the evening. I am the first clergyman who ever officiated on the Island." The next year, Reverend Marcus founded an Episcopal church on the site of a former Quaker meetinghouse on Broad Street.

Eight years after dissolving the first church, a new Episcopal church, called St. Paul's, was organized on Fair Street (pictured on the left, with the Unitarian Church on the right). In 1901, the church constructed a new stone building and commissioned Tiffany Studios to design stained-glass windows.

September 22

Eunice B. Paddock, the last Nantucket Quaker, died in 1900. In 1876, Paddock opened a sewing store on Main Street, where she also worked as a dressmaker.

Quakers, also known as the Society of Friends, had once dominated Nantucket religious culture. But by 1820, Quakerism on Nantucket was declining, and the Friends began to break into separate sects. The Friends' strict views, which ranged from refusing to participate in war to only marrying other Quakers, turned parishioners off. By the late 1860s, there were only a few Quakers on the island, and Paddock is believed to be the last.

Since 1939, members of the Religious Society of Friends have used the Quaker meetinghouse on Fair Street, owned by the Nantucket Historical Association, for worship, first during the summer and year-round since 2000.

September 23

American Revolutionary War naval commander and founder of the United State Navy, John Paul Jones, opened fire on the HMS *Serapis* and HMS *Countess of Scarborough* in 1779. Jones commanded a small squadron of American and French warships during the war and was captain of the *Bonhomme Richard*. On that day, two of Jones's crewmen killed in action were Henry Martin and Thomas Turner of Nantucket.

During the battle, the *Serapis* severely damaged the *Bonhomme Richard*, and Jones realized his only hope was to board the British vessel. So he rammed the enemy and drew alongside. The *Bonhomme Richard* crew bound the two ships together with grappling hooks as both continued firing into each other. Moving along the two ships' yardarms, the crew members of the *Bonhomme Richard* were able to cross over to the *Serapis* and drove the enemy crew members from their stations. During the battle, Jones famously said, "I have not yet begun to fight!" in response to the British demand that he surrender his ship.

In total, fourteen Nantucket men served with Jones during the American Revolution, later operating as French privateers. After the battle, Jones scuttled the damaged *Bonhomme Richard* and transferred his command to the *Serapis*. One of the greatest prizes taken by the Continental navy, the *Serapis* was soon transferred to the French for political reasons. The battle proved a major embarrassment for the Royal Navy and cemented Jones's place in American naval history.

September 24

Mildred Carpenter Jewett, born in 1907, disliked water and could not swim, yet she became famous for assisting mariners in distress and was a beloved volunteer coast guardsman and unfaltering friend to those in need, both animal and human.

In 1911, her family moved to her grandmother's farm in Madaket, where she lived for the rest of her life and acquired the nickname "Madaket Millie." The daughter of a fisherman and scalloper, Jewett was a skilled boat navigator and pilot and excelled at fishing. During World War II, she became a Coastal Defense specialist for the U.S. Coast Guard and patrolled Nantucket's beaches, keeping watch for German submarines. She also trained dogs for the U.S. Coast Guard and helped them in their rescue efforts. Jewett died in 1990 at age eighty-two at her home in Madaket, surrounded by her beloved animals, having assisted the U.S. Coast Guard in a variety of capacities for most of her life.

September 25

The newly formed Massachusetts Institute of Technology held its first faculty meeting in 1865 to elect a secretary and discuss programs and fees. Geometry professor William Watson was in attendance.

Watson, born on Nantucket in 1834, received his love of math from his mother, Mary Macy Watson, who guided his studies as a youth. Watson graduated from the Coffin School and attended the Bridgewater State Normal School and taught for two years. Using his teaching earnings, he attended Harvard College, where he was both a student and a teacher. By the time he left Harvard in 1858, Watson had received two math degrees.

He studied and traveled extensively in Europe and in 1862 received a PhD from the University at Jena. Back in America, Watson became involved in a growing discussion among Boston educators hoping to open a school of industrial science. With colleagues William Barton Rogers and John Runkle, Watson opened the Massachusetts Institute of Technology and started classes in February 1865. Watson wrote the first geometry textbook for his MIT classes. Both the United States and European countries honored Watson for his expertise in civil engineering, and he lectured frequently on technical subjects.

Watson kept in touch with his alma mater, the Coffin School, and he donated four lathes and woodworking tools. He also befriended Coffin School teacher Alvin Paddock and trained him in technical drawing.

September 26

The *Inquirer* notified the island of the passing of influential newspaper editor, politician and activist Samuel H. Jenks, who died in Boston in 1863.

Born in 1789, Jenks buried three wives before coming to Nantucket in 1819, where he married again to Martha Coffin. He became editor of the *Inquirer* in October 1821. Under his leadership, the paper grew successful, and Jenks used it to advance his causes. Jenks left the *Inquirer* in 1841 to become postmaster but became involved in the *Warder*, another newspaper. In 1846, the Great Fire in July destroyed his competitor's printing presses, and Jenks allowed the rival paper to use his so it could report on the disaster.

Jenks opened a Commercial Reading and Newsroom in 1823. For an annual fee, members could read newspapers, magazines and books. In 1826, he persuaded English admiral Sir Issac Coffin to fund a school for all Nantucket Coffin descendants, and he helped found the Nantucket Atheneum in 1834. Off-island, he served in both houses of the Massachusetts legislature, was the state insurance commissioner and edited several newspapers in Boston.

But on Nantucket, his biggest contribution was his dogged pursuit of establishing public education for island children. In 1827, Jenks lead the contentious fight to create free public schools, which eventually succeeded.

Jenks also lobbied to do away with the custom of imprisoning people for not paying their debts and lived to see the state outlaw the practice.

September 27

Walter N. Chase, grandson of the whale ship *Essex*'s first mate Owen Chase and keeper of the Coskata Life-Saving Station, died in 1929.

Chase was made keeper of the Coskata station in 1886, three years after it opened. For the next ten years, Chase led one of the best crews of "surfmen" in the U.S. Life-Saving Service. In 1893, he and his crew members were awarded medals for their heroism and skill in saving the crew of the schooner *H.P. Kirkham*. On January 20, 1892, the schooner was wrecked on Rose and Crown Shoal, about fifteen miles off Great Point, during a heavy gale. Captain Chase and his men rowed twenty-six hours to get to the crew and save the men.

At one time, there were 279 manned United States Life-Saving Service stations, and 5 were located on Nantucket.

September 28

While New York City prepared for an ornate funeral for Civil War hero Admiral David Farragut, the steamship carrying his body went aground off Great Point in 1870. The frigate *Guerriere* had been transporting Farragut's body from New Hampshire, where he died suddenly while on vacation.

David Glasgow Farragut was a native of North Carolina, but he fought for the Union during the Civil War and coined the popular saying, "Damn the torpedoes, full speed ahead!" in 1864. He was the first rear admiral, vice admiral and admiral in the United States Navy.

After the *Guerriere* grounded, Nantucket captain Alexander B. Dunham brought the steamship *Island Home* to the stranded vessel. The *Island Home* pulled the ship off the shoal the next day and brought it to Nantucket Harbor. The *Island Home* then transported the admiral's body to Hyannis, where it was brought to Fall River and sent to New York on another steamship, accompanied by a delegation from the city council of New York, a tugboat and a guard of marines.

The funeral party arrived in New York in time for the ceremonies. Admiral Farragut was brought ashore by the navy as city forts fired their guns in salute. Onshore, military officers marched with the coffin through the streets of Manhattan as thousands of Civil War veterans, students and members of maritime organizations stood along the parade route to honor him. Admiral Farragut's body was buried at Woodlawn Cemetery in the Bronx, and his grave site is listed in the National Register of Historic Places.

September 29

Ebenezer Gardner was born in 1764 and grew up in the shadow of the American Revolutionary War, as well as the suffering it inflicted on Nantucket. After witnessing the famine and the lack of fuel in 1780, caused when Nantucket mariners were not allowed to sail their ships to trade, Gardner set sail on a privateer. In the spring of 1781, at age sixteen, Gardner and four other Nantucket boys joined the *Saucy Hound*, a privateer visiting the island on a recruiting mission. Within days, the *Saucy Hound*, en route to Bermuda, boarded and captured a ship sailing for Britain.

But the luck of the *Saucy Hound* turned bad when a British ship captured it. Gardner and his Nantucket compatriots were taken to Sandy Hook, New York, where the British had established a base. He was put on the sloop *Rattlesnake* and forced to fight for England off Yorktown. He continued to fight for the British off the coast of America, in the West Indies and off the coast of Europe.

After twenty-eight months at sea, he was let off in England and paid for his service. He found his way back to Nantucket on a packet. After the war, Gardner went whaling in waters off Canada, Brazil and Africa, and he worked in other maritime trades, serving on ships in the Mediterranean Sea and returning to Britain on occasion. Gardner lived to be ninety-four years old and died in May 1859.

September 30

The Lighthouse Board installed new, experimental technologies on the lightships *Nantucket* and *Cape May* in 1934. A new type of short-range radio beacon was installed on the *Nantucket*, which allowed the lightship to send two radio signals, which gave passing ships the ability to calculate the time difference and find their position relative to the lightship. In 1917, the board installed radio beacons on lightships as  fog signals. In the early days of radio technology, a lightship sounded its foghorn and then also emitted a radio signal, providing two calculation points. But in time, engineers discovered emitting a series of radio signals was the most effective navigational tool for mariners.

At the lightship *Cape May*, the board installed the first sodium vapor lights. The lights, which flashed and rotated, were installed 165 feet above the water and could be seen for nineteen miles.

October 1

In 1847, Maria Mitchell stood on the roof of her parents' Main Street home and swept the sky with her telescope, as she frequently did, looking for anything unusual or interesting. At 10:30 p.m., she spotted a blurry, fuzzy light and realized it was a comet. She ran to get her father, William Mitchell, who confirmed it.

Female astronomers were very rare in 1847, and her discovery caused a sensation. The comet was named in her honor, the king of Denmark awarded her a medal and her story was told and retold in newspapers across America. Her life story is a history of firsts: she was the first woman to record a "telescopic" comet sighting, the first female professional to work for the federal government (for the Coast Survey and the Nautical Almanac) and the first woman elected into the American Academy of Arts and Sciences.

October 2

George F. Gaynor worked as a cable ship radio operator repairing the telephone cable that connected Nantucket to the mainland. In 1930, he sent a letter to his wife telling her about a large storm and about his life on the ship:

> *The name of the vicinity where we were hove-to, is known to sailors as "Hell-Hole." Guess the old man on the bridge must have seen Satan himself. During the storm I managed to take several pictures. The best one was a snap of the Chief Engineer coming down the ladder from the bridge, just as a big wave was coming over. A mess boy running along the deck saw the wave too and grabbed the Chief by the neck to save himself. They were both washed along the deck until the chief managed to get his arm around the rail. We are now moving along at a good clip and the sea is much calmer. The stars are out and except for rolling a bit the weather is good.*
>
> *Alone in the shack, I was sitting here looking out through the port thinking how uncanny and weird it seems out here. The water underneath, the sky overhead, and the swish as the ship cuts through the domain of Neptune and Davy Jones Locker. When all of a sudden I was startled by the soft thud of a small white object on the deck at my feet. It was a flying fish who had been attracted by the light in the shack.*

October 3

In 1874, the Boston publication *Woman's Journal* ran an article describing a "Women's Festival" called "the first public demonstration in favor of Woman's Rights" in Charlottesville, Virginia. The writer, Philena Carkin, was a friend of *Woman's Journal* co-founder Lucy Stone and colleague of Nantucket abolitionist Anna Gardner. Carkin taught alongside Gardner, a Quaker, for five years at the Charlottesville Freedman's School, which taught children of African descent.

Gardner worked at the school until 1871 and left when the city implemented public education. Carkin, who ran the school after Gardner left, described her as an "old time abolitionist" and, despite her upbringing, "a soldier by nature." An outspoken critic of social injustice, Carkin said Gardner encouraged female students to speak out and to serve the community outside the home.

Of the Women's Festival in 1874, Carkin wrote, "The women and girls who took part in the celebration numbered about fifty. Everything was done by them without any assistance from the other sex, because some of the young men had declared that we could do nothing without them. The room was filled at an early hour, a large number of the men and boys being present out of curiosity, and, perhaps, in hopes to witness a failure. At a given signal the women and girls appeared on the platform, and their appearance was hailed with applause by the audience. The exercises opened by the singing of 'Joy to the world the Lord has come,' in which the audience joined."

October 4

William Rotch, a prominent Nantucket Quaker and successful shipowner, was born in 1734. When the American Revolution began, Rotch, like most of the rest of Nantucket, declined to fight. Rotch, and the island, suffered at the hands of both the British and Americans who couldn't decide where the island's loyalty lay. The British ransacked Rotch's ships and harassed island citizens. The Americans refused to let Nantucket mariners sail.

In 1779, Rotch was part of a town-appointed committee that appealed directly to the British commanders and got them to agree to stop attacking Nantucket ships. But Rotch's problems were not over. Nantucket citizen and Patriot Thomas Jenkins charged the committee with treason for going to a British port without permission. A joint committee of the House and Senate heard the complaint in 1780, and Rotch and his fellow committee members were not given full liberty until the war ended.

In 1785, Rotch and his son Benjamin traveled to England to petition the British government to move Nantucket's whale fisheries operation to England. When the English didn't take his proposal seriously, Rotch turned to France and established a whaling venture in Dunkirk that operated from 1786 to 1794.

With the outbreak of the French Revolution, Rotch's son moved the Dunkirk operation to Milford Haven, England. The senior Rotch eventually retired to New Bedford, leaving a prosperous legacy to his sons. Rotch died in New Bedford on May 16, 1828.

October 5

In 1881, a severe two-day storm pounded Nantucket with cold temperatures, high wind and occasional snow flurries. When the gale had passed, island citizens discovered six schooners had run aground in local waters.

The *Malabar*, traveling to Belfast, Maine, from New York City, struck a sandbar near the entrance to the harbor. The crew members abandoned the ship and set out in a leaky boat. They were rescued by a lifesaving crew. The *Malabar* was stripped of its spars and rigging, but the vessel broke up.

The *Edwin I. Morrison*, headed for Philadelphia, Pennsylvania, came ashore on Coatue. A wrecking crew refloated the ship, and the steamship *Island Home* towed it into the harbor.

The *Eliza J. Raynor*, of Oyster Bay, New York, went ashore in the Chord of the Bay. It was refloated three days later with the assistance of people on shore.

The HS *Billins*, of Ellsworth, Maine, went ashore on Great Point. The crew abandoned it and boarded a passing ship. A portion of the cargo was saved, but the vessel was a loss.

The *GF Hathaway*, of St. John, New Brunswick, ran into trouble near *Handkerchief* lightship and sank. The crew set out in a lifeboat and landed in Siasconset.

The *R. Baker Jr.*, from New York City sailing to Thomaston, Maine, went aground on the Nantucket Bar and sank. When the vessel struck the shoal, a kerosene lamp exploded and burned out the interior. The crew climbed the masts to wait for help. The cargo, spars and rigging were saved, and the hull was sold at auction for thirty-seven dollars.

October 6

Builders poured the concrete walls of the Nantucket Historical Association's new museum on Fair Street in 1904. One of the first poured-concrete buildings constructed in Massachusetts, the NHA attached it to the Quaker meetinghouse. The *Inquirer & Mirror* praised the project, saying, "The structure will be just what the association has long needed, and will provide a place of safety for the constantly increasing and valuable collection of antiques."

Henry Wyer headed the committee in charge and reported to the membership that his colleagues needed to be convinced that poured concrete was a viable option. "Not one of the persons engaged in our work had ever seen a concrete building, with the single exception of the Harvard Stadium," he said.

Today, the NHA houses its research library in the historic structure.

October 7

In 1916, while much of Europe fought World War I, a German submarine surfaced in Newport, Rhode Island Harbor for three hours. The next day, the *U-53* sank six non-American ships within a mile of the *Nantucket* lightship and forty miles south of Nantucket. The attacks occurred in international waters, but Europe's war suddenly felt very close to home.

Clifton Smith, captain of the *Stephano*, spotted the German submarine around 6:00 p.m.

"We were about three miles east of the *Nantucket* Lightship, and about 42 miles from the mainland when I first saw the submarine…it was a little dark. But I could make her out plainly. She was about half a mile away, and was lying next to a fairly large ship, which was apparently a supply ship," he told the *New York Times*.

"She fired a shot across our bow and I slowed down. There were four such shots fired by her altogether. About two minutes apart. None of them hit us. There were two American destroyers nearby about this time. I ordered the boats lowered, and prepared to abandon the ship…While we doing this the submarine went under the lee of the *Stephano*. I could not see much of her, but I could tell by her lights that she was going alongside the ship," Smith said.

The *U-53* left and sank a freighter before returning. The submarine then fired thirty shots and later a torpedo into the hull, which sank the *Stephano* in seven minutes.

October 8

Erica Wilson, who helped NFL star Rosey Greer learn how to embroider, was born in 1928. Raised in England and a graduate of the Royal School of Needlework, Wilson was invited to teach in the United States in 1954 and stayed. Over time, she expanded her offerings to include sixteen books, a syndicated column, DVDs and television shows for PBS and the BBC. She had many celebrity clients, including Julie Nixon, Dorothy Doubleday and  football star Greer. She opened a store on Main Street in the 1960s and spent summers on Nantucket with her husband, furniture designer Vladimir Kagan, and their children. Wilson designed and manufactured exclusive needlepoint kits for the Metropolitan Museum of Art, as well as her own collection, which was sold at needlework shops.

Wilson died in December 2011. In announcing her passing, the *New York Times* called her, "The Julia Child of Needlework."

October 9

In 1775, lawyer and smuggler Phineas Fanning left Shelter Island, New York, in the middle of the night bound for Nantucket with illicit goods. With the colonies at war and all commercial ship trade halted, Nantucket's people were starving. Many began to grow food and catch fish, and some began to smuggle. Fanning, along with his partner and future mother-in-law, Kezia Coffin, were among them.

Born in 1759, Keziah Coffin's astute grasp of business made her a powerful force on Nantucket at the time of the American Revolution. She and her husband, John Coffin, were among the island's wealthiest citizens. She was the first to hire a lawyer to help her with her businesses.

Coffin's daughter, also named Keziah, chronicled Fanning's trips in her journal. Fanning left Shelter Island in the middle of the night and arrived on Nantucket just before midnight the following day. He brought "60 to 70 weight of butter, as much cheese, one cow (dead), 2 bbls of cider" and many bushels of fruit. In December, Fanning made another run, and Keziah the younger wrote, "Our house has been like a tavern, people coming after provisions." In 1777, Fanning and the daughter Keziah married.

Along with being wealthy, Keziah the elder was also controversial. In 1773, she left the Quaker meeting after being disciplined for keeping a spinet. After the war, she was charged with treason, in part for smuggling. Although her name was cleared, litigation and discord would plague her until she died in 1820.

October 10

The whale ship *Charles Carroll*, built on Nantucket for its captain Owen Chase, left home on its first trip in 1832. Chase, who had survived the whale ship *Essex* disaster in 1820, continued to hunt whales and by the 1830s had established himself as a successful captain.

He stayed home for two years to supervise the construction of the *Charles Carroll* at a Brant Point shipyard. After he left, his wife, Nancy, died several weeks after giving birth. Chase learned of his wife's death almost two years later when he met his brother at sea in the Pacific. Chase returned in March 1836 and married Eunice Chadwick in April. Four months later, he departed on a long whaling voyage, and sixteen months later, Eunice gave birth to a son.

Chase learned of his wife's infidelity while at sea. Herman Melville, aboard the whaler *Acushnet* at the time, wrote of hearing the news: "For, while I was in the *Acushnet* we heard from some whale ship that we spoke, that the captain of the *Charles Carroll*—that is Owen Chace—had recently received letters from home, informing him of the certain infidelity of his wife…We also heard that this receipt of this news had told most heavily upon Chace, & and that he was of the deepest gloom."

Chase returned in 1840 and filed for divorce, which was granted five months later.

October 11

In 1814, the *Prince de Neufchatel* schooner, operating as a United States privateer during the War of 1812, engaged in one of the most violent clashes of the war five miles south of Nantucket.

The *Nuefchatel* had captured a British vessel when the captain of another British ship, the HMS *Endymion*, noticed the American vessel was floundering due to a lack of wind. *Endymion* captain Henry Hope sent 111 British men in five boats to attack the *Prince de Neufchatel*, which was defended by 40 Americans. After thirty minutes of harsh fighting, the Englishmen surrendered. British casualties amounted to 28 killed, 37 wounded and 28 taken prisoner. The Americans reported 5 killed and 24 wounded. The *Nuefchatel* pilot, Charles J. Hillburn of Nantucket, was one of the Americans killed.

On the island, residents reported hearing cannon fire and seeing light flashes from Tom Nevers. *Prince de Neufchatel* captain John Ordronaux dropped most of the wounded and the British prisoners on Nantucket and left for Boston.

The *Neufchatel* operated mainly in European waters, damaging British shipping during the War of 1812. Noted for its speed, at one time it outran seventeen men-of-war. In 1813, operating in the English Channel, it took nine British ships as prizes. The ship also delivered a crushing defeat to the boats of a British frigate that tried to capture it. The British finally captured the vessel in December 1814 and destroyed it in 1815.

October 12

Merle Turner Orleans, Nantucket's quintessential newspaperwoman, was born in 1911. She was the daughter of Harry Turner, owner and editor of the *Inquirer & Mirror*, and used to say, "I have printer's ink, not blood, in my veins." She began working for her father as soon as she was able to ride a bicycle. Orleans received a master's degree in French from Wheaton College in 1934 and then returned to Nantucket to write for the paper.

After her father died, Orleans and her brother, Gordon Turner, ran the newspaper until they sold it in 1958.

Orleans continued to work at the *Inquirer & Mirror*, writing the "Here and There" and "Looking Backwards" columns, as well as the newspapers obituaries and wedding announcements. She was also the medical librarian at the Nantucket Cottage Hospital in the 1960s and 1970s.

Orleans died on October 31, 1995.

October 13

In 1842, the vessel *Peru* was the first fully loaded Nantucket whale ship transported over a sandbar using devices designed by Peter F. Ewer called "camels." As the ship glided into Nantucket Harbor, it was welcomed with cannon fire, steam whistles and the ringing of church bells.

The constantly moving sands around Nantucket had slowly placed a shoal at the mouth of Nantucket Harbor, and Ewer, a Nantucket native who made his fortune in the maritime trades, decided to reproduce a device he had seen in Holland. He designed and created floating dry docks, which he called camels, that lifted heavily laden ships and floated them through the shallow water.

Ewer's camels were two 135-foot pontoon-like hulls, shaped to conform to a ship's hull. The camels were partitioned into sections, filled with water, sunk below the ship and secured to it with heavy chains.

Ewer's venture began taking ships in and out of the harbor and had some success when the island was hit hard by the Great Fire of 1846. The fire sped up the island's already declining whaling industry and proved to be the end of Ewer's camels. Historian Edouard Stackpole noted, "Had this device been adapted earlier to Nantucket whaling procedures during the critical 1835–1855 period, the whaling merchants of Nantucket might have been enabled to keep the industry in competition with its rivals for a quarter century more."

October 14

A Canadian ship loaded with illegal alcohol clashed with the U.S. Coast Guard near the *Nantucket* lightship in 1930. The rumrunner was anchored near the lightship but was still outside the jurisdiction of the coast guard. Nonetheless, the coast guard patrol boat pulled in close to the ship's stern to prevent smugglers with shore

boats (like the one pictured here) from taking on cargo.

The captain, angered by this, turned his boat to face the patrol boat and ran on deck screaming curses and challenging the coast guardsmen to a shootout.

The coast guard crew members responded by setting up a machine gun on their deck and aiming it at the captain. The two boats spent the rest of the day in a standoff. At nightfall, the coast guard destroyer *Casson* took over and kept a searchlight on the rumrunner as it left and headed north.

October 15

Nantucket businessman and heir to the S&H Green Stamp fortune, Walter Beinecke Jr., had lunch with President Lyndon B. Johnson in 1968 to discuss historic preservation.

Beinecke combined business and historic preservation on Nantucket by purchasing and restoring the waterfront and much of the downtown in the late 1960s. A lifelong summer resident, Beinecke's philosophy was to create a tourist destination for the wealthy.

In 1968, he told *Time* magazine his plan was to attract fewer people who would buy six postcards and two hot dogs and more who would rent a hotel room and buy a couple sports coats. Beinecke's philosophy and methods, often called elitist, were controversial but ended up creating the blueprint for the island's economy well into the twenty-first century.

Born in 1918, Beinecke left school at age fifteen to join the merchant marines. He never finished high school or attended college but worked at many corporate jobs. He died in 2004 at age eighty-six.

October 16

In 1910, the dirigible *America*, making a transatlantic voyage under the direction of American journalist and explorer Walter Wellman, communicated by radio to the Siasconset Marconi station. As it floated a few miles off shore, crew members of the *America* reported that all was well. But they would have to abandon the airship the following day after losing its engines and drifting almost to Burmuda.

In 1905, Wellman convinced his employer, the *Chicago Record Herald*, to fund an exploration to the North Pole in a dirigible, a hydrogen-filled airship. Wellman made two attempts to leave for the North Pole, and mechanical troubles grounded him both times. In 1910, he announced he would fly his airship *America* across the Atlantic Ocean and left Atlantic City, New Jersey, on October 15.

The Siasconset wireless operators began to pick up the *America*'s signal around 9:00 a.m. the next day. For the next three hours, the ship and Siasconset exchanged brief messages. The airship was trapped in a dense fog and couldn't give its bearings, although at one point the Siasconset operator guessed it was almost directly over Nantucket.

A day later, the *America*'s engines malfunctioned, and it was drifting perilously close to the sea. Wellman and crew abandoned it and were rescued in their lifeboat by a passing British mail ship.

Wellman built another dirigible the next year, and it exploded during a test flight, killing all five crew members on board. It was his last project using a dirigible.

October 17

Painter, writer, teacher and Nantucket summer resident Nathaniel Jermund Pousette-Dart died in 1965. Born Nathaniel Pousette in 1886, Pousette-Dart was the son of Swedish immigrants and grew up in St. Paul, Minnesota. He studied painting at the Art Students League in New York City and in Philadelphia under the painter Robert Henri and at the Academy of Fine Arts.

He married Flora Louise Dart in 1913, and they combined their last names to form Pousette-Dart. After school, he lived in St. Paul, where he became known for his Minnesota landscapes. Later, he lived in Valhalla, New York. He exhibited at the Metropolitan Museum of Art, the Whitney Museum of American Art and the Pennsylvania Academy of Fine Arts. He is the author of nine art books and contributed to *Art News*, *American Artist* and other art magazines.

The Pousette-Darts had two children, both painters, Richard Pousette-Dart and Maggie Meredith. His grandson John Pousette-Dart is a musician.

October 18

Sixteen-year-old David Whippey left Nantucket on board the whale ship *Hero* in 1816 bound as an apprentice for seven years. But he ran away in Peru and never returned. By 1825, Whippey had landed on the Fiji Islands, where he planned to collect turtle shells and sandalwood to sell in China. But the captain who left him there didn't come back for thirteen years.

Stranded in the South Pacific, Whippey decided to stay, learned Fijian and earned the local tribal chief's trust. He eventually established Fiji's first business and prospered building boats and acting as a local mediator to ships stopping at the islands.

Whippey met up with an old Nantucket playmate, William Cary, in Fiji. Cary was the sole survivor of a shipwreck there in 1825. Both participated in warfare with the natives, although probably not by their own choice. But they did not participate in the local tradition of cannibalism. Whippey's willingness to assimilate the local customs (except cannibalism) is probably what kept the local tribes from killing him.

In time, a small band of white settlers established a community there with approval from the local chief. As he grew into his life, Whippey also became active in local politics and served as vice-consul to the United States from 1846 to 1856.

Whippey fathered eleven children with four partners, some of whom he married. Whippy died in October 1871 at the age of sixty-nine.

October 19

In 1903, the U.S. Navy began to take control of radio communication onboard the *Nantucket* lightship and had accomplished it by October 1904.

The Italian-owned Marconi wireless system revolutionized the maritime world when the *New York Herald* installed it on the *Nantucket* lightship in 1901.

Understanding that radio communication would help save lives and protect the coast, the United States started experimenting with other radio systems, but none worked as well as the one invented by the Italian Guglielmo Marconi. By 1904, almost every ship equipped with a radio used Marconi's. But that monopoly was broken when the navy installed an American-made wireless station on the *Nantucket* lightship in 1904.

Shut out, the *New York Herald* accused the Germans of using diplomacy to get their radio companies into the American market (in July, the German ambassador had complained to the U.S. secretary of state that its ships, equipped with German radios, could not communicate with the *Nantucket* lightship).

The Marconi Company refused to cooperate with the navy, saying two systems would jeopardize its patent applications, and upgraded its Siasconset station with a more powerful system.

Ship captains scrambled to reestablish radio communication with the lightship, which, in three years, had become a vital necessity.

In January 1905, the navy announced new rules that allowed vessels to use information gathered from the *Nantucket* lightship and had worked out an arrangement with the Associated Press to share naval wireless communications with journalists.

October 20

In 1916, the Nantucket Cranberry Company was the first in New England to harvest berries using a machine, which proved faster and more efficient than picking by hand. The machine was invented by Nantucket Cranberry Company president Horace B. Maglathlin. Growers from all over New England took note of Maglathlin's machine, nicknamed the "horse-picker." Maglathlin, a resident of Kingston, Massachusetts, received a patent the following year.

Cranberries, which grow wild on Nantucket, have been harvested commercially here since 1857. The Nantucket Cranberry Company was formed in 1905 and over time created a large-scale agricultural business. By 1918, the Nantucket Cranberry Company controlled 2,672 acres and cultivated a 234-acre tract near Gibbs Pond, which made it the largest contiguous cranberry bog in the world at the time.

The property changed owners many times until 1969 when island residents Roy Larsen, Walter Beinecke Jr. and Arthur Dean purchased it, along with more than seven hundred acres of undeveloped land surrounding it. The men gave the land to the Nantucket Conservation Foundation (NCF) so that the NCF could generate income from the bogs. Today, the NCF cultivates twenty-four separate cranberry bogs totaling 195 acres and produces nearly 2 million pounds of cranberries every year. Part of the yield also comes from the NCF's organic operation at the Windswept bog.

October 21

In 1835, Reverend James E. Crawford, who would later lead the Nantucket Baptist Church, was walking on State Street in Boston when he saw an angry mob try to lynch William Lloyd Garrison, the leader of the antislavery movement. Witnessing the event instantly converted Crawford to the abolitionist's cause, and he said later in a speech that his "heart and soul became fully dedicated to the cause of immediate emancipation.

The Boston Female Anti-Slavery Society had announced it would hold a meeting at the local American Anti-Slavery Society offices and many speculated that George Thompson, an English abolitionist, would speak. For days, those who supported the South had passed out handbills offering $100 to the first person to attack Thompson. But he did not attend the women's meeting. Before they started, the mayor, nervous about the growing crowd on the street, asked the group to relocate to a home six blocks away. Arm in arm, African American and white women left the building together and walked through the crowd to their new destination. Although it was a tense moment, the crowd let the women pass. But then some of the mob entered the antislavery office, dragged Garrison out and attempted to lynch him. He was saved by the police and put in jail overnight for his safety.

The incident galvanized many in support of the antislavery movement and is considered a turning point in the history of the abolitionist movement in New England.

October 22

Lewis Temple, a former slave and inventor of a revolutionary whaling harpoon, was born in 1800. Temple was a slave in Richmond, Virginia, and went to New Bedford, Massachusetts, in 1829. By 1836, Temple was one of the 315,000 free African Americans in the United States, and owned a store that served whalers on the New Bedford waterfront.

Temple learned by talking to his customers that many whales escaped because simple barbed harpoons could not hold the struggling animals. In 1848, Temple invented a new type of harpoon with a movable head that locked into a whale's flesh and prevented the whale from slipping loose. Temple's invention functioned like an ancient Eskimo-style harpoon. It had a cutting edge and a sweeping barb on the other side, a style that became known as a toggle. Once the point had been firmly planted deep into the whale blubber, the whole tip could pivot and lock into place.

By the 1850s, blacksmiths all over New Bedford were replicating Temple's toggle irons. The new design remained the harpoon of choice in the American whale fishery until the end of whaling in the 1920s.

Temple never patented his invention, but he made a good living from his harpoon sales and built a blacksmith shop in New Bedford. Temple accidentally fell one night while walking near the construction site and never fully recovered from his injuries.

October 23

Composer Ned Rorem, called "the world's best composer of art songs," was born in 1923. Rorem, who spends part of the year on Nantucket, has written almost five hundred songs (including a set called "Nantucket Songs"), three symphonies, four piano concertos, numerous choral and chamber works, ten operas, ballets and musical theater. He is also a prolific writer and has published twenty books.

As a youth, Rorem trained in piano at the Music School of Northwestern University, the Curtis Institute in Philadelphia and the Juilliard School in New York.

He has lived in France and has taught at universities, received a Pulitzer Prize for Music in 1976 and has also received a Fulbright Fellowship, a Guggenheim Fellowship, an award from the National Institute of Arts and Letters, three ASCAP–Deems Taylor Awards and an ASCAP Lifetime Achievement award. In addition, the Atlanta Symphony's version of three Rorem orchestral works won the 1989 Grammy Award for Outstanding Orchestral Recording.

In 1979, while spending the summer on Nantucket, Rorem wrote in his journal on July 10, which was later published as a book, "Tomorrow Madame Tureck is due again, this time with the young guitarist Sharon Isbin. They're coming at 5:45, the hour at which a violent chunk of hardware called Skylab in outer space is scheduled to whirl into our atmosphere and crash, probably on Nantucket, splattering our teacups and innards."

October 24

In 2007, after six weeks of precarious work moving the seventy-foot brick-and-granite Sankaty Lighthouse four hundred feet inland, workers focused on finishing a restoration of the historic 1850 light.

Congress approved $12,000 to build Sankaty Light in 1848, and it was one of the first in the country to be fitted with a Fresnel lens, a revolutionary new design that was thinner, lighter and easier to see. In its early days, a lighthouse keeper and his family lived at the light. Sankaty Light was electrified in 1933 and fully automated by 1965. In 1997, the light was listed on the National Register of Historic Places.

Operated first by the Light House Board and later by the U.S. Coast Guard, the Sankaty Lighthouse was purchased by the Siasconset Trust in 2007 and was moved away from its precarious position near the edge of the eroding bluff.

October 25

In 1859, the *Inquirer* ran an article discussing the problem of sea worms eating through the wooden hulls of whale ships. Captain Calvin Swain of Nantucket, commander of the whale ship *Minerva* of New Bedford, realized the ship was leaking near the Bay of Islands, New Zealand The crew discovered that sea worms had bored holes right through the hull. They plugged and tarred the holes and then laid sheets of canvas and chains over that. The captain managed to get the ship to Sydney, Australia, and into a shipyard for repairs.

With its cargo of 1,500 barrels of whale oil still on board, *Minerva* was hauled out of the water and inspected. The worms had found a worn section of the ship's copper sheathing and bored through two eight-foot planks to about an eighth of an inch.

The newspaper praised Captain Swain for saving the ship: "The prompt action of Capt. S. and perseverance in carrying the ship into port, notwithstanding the repeated entreaties and threats of his crew, who were perfectly exhausted by pumping, when she arrived, certainly establishes the fact that he is a man of the right stamp, a true representative of a Nantucket whale man, and we doubt not the underwriters of the property will present him with some fitting testimonial of their gratitude and respect."

October 26

An arsonist torched the Nantucket-built whale ship *Planter* in 1859 while it was being repaired at a Brant Point shipyard. The fire was discovered at 11:30 p.m., and firefighters thought they had limited it to the stern. But flames began to emerge from the forward hatches, and quickly the *Planter* was a total loss.

In order to save surrounding buildings, firefighters removed the ship supports on the east side. "The ship careened slowly and gracefully on her side. While the flames, fanned by the breeze, spread wildly over her, presenting a grand spectacle," said an article in the *Inquirer.*

The newspaper thanked James F. Chase, keeper of the Brant Point lighthouse, for serving hot ginger tea to the firemen.

The newspaper reported that a suspicious person had been seen leaving the shipyard shortly before the fire was discovered and stated, "The fire was probably the work of an incendiary."

Built in 1818 and under sail on its first voyage on September 25 of that year, the *Planter* sailed for forty-one years in the Pacific and Brazil whaling grounds. In 1840, a storm drove it onto the beach on Nantucket. And in 1850, the *Planter* crew left its captain on a tiny Micronesian island after he killed a crew member during a mutiny.

October 27

Well-to-do businessman Thomas Macy wrote a letter to the General Court in 1659 as his last official act as Salisbury town clerk. Within days, Macy and his family set out in a small boat for Nantucket.

Macy was born in England in 1609 and came to America in 1635. He settled in Newbury, Massachusetts, and five years later was granted land in nearby Salisbury. But despite his prosperity, Macy, a lifelong Baptist, was at odds with the Puritan church, which dominated the politics and social fabric of his town.

In 1657, Macy let four Quakers take refuge in his home for an hour during a heavy rainstorm. His neighbors reported the act, and Macy was fined thirty shillings for breaking a law prohibiting anyone from harboring "any of the cursed sects."

Prior to leaving Salisbury, Macy and several other townsmen had been investigating Nantucket for some months. Macy, Tristam Coffin and John Coleman visited the island in 1663 and witnessed the local Native American chiefs selling land to Thomas Mayhew. Macy and Coffin convinced Mayhew to sell them his ownership of Nantucket land, and they began to plan their pioneering move. At the time, the island was part of New York State, which had less strict laws about religion than Massachusetts.

Macy became a chief magistrate on Nantucket in 1676 and remained a staunch Baptist until his death in 1682.

October 28

Formed in April, the Nantucket Agricultural Society held its first Agricultural Fair in 1856. The society said its mission was to "disprove the oft-repeated assertion that Nantucket is a barren sand heap," educate island farmers and help create a new source of economic prosperity as the island

grappled with the loss of its whaling trade.

At the fair, high school principal A.B. Whipple explained the importance of those goals: "The great benefit…of these fairs, is not all in improved stock, and improved fruits, but in improved minds, improved tastes, improved sensibilities to whatever is beautiful; thereby improving our life and augmenting our happiness."

The first fair proved so popular that it was held open for two additional days. The society showed animals in an open lot in town and showed exhibits of vegetables, fruits, "fancy articles" and "manufactured articles" inside the Nantucket Atheneum.

The Agricultural Fair ran annually into the 1890s.

October 29

In 1768, postmaster for the colonies Benjamin Franklin was stationed in London and wondered why it took mail packets longer to reach New York than it took merchant ships to reach Newport, Rhode Island.

Franklin asked his cousin Timothy Folger, a Nantucket whaling captain, who told him that the merchant ships avoided an eastbound, mid-ocean current. But mail packet captains sailed right into it. Franklin and Folger created a chart of the current and named it the Gulf Stream.

In 1769, Franklin discussed the Gulf Stream in a letter:

> [T]*hat the Whales are found generally near the Edges of the Gulph Stream, a strong Current so called, which comes out of the Gulph of Florida, passing Northeasterly along the Coast of America, and then turning off most Easterly, running at the rate of 4, 3½ , 3, and 2½ miles an Hour, That the Whaling Business leading these People to cruise along the Edges of the Stream in quest of Whales, they are become better acquainted with the Course, Breadth, Strength, and Extent of the same, than those Navigators can well be who only cross it in their Voyages to and from America, that they have Opportunities of discovering the strength of it when their Boats are out in the pursuit of this Fish, and happen to get into the stream while the Ship is out of it, or out of the Stream while the ship is in it, for then they separated very fast and would soon lose sight of each other if care were not taken.*

October 30

The most destructive storm ever to hit Nantucket landed in 1991. It has no official name but has been called the "No Name Storm" and the "Perfect Storm." It began as a nor'easter and evolved into a hurricane.

On Nantucket, high winds and seas battered the shoreline and caused up to $30 million in damage. Waterfront wharves and buildings were destroyed, and boats sank or came to rest in yards and parking lots. The flooding went deeper into the island's interior than anyone had ever seen.

Storm waters split a portion Great Point off from the rest of the island and created an island of it for five months. At one point, the gap between Great Point and Nantucket was a quarter mile wide and six feet deep. Shifting sands eventually filled it and reconnected it to the island.

October 31

In 1915, the U.S. Department of Agriculture and the Massachusetts Department of Health sent agents to Nantucket to get water samples and devise a system to prevent scallopers from bulking up their catch by adding water. That year, the Massachusetts courts ruled that oystermen could not soak their oysters in water, and regulators decided to extend that policy to scallopers. According to government inspectors, it was common practice for fishermen to put four and half gallons of scallops in a seven-gallon keg and add water. Within a few hours the scallops had swelled to fill the keg.

Inspectors used water samples taken from Nantucket to set a baseline using an Abbe refractometer, which measures light through a prism. Scallops without added water refract light at a higher level than those soaked in water, partially due to the fact that added water brings out a milky liquid.

Nantucketers have collected scallops, which grow in the island's calm sandy harbors, for as long as man has inhabited the island. People fertilized their crops using the entire scallop and eventually realized the interior "eye," or muscle that joins the two shells, could be eaten.

The commercial scallop season runs from November 1 to March 31, although families may start collecting them on October 1. Regulations prevent all scallopers from taking small "seed scallops," and fishermen have a limited number of bushels they are allowed to take each day.

November 1

Benjamin Sharp was born in Philadelphia in 1858 and studied at the Coffin School on Nantucket. Sharp studied medicine at the University of Pennsylvania and studied in Europe, where he received a PhD in zoology.

Sharp never practiced medicine, but he taught zoology at the University of Pennsylvania and established himself as a scientist of note. He accompanied Robert Perry to Greenland in 1891 and three years later conducted research in Alaska, Siberia and the Arctic. That same year, he was elected to the Academy of Natural Sciences.

In the 1870s, Sharp purchased a Nantucket home and became active in many island organizations. He helped found the Nantucket Historical Association and the Nantucket Cottage Hospital. He was also a director at his alma mater, the Coffin School.

Sharp was also a state representative from 1910 to 1913 and chairman of the Fisheries and Game Commission.

November 2

Fearing a deadly outbreak of influenza would travel from New Bedford to the island, nurses and doctors were placed on steamships traveling to Nantucket in 1918. Along with being observed by medical staff, selectmen also required all passengers coming to Nantucket to bring a note from a physician declaring them to be healthy.

For weeks, Nantucket had followed state protocols designed to prevent an epidemic: the Dreamland stopped showing movies, church services and public gatherings were cancelled and the Red Cross House, located on Union Street, gave out influenza masks.

But despite their vigilance, influenza did strike the island hard, and by mid-November, there were 337 cases, with nine related deaths. The town cancelled schools, prohibited funerals, required soda fountains to use paper cups and closed pool halls. The Nantucket Board of Health took over the operation of Nantucket Cottage Hospital. The state sent three nurses and three doctors to the island to help care for the sick, who made hundreds of house calls and worked at the hospital.

Declaring the epidemic under control, the town returned management of the hospital to its trustees on November 17. On November 23, selectmen held an emergency town meeting, and voters agreed to appropriate $1,200 to pay for the emergency. When the accounting was done, the influenza outbreak cost island taxpayers $885, and selectmen honored members of the board of health for swiftly bringing the crisis under control.

November 3

For twenty-two years, the wireless radio station in Siasconset made headlines reporting the news, saving lives and keeping the East Coast safe during wartime. But in 1923, the station's owner, Radio Corporation of America, closed the historic station for good.

The *New York Herald* first built wireless stations in Siasconset and on the *Nantucket* lightship in 1901 as a way to report on shipping news faster. The Siasconset station sent its first message in August 1901 and in the following years would help assist ships in distress, most notably the victims on the sinking of the SS *Republic* and the *Titanic*. Later, the Marconi Company operated the Siasconset station.

In September 1914, the government took over the station for an alleged violation of neutrality laws and reopened it in January 1915 under navy control.

In 1920, the International Wireless Telegraph Company built a large station just south of Sankaty Golf Club. This third, short-lived station had the latest equipment and could communicate with vessels as far away as 1,800 miles.

In August 1921, RCA took over the Siasconset station. But the corporation elected to make extensive improvements to its Chatham station and closed Nantucket in 1923.

November 4

In 1824, the whale ship *Oeno* left Nantucket bound for the whaling grounds in the Pacific Ocean. While out hunting, Captain George B. Worth discovered an island in the Pitcairn Island group and named it Oeno.

But in April 1825, the *Oeno* struck a reef near Turtle Island, in the Fiji Islands, and quickly sank. The twenty-four members of the crew escaped onto their lifeboats and were lured onto a nearby island by what seemed like friendly natives. But two weeks after landing, a competing tribe from another island massacred them all except for the cooper, William S. Cary.

Adopted by one of the chiefs, Cary had been essentially held captive for a year before running into his former Nantucket playmate David Whippey, who had settled by choice on another Fiji island and earned the trust of the local tribal chief there.

Two and a half years after the wreck of the *Oeno*, Cary began the long trip back to Nantucket. While traveling on the *Glide*, Cary relived events when the ship first struck a reef and then later natives of the area attacked the crew and killed two men. Eventually, Cary made it back to Nantucket in 1833.

In 1887, a Nantucket newspaper reprinted Cary's logbook entries that described his adventure and named it "Wrecked on the Feejees: Experience of a Nantucket Man a Century Ago, Who Was Sole Survivor of Whaleship 'Oeno' and Lived for Nine Years Among Cannibals of South Sea Islands."

November 5

In 1851, Nantucketers were reminded of the loss of the whale ship *Essex* thirty-one years earlier when they read of the sinking of the New Bedford ship *Ann Alexander* in the *Inquirer*. The article described how a wounded male sperm whale attacked and sank the whale ship, an event eerily reminiscent to the loss of the *Essex* and much of its crew.

The *Ann Alexander* left New Bedford in 1850 and was hunting whales in the Pacific in August 1851 when the first mate harpooned a sperm whale. The whale turned, opened its jaws, attacked and destroyed the small whaleboat containing six men. The men were rescued, and the crew attacked two more times and managed to lodge harpoons in the whale's body but did not kill it. With the sun setting, the captain decided to stop his pursuit. But the whale did not stop his.

It rammed the *Ann Alexander* at a speed of roughly seventeen miles per hour and put a hole in the hull two feet below the water. As the ship quickly began to sink, twenty-two crewmen took to two leaky whaleboats. They had escaped with twelve gallons of water, a sextant, a chronometer and a chart. The boats headed north, hoping to enter an area with more rainfall to augment their meager water supply. Two days later the crew was rescued by the whale ship *Nantucket*, of Nantucket. The men were delivered to Peru, where they found passage home.

November 6

Alexander Starbuck, editor, author and historian, was born on Nantucket in 1841. He was a descendant of Edward Starbuck, an original English settler who immigrated from Derbyshire, England, to Dover, New Hampshire, and then to the island.

Starbuck attended public school and became a store clerk. In 1859, he went to work for Andrew Warren, a watchmaker and jeweler in Waltham, Massachusetts. He would sell or manufacture watches until 1883, but his skill as a writer and ranging curiosity eventually steered him toward journalism.

In 1885, Starbuck became editor of the *Waltham Free Press*, a weekly newspaper, which became a daily in 1888. In 1897, it was consolidated with the *Waltham Tribune* as the *Daily Free Press-Tribune*. Starbuck retired from the *Tribune* in 1922.

Now best known as a historian, he published the *History of the American Whale Fishery* (1878); *A Century of Free Masonry in Nantucket* (1903); *A History of Monitor Lodge, A.F. and A.M., of Waltham* (1921); and *History of Nantucket* (1925).

November 7

In 1937, controversy continued to stalk the abdicated king of England, the Duke of Windsor, and his new wife, Wallace Simpson, the American divorcée. The pair decided to postpone a trip to America when journalists circulated nasty speculation about their motives. But Nantucket saw opportunity in the chaos. On this day, the Australian newspaper the *Perth Sunday Times* ran an article with the headline, "Nantucket Wants Windsor as King."

It said:

> *Amid all the clamor for and against the Duke of Windsor's visit, the plain little island of Nantucket (off the coast of Massachusetts) stands out in monumental fashion.*
>
> *The Nantucketers decided that the island was in favor of a constitutional monarchy, with the Duke of Windsor as head. They consequently cabled the Duke an invitation to "visit our Utopia" and pointed out that "no place on Earth offered the peace and happiness of Nantucket Island." They also cabled Mr. Bassett Jones, a New York engineer and writer, and a close friend of John Fails, with whom the Duke and Duchess spent part of their Austrian honeymoon, asking him to use his influence with the Duke to accept their invitation.*
>
> *This is one of the matters on which the Windsors definitely refuse to be drawn into a controversy.*
>
> *Nantucket's is the second kingship offered the Duke of Windsor since he left England, an unofficial invitation from Poland already having been rejected.*

November 8

In 1893, Nantucket educator and social justice advocate Anna Gardner wrote Frederick Douglass a long letter discussing the death of women's rights leader Lucy Stone and reminisced about Douglass's visits to Nantucket.

In 1841, at age twenty-five, Gardner had organized a series of antislavery conventions on Nantucket. She witnessed Douglass's first public lecture and later watched him emerge as an international star of the abolitionist movement. In addition, Douglass was a vocal supporter of a woman's right to vote and famously defended that right with eloquence at the Seneca Falls Convention in 1848. Douglass lectured on Nantucket a total of five times; his last visit was in 1885 at age sixty-seven.

Now seventy-seven, Gardner seemed to be taking stock and wrote that she wished Douglass would visit the island again but acknowledged that their advanced ages would probably prevent it. At the time of her letter, Douglass represented Haiti at the Chicago World's Fair, and Gardner sent advice on ways to protect his health.

In closing, Gardner discussed Lucy Stone's contribution: "I have just finished writing a paper for our Unity Club on Lucy Stone. Forty years ago or more, she spoke in our Atheneum. Nantucket was one of the first places she visited after entering the lecturing field. Since then, how marvelous is the change in public sentiment!"

November 9

Nantucket newspaperman and editor of the *Inquirer & Mirror* for forty-one years, Harry B. Turner died in 1948.

Born on Nantucket in 1877, Turner began working at the *Inquirer & Mirror* at age sixteen while still in school as an apprentice setting type by hand.

After a three-year apprenticeship, Turner worked at various mainland newspapers and returned to Nantucket in 1896 to work at the *Inquirer &*

Mirror. In 1907, Turner's mentor, Roland B. Hussey, stepped down as editor. Turned would be the newspaper's editor until his death. Under Turner's leadership, the *Inquirer & Mirror* published the first *Argument Settlers* book, which is still in print. In 1921, the newspaper celebrated its centennial anniversary with a book titled *100 Years on Nantucket*.

Turner was active in many organizations and served as vice-president of Pacific National Bank and as a life councillor at the Nantucket Historical Association and wrote a history of the Union Lodge.

November 10

In 1861, two federal officers walked into the Nantucket post office and asked to speak with the island's state representative, Elisha Smith, and justice of the peace William C. Folger. Ensuing events lead to the arrest of twenty-two-year-old Charles Backus, who had been forging the men's signatures in the hopes of receiving government pensions and surplus federal land.

The *Inquirer* reported, "Our usually quiet community was thrown into quite an up-splutter a few days since, by the deliberate and authoritative walking in to the Post Office of a couple of strangers, who has just arrived in the steamer. One of them, who proved afterwards to be an officer from the Pension Bureau at Washington, began to inquire for some very respectable citizens, and required of the Postmaster that they be summoned immediately."

Smith and Folger denied signing any of the documents shown to them by the authorities. A short time later, a U.S. deputy marshal, accompanied by local police, went to David Smith's farm in search of Charles Backus. When they arrived, Backus ran into the barn, and after a lengthy search, the authorities routed him from under a pile of hay. The next day, Backus was taken off-island.

The newspaper reported that Backus had been in the forging business for a while and had been trained in Boston. The *Inquirer* concluded, "Backus is about twenty two years old and looks as green as a squash."

November 11

A Broadway musical called *The Girl from Nantucket* played at the Adelphi Theatre in 1945. It was written by Hi Cooper, Harold Sherman and Paul Stamford, with music by Jacques Belasco and lyrics by Kay Twomey. The show opened on October 8, closed on October 17 and lost $365,000.

George J. Nathan, in *The Theatre Book of the Year*, wrote:

> *Second only to* Hairpin Harmony *and* The Duchess Misbehaves, *produced respectively in the 1943–1944 season and in the one here considered, this is the worst musical show of the decade. Its book, which has to do with a house-painter mistakenly commissioned to do the murals for a museum, reaches its highest humor in the remark, "I appeal to you as a woman," with the retort, "You don't even appeal to me as a man."*
>
> *…The music is an orchestration of the mellifluous sounds produced by hitting a wash-boiler alternately with a saxophone and potato masher. The costumes were apparently designed by the composer…The orchestra, under the direction of Harry Levant, played the numbers over its left shoulders, with its eyes roaming the audience. And the performers were for the most part out of the road grab bag.*

November 12

In 1844, William Hadwen, made wealthy by a fortuitous marriage and a profitable whaling industry, purchased property at the corner of Main and Pleasant Streets. Hadwen commissioned Frederick Brown Coleman to build a Greek Revival mansion with a five-bayed façade, colossal pilasters and a pedimented ionic portico.

The building, and its twin next door, were the most ostentatious private dwellings the island had ever seen and a symbol of the wealth and prosperity.

Originally a jeweler in Rhode Island, Hadwen met his future wife at her sister's wedding in 1820. After he married Eunice Starbuck, he entered the whale oil and spermaceti candle business with his new brother-in-law. Their mutual father-in-law, Joseph Starbuck, was the island's most prosperous whale oil merchant.

Hadwen's home at 96 Main Street was donated to the Nantucket Historical Association in 1965 and is now open to the public.

November 13

American author Nathaniel Benchley was born in 1915. The son of humorist Robert Benchley, he wrote many books for children and young adults, as well as a biography of his father, and his first novel, *Sail a Crooked Ship*, was filmed by Columbia Pictures in 1961.

Director Norman Jewison made Benchley's novel *The Off-Islanders* into a motion picture called *The Russians Are Coming, the Russians Are Coming*, for which Benchley received an Academy Award nomination. Much of his material was drawn from his life in New York and Nantucket, where the family had a summer home. He found the small-town life in Nantucket was rich in characters, and *The Off-Islanders* is the story of a Russian submarine run aground on a small New England island.

In 1974, his son, Peter, published his first novel, *Jaws*, based on his experiences fishing off Nantucket in his youth.

November 14

Herman Melville's sixth book, *Moby-Dick; or, The Whale*, was published in 1851. The story of Captain Ahab's obsessive quest for the white whale was not a commercial success, and the book was out of print by the time Melville died.

The author D.H. Lawrence revived *Moby-Dick* in the 1920s by calling it "the greatest book of the sea ever written." Today it is considered one of the Great American Novels and a leading work of American Romanticism.

Melville, who went whaling on several voyages, first heard of the voyage of the Nantucket ship *Essex* while at sea. He obtained an account of the story written by *Essex* first mate Owen Chase, which described how a sperm whale attacked and sank the ship and left its crew to drift in the Pacific Ocean for months without food or water. Melville scholars attribute the author's fascination with the wreck of the *Essex* and another whaling story, the story of an albino whale named Mocha Dick, as the basis for the novel.

Already a well-regarded author for his books *Omoo* and *Typee*, Melville considered *Moby-Dick* his masterpiece and was bruised by critics' harsh analysis and the public's lack of interest. In 1852, he published *Pierre*, another commercial disappointment, and then stopped writing novels. He worked as a clerk at the New York Customs House and privately wrote poetry.

When he died in 1891, Melville was almost completely forgotten as an author.

November 15

In 1850, the crew of the Nantucket whale ship *Planter* left Captain Issac B. Hussey on an island in Micronesia after he shot and killed a crewmember during a mutiny. The *Planter* left Nantucket in 1847 and headed for the Pacific Whaling Grounds. On the trip, Captain Hussey and his nephew fifteen-year-old William C. Paddock spent three months in the Gilbert Islands negotiating to purchase coconut while the *Planter* hunted for whales.

Later in the voyage, some of the crew threw a cask of beef overboard. Captain Hussey announced that no more beef would be served until those who committed the act came forward. Some of the crew refused to work, and as Paddock recalled years later, Captain Hussey was decisive. When the men refused to work, he shot one of the ringleaders in the head. The mutiny ended, and the three hundred Pacific islanders traveling with them were so frightened they jumped overboard.

While Hussey remained on Morgan's Island, the first mate sailed the *Planter* home, and Paddock was instructed to return with the captain's wife. But when Paddock reached Nantucket, he learned that Mrs. Hussey had died and decided to stay put.

In 1853, Captain Hussey left Micronesia in command of the San Francisco brig *William Penn* and headed for America. While off the Gilbert Islands, the crew mutinied and killed Hussey and the ship's cook. The mutineers stole everything on the boat, left and never were apprehended. The wounded ship's mates buried Hussey and the cook at sea.

November 16

The Nantucket Weather Station closed after seventy-nine years of service to the United States Weather Bureau. From 1827 to 1861, William Mitchell recorded weather observations from his home on Vestal Street and later from the Pacific National Bank on Main Street. Henry Paddack continued the practice until 1886 from his home at 9 Vestal Street.

The United States Army Signal Service began the first formal observing program in 1886 after the island had been connected to the mainland by a telegraph cable. The United States Weather Bureau took over in 1891, working from the Pacific Club Building. In 1904, the bureau moved to a newly built Weather Bureau Building at 46 Orange Street. With a growing need for weather information for aviation, the bureau was moved to the airport in 1946. The program was turned over to the Federal Aviation Administration on this day in 1970.

November 17

Nantucket town crier Billy Clark was born in 1846. The island had three town criers in the 1860s, but Billy Clarke is the most notorious. A self-appointed town crier who made a modest living, Clark prowled the town with his tin horn and sold newspapers and his services to those in need of an announcement.

In 1882, Edward Godfrey published *The Island of Nantucket: What It Was and What It Is* and recounted this story:

During the war, then as now, combining the business of newsboy with that of town crier he [Clark] *had occasion to announce a meat auction, Manassas Junction had just been evacuated, and William, upon the arrival of the boat, with that zeal which has always characterized him seized his papers and rushed through the streets vociferously shouting*

> *"Great battle at Molasses Junction"*
> *"Great many killed and wounded"*
> *"Meat auction tonight"*

November 18

Twelve-year-old George W. Gardner Jr. departed Nantucket for his first whaling voyage in 1822. Gardner sailed to Haddam, located on the Connecticut River, to board a new boat called *Maria*. At the end of his whaling career, Captain Gardner remembered his first voyage this way:

> *When we arrived at Haddam the* Maria *was still in the stocks at the shipyard. The contractor and builder were ill, and the carpenters had stopped work for fear they would not be paid. But one of the owners being on the scene now assured their pay, and work resumed. The officers and crew of the ship assisted in carrying on board the new deck beams…Finally, after considerable delay, the new ship was launched and delivered to the owners. I believe the contract price was $9,600, and she was 362 tons burthen.*
>
> *The master, Captain George W. Gardner Sr., (my father) and W officers and part of the crew now took charge of the* Maria. *Her low masts were stepped, and she was "hove down" and sheathed and bottom coppered. Then her topmasts were sent up and she was completely rigged. Her ground tier (lower hold) was filled with cask water from the river for ballast.*
>
> *…On November 18, 1822, just four months and eight days from the day we had left Nantucket in the old ship* Globe, *we took our departure from Edgartown, passed through Vineyard Sound by Gay Head, and out into the broad Atlantic, bound for Cape Horn and the Pacific Ocean.*

November 19

In 1885, the United States Signal Service connected Nantucket to the mainland by a telegraph cable for the first time. The cable was intended to assist the U.S. Weather Bureau in its reporting but also had the effect of joining the island to the world. The cable originated in Woods Hole and ran to Martha's Vineyard and then to Nantucket.

By June 30, 1885, there were 489 bureaus and volunteer citizens sending telegraphic reports daily, including 25 from Canada. Prior to installing the Nantucket cable, telegraph lines stretched 2,779 miles along the Atlantic coast from North Carolina to New Jersey.

In his 1885 report to Congress, the U.S. secretary of war reported:

> *The telegraph cable has proved of great value to shipping and affords a means of rapid communication when assistance may be required. Portions of this line are now used as a telephone line by the lifesaving service and, in cases of wreck, the crews of lifesaving stations are enabled to more promptly reach the scene of the wreck. A contract has been made for the manufacture and laying of the cable authorized by Congress to connect Nantucket with the mainland and it is believed that telegraphic communication will be established with this island during the present year thus adding to this service a most valuable station for the display of storm signals.*

November 20

In 1820, the Nantucket whale ship *Essex* was attacked and sunk by a male sperm whale in the Pacific Ocean. After drifting in whaleboats for three months, eight crew members survived.

The *Essex* left Nantucket in 1819, and two days later, a squall almost sank it. Despite the loss of a sail and two whaleboats, Captain George Pollard continued on. On this day, a lookout spotted a pod of whales, and three whaleboats set out in pursuit. After having his boat damaged by a whale, first mate Owen Chase returned to the *Essex* to repair it. There he noticed a very large sperm whale idling in the water near the 238-ton vessel. With alarming speed and power, the whale rammed the bow of the ship and shattered it.

The crew had very little time to gather supplies before abandoning the sinking *Essex* in three whaleboats. Two thousand miles west of South America and adrift in small, open boats, the crew had virtually no food or water. For ninety days, the *Essex* crew drifted in the South Pacific. Of the twenty men who left the sinking *Essex*, eight would survive the starvation and dehydration of the whaleboats. In the final days of their journey, one of the whaleboats disappeared and was never found. Members of the two remaining whaleboats resorted to cannibalism in order to stay alive. Later, author Herman Melville would read Owen Chase's account of the *Essex* disaster and use it as a basis for his novel *Moby-Dick*.

November 21

The American humorist, actor and author Robert Benchley died in 1945. Benchley's style of humor brought him respect and success as a columnist for *Vanity Fair* and the *New Yorker*.

After graduating from Harvard University, Benchley began at *Vanity Fair* with fellow Harvard alumnus Robert Emmet Sherwood, as well as Dorothy Parker.

The three presided over the Algonquin Round Table between 1919 and 1929, which grew to include Alexander Woollcott, playwrights George S. Kaufman and Marc Connelly, actor Harpo Marx and journalist/critic Heywood Broun. Benchley wrote over six hundred essays, which were compiled in twelve volumes, during his career. He also appeared in a number of films, including forty-eight short films that he mostly wrote or co-wrote and numerous feature films.

Benchley may be best remembered for his contributions to the *New Yorker*, and for his short film *How to Sleep*, which won Best Short Subject at the 1935 Academy Awards.

He appeared in Alfred Hitchcock's film *Foreign Correspondent*, in Walt Disney's *The Reluctant Dragon* and with Deanna Durbin in *Nice Girl?* He also appeared in films with Bob Hope, Bing Crosby and Fred Astaire.

Benchley spent summers with his family in Siasconset and is buried on Nantucket in Prospect Hill Cemetery.

November 22

The island's last blacksmith, Canadian-born Aquila Cormie, died in 1961. At the beginning of the twentieth century, Nantucket had many blacksmiths who repaired fishing gear, shod horses and made decorative ironwork for homes.

Cormie was born in New Brunswick and came to Nantucket as a teenager to work for his cousin. He returned for good two years later and apprenticed with local blacksmiths. When automobiles were finally allowed on Nantucket in 1918, Cormie installed the island's first gas pump on the sidewalk of South Water Street, sold tires and learned to do bodywork. One of several Canadian blacksmiths, he partnered with fellow Canadian Frederick Heighton. Heartbroken at the loss of his wife in 1930, Cormie went back to Canada. Two years later, Heighton asked him to come back to Nantucket, and Cormie agreed. Even after Heighton's death, Cormie continued to work as a blacksmith until he retired in 1955.

November 23

In 1908, Olive Dame Campbell and her husband, John, traveled through Appalachia surveying the social and economic conditions and hoping to improve schools there. In her diary, she describes their journey at the end of the day: "It was picturesque enough to see the night settle on the mountains—til finally we could only see the high mountain side on our left and a Virginia rail fence so close on the right I could almost touch it. Occasionally a light would glimmer at the foot of a distant hill—or we could see door and window chinked outlined in the flickering light of an open fire."

During the trip, Campbell noticed the local music closely resembled English and Irish ballads and began to write down songs as a way to preserve them. Campbell spent the rest of her life in the region and became an important reformer, but today she is best remembered for capturing the region's musical traditions. The film *Songcatcher* is loosely based on her life.

Born in West Medford, Massachusetts, in 1882, Olive Dame's family has summered on Nantucket for generations. She married in 1907 and became a widow twelve years later when John Campbell was killed in an accident. In 1925, she founded the John C. Campbell Folk School in Brasstown, North Carolina, which is based on the Scandinavian "folk school" tradition. She also helped found the Southern Highland Craft Guild.

Campbell continued to work in collecting ballads and handicrafts up until her death in 1954. The folk school continues today teaching art and crafts and celebrating Appalachian music, dance and art.

November 24

In 1855, the *New York Times* cited an article in the *Nantucket Inquirer* about an unusual island medical case involving a woman who swallowed needles:

> *Dr. E.P. Fearing, in a communication to the* Nantucket Inquirer, *gives an account of a remarkable surgical operation which he performed. He says: "In the early part of last July, I was called to visit Jane James, aged 44 years. I found her very ill with peculiar symptoms, involving an obscurity as to the nature of the disease. Soon after she came under my care, a needle or pin was discovered near the pit of the stomach, lying deep seated, flatwise. I operated and removed a perfect needle. Since that time to the Present, I have frequently removed needles—eight the greatest number in one day.*
>
> *The whole number removed amount to sixty-two needles, and a pin, supposed to be a breast-pin, with the head wanting. No doubt quite a number remain to be removed. They have been found in a scattered condition, in the region of the stomach, abdomen and left side. As the needles have been removed her sufferings have diminished. She is said to be a wo-man of truth, and says she has not the slightest recollection of ever having swallowed a needle or any-thing of the kind. However impossible it may seem, there cannot be a doubt but that she swallowed the needles, probably in papers, about twelve years ago, when in a state of insanity.*

November 25

Abram Quary died in 1854 at the age of eighty-two, the last male Wampanoag tribe member left on Nantucket.

Quary was born in 1768, five years after disease had decimated Nantucket's Wampanoag population. When he was young, Quary lived in a white home for several years and then went whaling. He married twice and lost a young child. Alone, Quary settled into a solitary life and often turned people away who came to see him. He spent his time weaving baskets, collecting herbs and clamming and frequently hosted clambakes. He would raise a white flag outside his house in Shimmo to signal that he was ready for visitors.

At the end of his life, concerned citizens convinced Quary to move to the asylum, where he lived his final two years. Within six weeks of his passing, Dorcas Honorable, the island's last Native American resident, also died.

November 26

In 1825, stranded in the Pacific and living with a local tribe, Nantucket whaler Cyrus M. Hussey knew that an American ship was nearby but had not yet learned that it was there to rescue him.

In 1822, Hussey sailed as a cooper on the whale ship *Globe*. He had witnessed a violent mutiny, including the murder of the captain as well as the lead mutineer. Finally, abandoned on Mili Atoll, local tribes had killed all his crew mates except for William Lay. The two lived with the tribe for almost two years.

After their rescue, Hussey and Lay wrote about their experiences. Hussey wrote, "On the next morning, 26th, the chief again questioned me respecting the vessel, but I could give him no particular information, as I had not seen her.—The natives then commenced knotting up leaves to inquire of their god, who, they said, would inform them what was best to be done. Towards night they departed, leaving me with my master, giving him strict orders not to let me go to the vessel, fearing that I should not only remain on board, but give information that my shipmates had been murdered. I was glad to see them depart, for I feared they would kill me.—The reader can have but a faint idea of my feelings at that time; nor will I attempt to describe them."

Four days later, the U.S. Navy had Hussey and Lay on board the ship *Dolphin* and set sail for South America and then home.

November 27

In 1878, the *Nantucket Journal* announced the arrival of construction crews who would build the Wannacomet Water Works.

At that point, islanders got their water by collecting rainwater and from neighborhood pumps. Firefighters used underground cisterns that were filled by diverting rainwater from nearby rooftops.

Twenty-year-old Moses Joy proposed a system to distribute water to every home. Residents strongly opposed it, saying that water could never be made to run uphill. But Joy persisted and moved forward with the Wannacomet Water Company. He built a steam-powered pumping station at Washing Pond and constructed a twenty-five-thousand-gallon, elevated storage tank there. Joy also laid down 16,286 feet of pipe around town. The Wannacomet Water Company began service in 1879 with 63 customers, which grew to 357 customers in five years.

Joy also installed the island's first fire hydrants. In 1878, the water company connected the first hydrant in front of the Congregational Church on Centre Street. Still battling the doubters, Joy announced he could spray water over the church steeple from the fire hydrant. When the Nantucket Fire Department turned down his request to borrow a hose for the demonstration, Joy got one from New Bedford. As water shot over the Congregational Church steeple, Joy finally persuaded Nantucket that an underground water system delivered by pipe would work.

November 28

In 1935, Anthony Frederick Sarg, known as "America's Puppet Master," unveiled his giant, inflatable puppets during the Macy's Thanksgiving Day Parade in New York City.

A German American, Tony Sarg, as he was known professionally, was a puppeteer and illustrator. In 1928, Sarg designed helium-filled balloons for Macy's Department Store and also created the store's window displays. Born in 1800, Sarg was raised with puppets and brought his interest in them to America. He exhibited his work at the 1933 Chicago World's Fair, which was the pinnacle of his career.

On Nantucket, he opened the Tony Sarg Shop on Centre Street in 1921 and spent summers on the island. In 1937, Sarg staged a hoax sighting of a sea serpent that ended with it appearing on South Beach (now Washington Street Extension—and not where it was intended to land!). It was one of Sarg's Macy's Day Parade balloons.

November 29

Susan Brock sailed with her husband, Captain Peter C. Brock, on the whale ship *Lexington* from 1853 to 1856. Her journal contains eighty-five poems, including the "Nantucket Girls Song," which she wrote down while visiting New Zealand:

Nantucket Girls Song

I have made up my mind now to be a Sailor's wife,
To have a purse full of money and a very easy life,
For a clever sailor husband is so seldom at his home,
That his wife can spend the dollars with a will that's all
*   her own,*
Then I'll haste to wed a sailor, and send him off to sea,
For a life of independence is the pleasant life for me,
But every now and then I shall like to see his face,
For it always seems to me to beam with manly grace,
With his brow so nobly open, and his dark and kindly eye,
Oh my heart beats fondly towards him whenever he is nigh,
But when he says Goodbye my love, I'm off across the sea
First I cry for his departure, then laugh because I'm free,
Yet I'll welcome him most gladly, whenever he returnes
And share with him so cheerfully all the money that he earns
For he's a loving Husband, though he leads a roving life
And well I know how good it is to be a Sailor's Wife.

November 30

In 1834, Reuben R. Pinkham, naval officer and Nantucket maritime merchant, sent a newsy letter to his parents in the Midwest telling them of island life and of his thoughts concerning his next post.

> *As for future courses I wait for the Government to mark them out, so far as I am concerned with the Navy. I had while in South America numerous offers, when if I would neglect the service, I would be sure of my thousand in years!*
>
> *But I have been ever careful of lifting that sheet anchor. Now is the time I can save a few dollars from my pay, but, as I think I explained in a former letter, I cannot do it if I am one of the officers who have to entertain half of the inhabitants of "Cape Town," the King, Chiefs, Queen Regent to Queen Dowager and suite at the Sandwich Islands, the Queen Pomaru of Otaheiti and suite, the various entertainments necessary to be given to keep up the national dignity abroad given and accepted in foreign ports!*
>
> *Repeat that our pay is not adequate to meet such extraordinary taxations. But I will dispense with a Jerimiad at this time, and only admit to such topics my way of assuring my dear Parents that I hold myself as much responsible to them for the acts of my life now. Aye, more than I did when I was the obstreperous age of fifteen!*

December 1

Nantucket's first Life-Saving Station opened on Surfside Beach in 1874. The site had hosted a Humane Society house for forty years. The Massachusetts Humane Society (established in 1786) built shoreline huts, which volunteers manned by keeping watch for ships in distress.

In 1871, the federal government created the U.S. Life-Saving Service and built one hundred Life-Saving Stations along the East Coast in its first decade. Eventually, it added Nantucket stations in Coskata, Madaket and Muskeget.

The government Life-Saving Stations were manned by a crew of paid "surfmen," although many of them were former Humane Society volunteers.

For several years, the U.S. Life-Saving Service and the Humane Society coexisted and often competed to be the first on the scene of a disaster. In 1915, the U.S. Life-Saving Service and the Revenue Cutter Service merged to form the U.S. Coast Guard. The Humane Society stopped its service in the 1930s.

December 2

In 1946, representatives from twelve governments met in Washington, D.C., and signed the International Convention for the Regulation of Whaling. The environmental agreement created an organization called the International Whaling Commission (IWC), whose mission was to regulate the hunting and killing of whales worldwide.

The agreement's preamble states, "The history of whaling has seen overfishing of one area after another and of one species of whale after another to such a degree that it is essential to protect all species of whales from further overfishing."

The IWC currently represents eighty-eight countries and was originally charged with protecting whale species, designating whale sanctuaries, setting limits on whale killings and prohibiting the capture of suckling calves and female whales accompanied by calves. The IWC also compiles statistical and biological records.

In 1986, the IWC established a moratorium on all commercial whaling, a mandate still in place today, although the commission allows aboriginal people the right to hunt whales for subsistence. Japan and Russia have refused to acknowledge the IWC's moratorium. Norway and Iceland have issued their own whaling quotas after protesting the IWC's ban on whaling.

December 3

In 1858, the *California Farmer and Journal of Useful Sciences* printed an article about Nantucket whalers who discovered six hundred pounds of ambergris inside a slain sperm whale. Once prized by perfumers for its fixative abilities, ambergris is created by a biological reaction in the intestines of a sperm whale. Because the beaks of giant squids have been found embedded in ambergris, scientists surmise it may be produced in the whale's gastrointestinal tract to ease the passage of hard, sharp objects. The sperm whale usually vomits the squid beaks, but if one travels farther down the gut, it will be covered in ambergris.

The journal speculated that the ambergris cache found by those on the ship *Watchman* was the biggest in history, writing, "The largest piece before known weighed 182 pounds, and was purchased of the King of Tidore by the Dutch East India Company. Another piece, found inside of a whale near the Windward Islands, was sold for £500 sterling...The quantity obtained by Captain Hussey was, upon his arrival, shipped to this city. The next day the entire quantity was sold to a firm of druggists in this city for the large sum of $10,000, the whale thus yielding $10,450, which is said to be the most valuable on record. The purchasers will probably realize $60,000. We learn that the article is destined for a foreign market."

Perfume manufacturers now use a synthetic fixative. In 1973, the use of ambergris was outlawed in the United States under the Endangered Species Act.

December 4

In June 1954, two men who were arrested for fishing in Long Pond without a license were let go because of a stipulation in the 1693 deed that transferred ownership of Nantucket from New York to Massachusetts. But the ramifications of that decision put the island in a bind six months later when deer hunting season arrived.

The two were represented in court by a lawyer paid for by the Nantucket Sportsmen's Club. The lawyer successfully argued that Nantucket has jurisdiction over its ponds because of the Colonial Act of 1693. In 1692, New York deeded Nantucket to Massachusetts and the act declared that Massachusetts had no authority over island ponds.

In response, state government officials removed the local warden, saying if Massachusetts law didn't apply to pond fishing, then the island didn't need state supervision. But six months later, on the eve of December deer hunting season, the sportsmen's club asked the agency to reconsider, and a temporary warden was sent for the one-week deer hunt.

Court cases and legal scuffles over control of island ponds started in the 1840s, and each time the legal authority hearing the case sided with Nantucket. In 1989, thirty-two Nantucket High School students cosponsored a bill to determine the pond status. The bill disputed the state fish and wildlife department's claim that licenses were required. The bill never made it out of committee, but to this day anglers can still fish island ponds without a license.

December 5

In 1981, a surprise nor'easter stranded about two thousand visitors on the island while at the same time, seventeen pilot whales came ashore on Nantucket's south shore beaches.

The storm began on Saturday during the annual Christmas Stroll celebration. By evening, the boats and planes were cancelled, and about two hundred people had no place to go. The police sent out an island-wide request for residents to take in people, and seventy-five people agreed to house about one hundred visitors. In addition, forty-two people spent the weekend at the Nantucket Cottage Hospital. The remaining visitors were able to find lodging at an inn or hotel. By Monday, all visitors were able to leave the island.

While emergency responders helped stranded people, the town game warden was trying to help the beached whales. The whales eventually died, despite attempts to rescue them. After the storm, scientists from New England Aquarium came to the island to perform autopsies on the whales. Although no one knows why they beached themselves, the scientists speculated that it was due to a parasite in their inner ears or due to the storm.

December 6

In 1839, the Whig Party held its first national convention, and Nantucket congressman Barker Burnell was there. Formed in the 1830s, the Whig Party coalesced around a mutual opposition to President Andrew Jackson and the Democrats. The Whigs believed Congress should have supremacy over the president. In its twenty-year history, two U.S. presidents represented the Whig platform, but its constituents could not agree on whether to expand slavery to the new territories, and the party faded from the political stage.

Born on Nantucket in 1798, Burnell was serving in the Twenty-seventh U.S. Congress when he died of consumption in 1843. On December 14, 1843, John Quincy Adams announced his death to Congress and made the following motions: "Expressions of sympathy to the surviving widow and relatives; the wearing of crepe on the left arm for 30 days and out of respect for his memory to adjourn until noon the following day."

Burnell began his political career at twenty-two years old, most notably convincing the Massachusetts legislature to end the practice of imprisoning citizens who were in debt. In his remarks to the House, John Quincy Adams recalled Burnell's energy and enthusiasm during his first session and Adams's own sadness at watching Burnell's health fail in the second. Records show him missing 397 of 967 roll call votes during the two years he was in Washington, D.C., most likely due to his fragile health.

December 7

Philip Murray, founder of Murray's Toggery Shop and home of the famous Nantucket Reds clothing line, died in 1959. Born in 1890 and raised on Nantucket, Murray began working at a men's clothing store at age fourteen. In 1945, he took over a store he managed and renamed it Murray's Toggery.

By the early 1950s, Murray and his son, Philip C. Murray, were running the family business. In the 1960s, the store began selling light red, cotton men's pants that were patterned after trousers worn in Brittany. With each laundering, the pants faded to a dusty rose. In 1980, *The Official Preppy Handbook* featured Nantucket Reds trousers, and they quickly became a popular summer status symbol.

Soon Murray's was selling fishing caps, sweaters, shorts and socks, as well as women's and children's clothing, in the Nantucket Red material. Today, Murray's markets the Nantucket Reds with the tagline "Guaranteed to Fade."

December 8

In 1852, the Nantucket sheriff raided four homes and shops and confiscated illegal liquor. In May of that year, the state legislature had outlawed the production and sales of all liquor.

A State Temperance Society complaint prompted search warrants for properties on Gunter Alley, Hussey Street, Federal Street and Rose Lane. A *New York Times* report said, "Some seven or eight barrels, one keg and some dozen or fifteen jugs, some full and others partially filled with liquor, were seized and are now held by the Sheriff for further orders. One or two suspicious places were searched, but no 'ardent' was found on the premises."

The judge dismissed one defendant for lack of evidence, fined the rest twenty dollars and ordered that the liquor be destroyed.

In 1838, Massachusetts banned the sale of fewer than fifteen gallons of alcohol per household per year but repealed the law in 1840. In 1851, a Nantucket Friends of Temperance group called for a law based on the "Maine Temperance Law." And Massachusetts did enact a similar a law in 1852, but it was struck down a year later by the Massachusetts Supreme Court. In 1855, the Massachusetts legislature passed a revised liquor law to avoid the constitutional flaws of the first.

December 9

One day after the United States declared war on Japan in 1941, the Nantucket Public Safety Committee, under state mandate, set up offices in the town building and began implementing safety procedures for the island.

High school girls were assigned a first- or second-grade student to escort home in the event that school was cancelled because of an air raid warning.

Local air wardens visited each house in their district and delivered a letter explaining the role of the Public Safety Committee. The committee instructed island residents how to black out windows to both prevent light from escaping and to protect people from shattering glass. Cars were not allowed on the roads at night unless they had special black-out lights.

Homeowners were told to put down three inches of sand on their attic floor in case a bomb came through the roof. The committee's instructions suggested that homeowners could cover the bomb in sand, wet down the floor near it and, if possible, throw it out onto the street. The committee also stacked sand bags in heavily populated areas and instructed residents, "You are to use them on incendiaries falling near you in the street. Pick up the bag and drop it on the bomb.

"Remember that in an incendiary attack a single plane can release over 2,000 bombs, each one a potential fire in itself, and that in the Town of Nantucket, we have exactly five pieces of apparatus."

December 10

A ship carrying six hundred barrels of whale oil landed in New York City in 1856 and prompted the *New York Times* to predict great changes for the New England whaling industry. The paper stated, "Those 600 barrels of oil were carried into Panama by a whaling vessel, transported across the Isthmus on the railroad, and landed here in less than one-fifth the time that would have been occupied in sending it home in the usual manner, around Cape Horn. If the oil taken in the Pacific can be sent to the Atlantic ports in this manner as cheaply as in the old way, it will put an end to the whaling business, which has been so prolific a source of wealth to New-England heretofore."

The newspaper predicted that the whaling industry would shift from New England to San Francisco and noted, "In San Francisco there are New-Englanders enough to build the whaling business up; several hundred young men from Nantucket emigrated to California on the first organization of the Territory; they have a perfect knowledge of the business, and a love for it, and they will probably carry it on there."

The *Times*' prediction was not inaccurate. By 1886, San Francisco surpassed New Bedford and Nantucket as the nation's largest whaling port. But the heady days of whaling were long over by that point. Gas, then electricity, had become the consumer's fuel choice for illumination.

December 11

In 1848, the Nantucket whale ship *Christopher Mitchell* left Nantucket to hunt in the Pacific whaling grounds. Unbeknownst to the crew, a green hand named George Johnson was really a woman.

In July 1849, while heading toward the Galapagos Islands, the captain suddenly turned the *Christopher Mitchell* around and headed for Paita, Peru. Johnson's identity had been discovered. She was nineteen-year-old Ann Johnson from Rochester, New York.

The captain put her off the ship, and Johnson was taken to the American consulate and sent home on the whale ship *Nantucket*.

In 1862, twenty-year-old Georgiana Leonard signed on to the whaling bark *America* as George Wheldon. She proved herself capable, and the crew liked her, although they noted George/Georgiana had a bad temper. In 1863, while pursuing whales, she got into an argument with another crewmember and pulled a knife on him. Her secret was revealed when the captain ordered her stripped to the waist and flogged.

That captain didn't head for shore but made Leonard the cabin boy and continued whaling. Six months later, the *America* landed on the island of Mauritius, and the captain found a job for Leonard as a stewardess on a clipper ship. A year later, the two crossed paths again in Mauritius, Leonard still a stewardess and the *America* still out whaling. Leonard told her former captain she was marrying her ship's second officer.

December 12

David Sarnoff, the Belarusian American pioneer of American radio and television, died in 1971. Born in 1891, Sarnoff immigrated in 1900 and went to work for the Marconi Wireless Telegraph Company of America in 1909. He rose from office boy to commercial manager and later to president of RCA. As part of his training, Sarnoff worked at the Marconi wireless station in Siasconset.

While at the Marconi Company, Sarnoff saw that radio technology had the potential to broadcast to masses of people, not just from one point to another. But his supervisors did not embrace the idea.

In 1919, the Radio Corporation of America (RCA) purchased the Marconi Wireless Company, and Sarnoff tried to convince his new bosses that radio could be used to entertain the masses. Again, they rebuffed him. Finally, in 1921, Sarnoff arranged to broadcast a heavyweight boxing match between Jack Dempsey and Georges Carpentier. More than 300,000 people listened, and broadcast radio was born. Sarnoff's stature rose quickly at RCA. In 1926, the company purchased a radio station and formed NBC. By 1930, Sarnoff was RCA president.

Brash and ambitious, Sarnoff negotiated the purchase of the Victor Talking Machine Company, which made records, and set the company up to manufacture both radios and records. By 1936, under Sarnoff's direction, RCA spent $50 million to develop television technology, which put the company in a position to dominate television sales in the post–World War II years.

December 13

Twenty-five Massachusetts regiments were engaged in the Battle of Fredericksburg in 1862. After two days of fighting from across the river, Major General Ambrose Burnside ordered soldiers to charge the city and the ferocious fight that ensued would be one of the Civil War's bloodiest. When it was over, the Union Army of the Potomac had suffered huge losses, and Burnside withdrew his army.

Eight Nantucket men were killed at Fredericksburg, and thirteen were wounded. Nantucket soldier Josiah Fitch Murphey was one of them and later wrote, "I got up rather faint, and a feeling of madness came over me, and a word in your ear gentle reader and let it go no further, I cursed the whole southern confederacy from Virginia to the Gulf of Mexico; but on second thought I realized it was war and banished such thoughts from my mind and made my way across the river to a hospital called the Lacy House, so named from its former occupants.

"While lying in the hospital on the 13th during the battle, a rebel solid shot struck it and made it tremble all over. It did no damage as far as I know but we held our breath expecting every minute another would come tearing through the walls and perhaps the room where we were lying, but none struck us."

Nantucket Union lieutenant Leander Alley was killed on December 13 and was so beloved by his company that the army paid to have his body brought back to Nantucket.

December 14

Twenty-seven-year-old Smith College graduate Cynthia Stuart was arrested at her New York City hotel in 1933 and charged with stealing jewelry from her hostess while visiting Nantucket the previous summer, as well as stealing jewelry from members of her socially prominent family.

According to the police, a ring was stolen from the purse of a New Jersey woman while she was sunning herself at the beach on Nantucket on July 28. The Nantucket police department alerted the New York City authorities, and detectives began looking in city jewelry stores and pawnshops. In November, they spotted the ring in a Fifth Avenue shop. The detectives also spotted a stolen diamond watch there and were told it all came from the same woman. Although she had given a fake name and address, the police were able to locate Stuart when they discovered the stolen watch belonged to her uncle. The police located and arrested Stuart at her residence in the Barbizon Hotel.

When asked why she stole the ring, Stuart said she "might need money sometime."

However, Stuart was released the following week when neither her family nor her former hostess would sign complaints against her.

December 15

In 1822, the Nantucket ship *Globe* left on a voyage to the Pacific whaling grounds. But it returned when a piece of the mast broke. The *Globe* left a second time on December 20. The ship had two coopers, both from Nantucket, Cyrus Hussey and Roland Coffin. By the time the voyage ended, Hussey would be one of seven survivors. Coffin would be killed by a native tribe in the Marshall Islands.

News of the *Globe* mutiny rocked the world in 1824, and on Nantucket, a rumor that Roland Coffin helped the mutineers created a stir.

Gorham Coffin, an owner of the *Globe* and Roland's uncle, was outraged. He wrote to Secretary of State John Quincy Adams "not wishing to extenuate his fault, if guilty, but to prevent if possible that aught may be set down in malice." He also wrote to Secretary of the Navy Samuel L. Southard, "While justice is stern, may not her sister virtue, mercy, be awed into silence, but be ready to extend her shield, over those who have been forced to yield to necessity, with a drawn sword over their heads. Having this letter forwarded to Commodore Hull and writing to Daniel Webster with the argument in Roland's defense as the crew was jealous of Roland due to his hard work and being related to owners of the ship."

After questioning the *Globe* survivors, the U.S. consulate in Chile arrested Joseph Thomas for having a role in the mutiny and let the four other survivors come home. The consulate also sent the U.S. Navy to the island where part of the crew had been abandoned. When they arrived, they found two survivors.

December 16

In 1773, more than one hundred demonstrators disguised as American Indians boarded three ships docked in Boston Harbor and destroyed a shipment of tea in a political protest of the Tea Act of May 10, 1773.

Two of the three ships were owned by the Rotch family, powerful Nantucket whaling merchants. The *Dartmouth* and the *Beaver* had delivered a shipment of whale oil to London and were looking for return cargos. Their captains unwittingly agreed to transport the British East India Company Tea to Boston. American colonists, furious over a British tax levied on tea, refused to let the cargo be unloaded. Thomas Hutchinson, chief British authority in Boston, refused to let the ships leave without unloading. Representing his family's interests, Francis Rotch tried to negotiate with Hutchinson. When Britain's representative refused to compromise, Samuel Adams addressed a tense crowd of Patriots, saying, "This meeting can do nothing more to save the country!"

With that, the Sons of Liberty, a secret, paramilitary organization that favored independence, enacted its raid plan.

The third ship, the *Eleanor*, was owned by Boston merchant and selectman John Rowe.

After the raid, both the *Beaver* and the *Dartmouth* delivered whale oil to London in 1774 and also carried witnesses who had been summoned to Whitehall to testify on the Boston Tea Party. The *Beaver* was sold in London at that time, and the *Dartmouth* was shipwrecked as it returned to America.

December 17

Poet, Quaker and ardent abolitionist John Greenleaf Whittier was born in Haverhilll, Massachusetts, in 1807. One of the country's most popular poets in his time, Whittier included a poem called "The Exile's Departure" in the 1840 book *The North Star: The Poetry of Freedom, By Her Friend.*

The poem was about Thomas Macy's 1660 conflict with the Puritan Church after he was fined for sheltering Quakers during a rainstorm. Macy, a Baptist, had already purchased land on Nantucket and soon left Amesbury to join other families and establish a new community there. Whittier used Macy's story to inspire abolitionists to defy the slavery laws and shelter fugitive slaves.

While a young man, *Newburyport Free Press* editor William Lloyd Garrison liked Whittier's poetry and published his first poem in 1826. Garrison also hired Whittier as a newspaper editor. In 1833, Whittier joined Garrison's antislavery cause and spent twenty years writing and lobbying in favor of freeing slaves. Throughout his life, he worked as a newspaper editor and published poetry. He also tried politics, but his radical positions on emancipation ruined his chances for election.

He helped found the Liberty Party and eventually participated in the evolution of the Liberty Party into the Free-Soil Party. In 1850, he convinced Charles Sumner to run on the Free-Soil ticket for the U.S. Senate.

Influential during his lifetime, Whittier is today best remembered for his softer poems like "Snow-Bound" and for writing the words to the hymn "Dear Lord and Father of Mankind."

December 18

In 1975, the U.S. Navy announced plans to close the Tom Nevers Navy Base. Established in 1955 during the Cold War, the navy described it as an "oceanographic research station," but in truth, the top-secret base was used to track Soviet submarine activity throughout the Atlantic Ocean. In addition, the government built a bomb shelter there in 1962 for President John F. Kennedy to use in the event of a nuclear attack while he was visiting his family home in Hyannisport.

In order to track the Soviets, navy personnel used a "hydrophone cable" that extended north and then northeast from Nantucket all the way to the Norwegian Sea.

The town bought the forty-acre base in 1980, and today it is used for many recreational purposes. The Nantucket Hunting Association leases the former bomb shelter.

December 19

In 1851, two schooners carrying Nantucket men were towed over the sandbar at the harbor entrance and began to make their way to the shipwrecked *British Queen*. The day before, a fire spotter stationed in the tower of the Unitarian Church saw the ship with its Union Jack flag flying upside down, the international signal for a vessel in distress. The *British Queen*, with 228 Irish passengers on board, was stranded in ice twelve miles off shore.

The *British Queen*, a former slave trader, left Dublin in October bound for New York City, where its passengers hoped to leave the deadly famine behind for opportunities in America. But as the ship neared its destination, a blizzard blew it off course and into Nantucket's Muskeget Channel. With the ship taking on water, passengers and crew members huddled on the deck to stay warm, but they lost two people during the night. Rescuers finally reached the ship, and the survivors were brought safely to Nantucket.

The island took them in, giving the passengers food and clothing and lodging them in churches and other large buildings. On Christmas Day, most of the passengers boarded the paddle steamer *Telegraph* and set off once again for New York City—all except Julia and Robert C. Mooney, who decided to stay on Nantucket. The Mooneys established several island farms. Julia never left the island again and died in 1893. Robert left once to attend the Brockton Fair with his children and died in 1908.

December 20

Massachusetts governor Michael Dukakis signed the Nantucket Islands Land Bank Bill into law in 1983. Nantucket town meeting voters accepted the legislation in January 1984 by a vote of 293 to 12. In recommending a yes vote, the Nantucket Finance Committee said, "It is probably the last chance to preserve for public use and enjoyment some open spaces and beaches of the Nantucket Islands."

The first program of its kind in the United States, the Nantucket Land Bank is funded by a local tax on property sales and acquires land at fair market value to preserve as open space forever. By 2014, the Land Bank had preserved more than 2,600 acres.

Due to the combined efforts of the Land Bank, the Nantucket Conservation Foundation, the Nantucket Land Council and the Massachusetts Audubon Society, half of Nantucket is preserved as open space.

In its thirty years, the Nantucket Land Bank has purchased or received as gifts property that provides access to beaches and ponds, large tracts of interior space and two golf courses. Charged with preserving open space for both human enjoyment and to protect wildlife habitat, the Land Bank is governed by an elected commission.

Its staff maintains walking trails, roads and parking areas on its properties, which are marked by a green striped post. The Land Bank has also served as a model for other towns seeking to protect open space from the pressures of development.

December 21

In 1979, the Liberian tanker *Argo Merchant* broke apart twenty-nine miles southeast of Nantucket and caused one of the largest marine oil spills in history.

The ship left Venezuela carrying 7.7 million gallons of fuel and ran aground on December 15, twenty-four miles off course. A combination of bad weather, malfunctioning equipment and a poorly trained crew accounted for the accident.

U.S. Coast Guard helicopters rescued the thirty-eight-member crew, but the shallow waters and weather conditions made it impossible to offload the oil or salvage the ship. When the *Argo Merchant* broke apart, it emptied enough fuel oil to heat eighteen thousand homes for a year. Fortunately for Nantucket, northwesterly winds blew the oil off shore, and coastal fisheries and beaches were spared the worst. Teams of scientists tracked the slick for months, and the disaster prompted the National Oceanic and Atmospheric Administration (NOAA) to create a hazardous materials team.

December 22

Grace Brown Gardner, a teacher and historian, died in 1973. Gardner was born on Nantucket in 1880, attended Nantucket schools and received a bachelor's degree from Cornell University and a master's degree from Brown University. She taught in New Bedford and Fall River and moved on to the Framingham Normal School in 1918. She taught science and botany there for twenty-three years and retired to Nantucket.

Gardner inherited a love of Nantucket history from her father, a newspaperman and politician. Her mother was the island's first female tax collector. Gardner was a vice-president of the Nantucket Historical Association for almost twenty-five years and spent hours creating her famous scrapbooks. Now part of the NHA's collection, the scrapbooks document all aspects of Nantucket history. In addition, Gardner wrote columns for the *Inquirer & Mirror* and served on the boards of the Nantucket Atheneum and Maria Mitchell Association.

December 23

Twenty-nine-year-old German POW Fred Kammerdiner escaped from Fort Devens in 1944 and was discovered living in Siasconset a year and a half later. While at Fort Devens, in central Massachusetts, Kammerdiner had become acquainted with Anna Hamilton, a forty-year-old civilian truck driver. The two had exchanged notes in which Kammerdiner professed his love for her.

After escaping, the German contacted Hamilton, she purchased a cottage in Siasconset in February 1946 and the two settled there. Kammerdiner used the name Robert LaForge and told people he was a Swiss handyman. On July 24, 1946, the FBI, acting on a tip, discovered the escaped German POW and deported him. Hamilton was arrested and given probation.

Kammerdiner continued to write to Hamilton from Germany and said he wanted to return to America. After repeated marriage proposals, the two were married in 1948 in Germany. Kammerdiner stayed behind for a time, and his new wife sent him money, food and clothing. Eventually, she paid for him to come back to Siasconset but was dismayed by his refusal to consummate the marriage and his negative attitude. In 1949, the couple moved to Boston, and Kammerdiner disappeared.

In 1950, Anna Hamilton Kammerdiner petitioned the court for an annulment. During the hearing, she testified that Kammerdiner told her he had fathered a child in Germany and that he was distraught to learn that marrying an American did not automatically grant him citizenship.

December 24

Jose Formoso Reyes, a Filipino schoolteacher who popularized the Nantucket lightship basket as a purse, died in 1980.

The origin of Nantucket lightship baskets, which have a wooden base and are constructed over a mold, began on whale ships in the early 1800s. By the 1850s, crews of men stationed on the Nantucket lightship took up basketry as a way to relieve their boredom. In 1900, the government prohibited lightship crews from making baskets while on duty, but many islanders continued making them.

The early baskets were open and used for shopping and storing household items. In 1948, Reyes, who learned to make baskets from Mitchell Ray, created a lidded basket, and it became a tradition for girls to receive a lightship basket purse as a gift after graduating from Nantucket High School.

Today, Nantucket lightship baskets are mass-produced in China and also made by hand by a small group of artisans.

December 25

In 1909, four-year-old Alma Bigelow was treated to a special Christmas celebration by the crew and passengers of the Belgian ship that had rescued her from a sinking ship off Nantucket three weeks before.

Captain Edgar E. Bigelow, his family and crew were on the schooner *Eugene Borda* when it began to sink off Nantucket's coast on November 29. The *Eugene Borda* was traveling from Nova Scotia to Philadelphia, Pennsylvania. The ship *Vaderland*, of Antwerp, had just left New York City bound for Belgium when a crew member spotted the sinking schooner.

In a strong gale and heavy seas, the *Vaderland* sent a lifeboat and both crew and passengers watched anxiously as all aboard were rescued. When the last person set foot on the *Vaderland*, a loud cheer went up. The ocean liner continued on its course for Europe with the survivors on board.

When Christmas Day came, the *Vaderland* captain and officers, as well as the two hundred passengers on board, decided to give the child a Christmas to remember. They decorated the ship and put up a Christmas tree. The captain told Alma that Santa Claus had dropped off a gift for her, which turned out to be a set of furs. Everyone ate a sumptuous Christmas dinner.

The *Vaderland* delivered the captain of the *Eugene Borda* and his family to New York City on December 27.

December 26

David Ruggles, a radical African American abolitionist who was once thrown off a Nantucket steamship, died in 1849.

Born in 1810, Ruggles moved to New York City at seventeen and was an officer of the New York City Temperance Society by age twenty-one. In 1834, he was one of five African American agents of the *Emancipator*, the official voice of the American Anti-slavery Society. He was the editor of the first African American magazine, the *Mirror of Liberty*, which first published in 1838.

Ruggles also helped more than one thousand fugitives escape on the Underground Railroad and assisted hundreds of runaways, including Frederick Douglass. If fugitive slaves were recaptured, Ruggles visited them in jail and attended their trials to serve as a public witness to their fates.

In 1841, he refused to sit in the "blacks-only" section of a steamship headed for Nantucket. A month later, he boarded a "white car" at the railway station. When he was removed, he filed a lawsuit against the company. This provoked other anti-discrimination suits, unfavorable publicity and acts of civil defiance by others. Ruggles was jailed many times before he was thirty years old, and those experiences broke his health and seriously affected his vision.

Ruggles underwent hydrotherapy for his blindness and then started a new career as a hydrotherapist in Northampton, Massachusetts. He treated such celebrated people as Sojourner Truth and William Lloyd Garrison. David Ruggles died in Florence, Massachusetts, at age thirty-nine.

December 27

In 1890, the *Inquirer & Mirror* published an obituary for Nantucket native Captain Laban Coffin. Coffin died in Oregon at age sixty-six. After living a peripatetic life traveling the world on whale ships and clipper ships, living in Spain while recuperating from a whaling accident and running a business in Hong Kong, Coffin moved to the West Coast and helped settle Oregon as a miner and agent of the U.S. Land Office.

In fact, the history of Pacific Coast pioneers contains the names of many Nantucket men who acquired both a wanderlust and superior nautical skills aboard Nantucket whale ships and in the East Coast merchant trade.

Engineer Charles Tracy was born on Nantucket in 1853 and worked on steamships all along the West Coast from Washington State to Mexico. Walter Swain was born in 1855, reached California in 1881 and, in 1887, went to Seattle, Washington, where he worked on steamships. Engineer Alexander C. Riddell was born in 1852 and moved west in 1874 to work on steamships in San Francisco, California, and Seattle and Olympia, Washington until his death at age fifty-three. Captain Samuel B. Randall was born in 1840, married in Australia and moved to San Francisco, California. Later, he operated tugboats in the Pacific Northwest in Puget Sound and on the Columbia Bar.

December 28

In 1854, Henry David Thoreau, writer and leader of the transcendentalist movement, delivered a speech at the Nantucket Atheneum titled "What Shall It Profit?"

On a visit to Siasconset, Thoreau wrote in his journal, "Half way to Siasconset I saw the old corn hills where they had formerly cultivated—the authorities laying out a new tract for this purpose each year. This island must look exactly like a prairie except that view in clear weather is bounded by the sea."

The next day he wrote, "Nantucket to Concord at 7½ AM—still in mist. The fog so thick that we were lost in the water—stopped and sounded many times...Whistled and listened for the locomotive's answer—but probably heard only the echo of our own whistle at first—but at last the locomotive's whistle & the life boat bell."

December 29

A temporary Nantucket crew was rescued from the sinking *Cross Rip* lightship in 1866. On December 28, a heavy gale had pulled the *Cross Rip* lightship from its mooring near Martha's Vineyard and Nantucket and carried it out to sea.

The lightship was being manned by a Nantucket crew while the assigned captain and crew were ashore on liberty. No one heard anything from the *Cross Rip* for six weeks, and all had assumed the crew was lost when a letter arrived from New Orleans, Louisiana. The letter said the Nantucket crew had arrived in the Crescent City at the end of January aboard the *Henry L. Richardson* of Thomaston, Maine, which had spotted the distressed lightship and come to the rescue.

First stationed in 1828, the vessel was originally positioned near the entrance to Nantucket Harbor. In 1858, the vessel was moved west to Cross Rip Shoal.

December 30

In 1865, a Nantucket resident submitted a letter to the *Boston Journal* that told of two tragic Christmas shipwrecks:

> *Within the last few days our Christmas season on the island had been saddened by two shipwrecks. Last Friday night a fine, trim-looking schooner was driven on shore near the head of Hummock Pond…not one of the crew remained by her and not one of them was saved.*
>
> *If we felt here that this shipwreck was a sad introduction to the merrymaking of Christmas the feeling was most impressively deepened by a second shipwreck.*
>
> *Early Monday morning our Christmas greetings were checked by the news—"Another wreck on shore—a dead body found."*
>
> *The wreck proved to be that of the ship* Newton, *of Hamburg, which cleared from New-York last week on the 21st inst.*
>
> *Two bodies supposed to belong to the crew of this vessel have been found.*
>
> *Who shall answer for the others who were passengers on board, or composed the crew of the ill-fated vessel? The deep voice of the waves gives no answer, nor can they till the sea surrenders up the dead.*
>
> *Sad thoughts have come into our Christmas festivals—thoughts whose sadness could only be relieved by a living faith in him whose advent we commemorate, and by whom life and immortality are brought to light.*

December 31

By New Year's Eve 1999, scientists had not conclusively answered the question of whether Nantucket's eastern shore or Lubec, Maine, the country's easternmost point, would be the first continental American town to see the sunrise on the first day of the new millennium.

The national media bet on Maine. The U.S. Naval Observatory called it a draw. But on Nantucket, Maria Mitchell Association astronomer Vladimir Strelnitski predicted Siasconset would see the sunrise first.

More than two thousand people went to Siasconset to observe, and a cheer rose up when Strelnitski announced that Nantucket had seen the sunrise ninety-three seconds before Maine.

The *New York Times* (whose reporter was stationed in Lubec) reported:

> *Lubec's claim to the millennium's first light had been based on expectations that the sun would rise here at just after 7:04 a.m., theoretically beating out by milliseconds competitors on Cadillac Mountain in Bar Harbor, Me., and on Nantucket Island in Massachusetts.*
>
> *But the sun's upper tip could not be seen flaring above Grand Manan Island on the Bay of Fundy until about 7:09; and plans to compare sunrise moments in real-time with people in Nantucket and Bar Harbor*

failed because of spotty cell-phone reception. (The U.S. Naval Observatory declared a tie between Lubec and Bar Harbor, while Nantucket claimed the sunrise prize at 7:04:19 a.m.).

PHOTO COURTESIES

January 1: Amy Jenness

January 4: (*Top*) Library of Congress, Prints & Photographs Division; (*Bottom*) Amy Jenness

January 8: Alanson S. Barney, Nantucket Historical Association

January 9: Library of Congress, Prints & Photographs Division

January 11: Nantucket Historical Association

January 15: Nantucket Historical Association

January 22: Photo by Louis Davidson, courtesy of the Nantucket Atheneum

January 25: Library of Congress, Prints & Photographs Division

January 26: Amy Jenness

January 27: Library of Congress, Prints & Photographs Division

January 28: Nantucket Historical Association

January 29: Photo by Louis Davidson, courtesy of the Nantucket Atheneum

January 31: Photo by Louis Davidson, courtesy of the Nantucket Atheneum

February 4: Nantucket Historical Association

February 7: Nantucket Historical Association

February 8: Nantucket Historical Association

February 9: Photo by Louis Davidson, courtesy of the Nantucket Atheneum

February 13: Photo by Louis Davidson, courtesy of the Nantucket Atheneum

February 14: Library of Congress, Prints & Photographs Division

February 16: Nantucket Historical Association

February 18: Nantucket Historical Association

February 22: Nantucket Historical Association

February 24: Nantucket Historical Association

February 27: Nantucket Historical Association

February 28: Louis Davidson, courtesy of the Nantucket Atheneum

March 1: Library of Congress, Prints & Photographs Division

March 3: Library of Congress, Prints & Photographs Division

March 8: Amy Jenness

March 12: Louis Davidson, courtesy of the Nantucket Atheneum

March 13: Library of Congress, Prints & Photographs Division

March 17: Library of Congress, Prints & Photographs Division

March 18: Nantucket Historical Association

March 24: Library of Congress, Prints & Photographs Division

April 9: U.S. Department of the Interior, National Park Service

April 11: Amy Jenness

April 12: Library of Congress, Prints & Photographs Division

April 16: U.S. Navy

April 19: Nantucket Historical Association

April 22: Nantucket Historical Association

April 24: Nantucket Historical Association

April 26: Library of Congress, Prints & Photographs Division

April 27: Nantucket Historical Association

April 29: Library of Congress, Prints & Photographs Division

April 30: Library of Congress, Prints & Photographs Division

May 4: Library of Congress, Prints & Photographs Division

May 6: Nantucket Historical Association

May 7: Nantucket Historical Association

May 9: Nantucket Historical Association

May 10: Louis Davidson, courtesy of the Nantucket Atheneum

May 15: public domain

May 17: Nantucket Historical Association

May 18: Nantucket Historical Association

May 19: Library of Congress, Prints & Photographs Division

May 22: Nantucket Historical Association

May 28: Nantucket Historical Association
May 30: Nantucket Historical Association
June 6: Nantucket Historical Association
June 7: Office of the National Archives
June 8: Library of Congress, Prints & Photographs Division
June 13: Nantucket Historical Association
June 16: 1907 photograph by A.F. Bradley
June 19: Nantucket Historical Association
June 21: Library of Congress, Prints & Photographs Division
June 22: Library of Congress, Prints & Photographs Division
June 23: Library of Congress, Prints & Photographs Division
June 24: Nantucket Historical Association
June 26: Nantucket Historical Association
June 28: Nantucket Historical Association
June 29: Louis Davidson, courtesy of the Nantucket Atheneum
June 30: Nantucket Historical Association
July 4: Library of Congress, Prints & Photographs Division
July 5: Library of Congress, Prints & Photographs Division
July 6: Library of Congress, Prints & Photographs Division
July 7: Library of Congress, Prints & Photographs Division
July 8: Library of Congress, Prints & Photographs Division
July 11: Nantucket Historical Association
July 16: Nantucket Historical Association
July 20: Nantucket Historical Association
July 25: Nantucket Historical Association
July 30: Nantucket Historical Association
July 31: Ben Frantz Dale

August 1: *Popular Science Monthly* (1907)

August 3: Nantucket Historical Association

August 4: Nantucket Historical Association

August 6: Nantucket Historical Association

August 8: Library of Congress, Prints & Photographs Division

August 14: Nantucket Historical Association

August 15: Amy Jenness

August 16: Photo by Louis Davidson, courtesy of the Nantucket Atheneum

August 18: Library of Congress, Prints & Photographs Division

August 21: public domain

August 24: Nantucket Historical Association

August 26: Nantucket Historical Association

September 1: Nantucket Historical Association

September 2: Nantucket Historical Association

September 8: Library of Congress, Prints & Photographs Division

September 9: Nantucket Historical Association

September 11: Library of Congress, Prints & Photographs Division

September 14: Nantucket Historical Association

September 15: Nantucket Historical Association

September 17: Photo by Louis Davidson, courtesy of the Nantucket Atheneum

September 18: Henry Zbyszynski

September 21: Nantucket Historical Association

September 22: Nantucket Historical Association

September 24: Louis Davidson, courtesy of the Nantucket Atheneum

September 30: Library of Congress, Prints & Photographs Division

October 1: Nantucket Historical Association

October 6: Library of Congress, Prints & Photographs Division

October 8: Louis Davidson, courtesy of the Nantucket Atheneum

October 12: Louis Davidson, courtesy of the Nantucket Atheneum

October 14: Nantucket Historical Association

October 15: Louis Davidson, courtesy of the Nantucket Atheneum

October 17: Louis Davidson, courtesy of the Nantucket Atheneum

October 24: Nantucket Historical Association

October 28: Nantucket Historical Association

October 30: Nantucket Historical Association

November 1: Nantucket Historical Association

November 6: Nantucket Historical Association

November 9: Louis Davidson, courtesy of the Nantucket Atheneum

November 12: Library of Congress, Prints & Photographs Division

November 13: Louis Davidson, courtesy of the Nantucket Atheneum

November 16: Courtesy of National Oceanic and Atmospheric Association (NOAA)

November 17: Nantucket Historical Association

November 22: Louis Davidson, courtesy of the Nantucket Atheneum

November 25: Nantucket Historical Association

November 28: Nantucket Historical Association

December 1: Library of Congress, Prints & Photographs Division

December 7: Louis Davidson, courtesy of the Nantucket Atheneum

December 18: Nantucket Historical Association

December 21: Courtesy of NOAA

December 22: Photo by Louis Davidson, courtesy of the Nantucket Atheneum

December 24: Photo by Louis Davidson, courtesy of the Nantucket Atheneum

December 28: 1856 Benjamin D. Maxham, National Portrait Gallery

December 29: Nantucket Historical Association

Author Photo: Laura Pless

BIBLIOGRAPHY

Books

Beegel, Susan F. *The Nantucket Reader*. Nantucket, MA: Mill Hill Press, 2009.

Brown, Diana, and Colin Brown. *The Whaler and the Privateer*. Nantucket, MA: Letter of Marque Press, 1993.

Butler, Karen. *Nantucket Lights*. Nantucket, MA: Mill Hill Press, 1996.

Campbell, Olive Dame. *Appalachian Travels: The Diary of Olive Dame Campbell*. Lexington: University Press of Kentucky, 2012.

Catalogue of Nantucket Whalers: and Their Voyages From 1815 to 1870. Nantucket, MA: Hussey & Robinson, Printers and Publishers, 1876.

Douglass, Frederick. *Life and Times of Frederick Douglass.* Hartford, CT: Park Publishing, 1882.

Folger, Peleg. *Remarkable Observations: The Whaling Journal of Peleg Folger, 1751–54.* Nantucket, MA: Mill Hill Press, 2006.

Lancaster, Clay. *The Far-Out Island Railroad.* Nantucket, MA: Pleasant Publications, 1972.

Macy, Obed. *The History of Nantucket.* Boston, MA: Hilliard, Ray & Co., 1835.

Mann, Horace. *The Life and Works of Horace Mann.* Vol. 2. Boston: Lee and Shepard Publishers, 1891.

Miller, Robert F., and Robert F. Mooney. *The Civil War: The Nantucket Experience.* Nantucket, MA: Wesco Publishing Company, 1994.

Palmer, Beverly Wilson. *Selected Letters of Lucretia Coffin Mott.* Champaign: University of Illinois Press, 2002.

Philbrick, Nathaniel. *Away Offshore.* Nantucket, MA: Mill Hill Press, 1994.

Rusk, Ralph L. *The Letters of Ralph Waldo Emerson.* Vol. 3. New York: Columbia University Press, 1939.

Stackpole, Edouard A. *Life Saving Nantucket.* Nantucket, MA: Nantucket Life Saving Museum, 1972.

———. *Whales & Destiny*. Amherst: University of Massachusetts Press, 1972.

Starbuck, Alexander. *The History of Nantucket: County, Island and Town*. Rutland, VT: Charles E. Tuttle Co., 1969.

Turner, Harry. *Nantucket Argument Settlers: Island History at a Glance*. Nantucket, MA: *Inquirer & Mirror*, 1994.

White, Barbara Ann. *A Line in the Sand: The Battle to Integrate Nantucket Public Schools, 1825–1847*. New Bedford, MA: Spinner Publications, 2009.

Newspapers

California Digital Newspaper Collection. http://cdnc.ucr.edu.
Cape Cod Times. www.capcodonline.com.
The Library of Congress Chronicling America Historic American Newspapers. chroniclingamerica.loc.gov/.
Nantucket Atheneum Digital Newspaper Archive. www.nantucketatheneum.org.
National Library of Australia Trove. trove.nla.gov.au/.
National Maritime Digital Library. nmdl.org.
New York Times. http://www.nytimes.com.

Websites

City of New Bedford. www.newbedford-ma.gov.

Creative Commons. creativecommons.org.

Foreign Ships in Micronesia. www.micsem.org.

Hathi Trust Digital Library. www.hathitrust.org.

History of American Women. www.womenhistoryblog.com.

The Library of Congress. www.loc.gov.

The Massachusetts Studies Project. http://www.msp.umb.
  edu/afam/AfAmTimelines.html.

Nantucket Atheneum. www.nantucketatheneum.org.

Nantucket Historical Association. www.nha.org.

New Bedford Whaling Museum. www.whalingmuseum.org.

Prospect Hill Cemetery. www.prospecthillcemetery.org.

Sturgis Library. www.sturgislibrary.org.

U.S. Coast Guard. www.ucsg.mil.

Wikipedia. en.wikipedia.org.

ABOUT THE AUTHOR

Amy Jenness works at the Nantucket Atheneum, the island's public library, where she is in charge of adult programs and facilitates a writing group. She has also been employed at the Nantucket Historical Association and the *Nantucket Inquirer & Mirror.*

Amy's journalism has appeared in many island publications, and she was the associate editor of *N Magazine* and managing editor of *Vermont Business Magazine*. She belongs to the Moors Poetry Collective, based on Nantucket, and her poetry has appeared in three of the group's anthologies.